CALLED
TO
TEACH

"Justin McClain's daily reflections will help keep Catholic school teachers focused on the importance of faith witness to students, which is essential to Catholic education."

Tom Burnford
Secretary for Education
Archdiocese of Washington

"I pray that this book reaches and helps many teachers in their mission to form students as missionary disciples."

Andrew Lichtenwalner
Catholic systemic and moral theologian

"Justin McClain's *Called to Teach*, the fruit of his own meditation on the vocation of teaching, is a wonderful resource for the men and women who teach in our Catholic schools. The brief, practical daily reflections—well grounded in actual experience—can motivate even the busiest among us to ponder, 'How can I invite the Lord into my classroom?'"

Br. John Paige, C.S.C.
President of Holy Cross College

"This book is the perfect fit for that teacher in all of us, and specifically to those in the Catholic school classroom."

Patrick Rivera
Director of Young Adult Ministry
Diocese of San Diego

"This book is a blessing to those both in and out of the classroom because its reflections are inspiring, theologically rich, and remarkably insightful. While the reflections are quick and easy to read, they are also simultaneously practical and relevant and will be greatly appreciated by anyone charged with the immensely beautiful vocation of teaching. Justin McClain has given us a wonderful book that I will be using daily in my classroom for years to come!"

Katie Prejean
Catholic speaker, theology teacher, youth minister, and author of *Room 24*

"Justin McClain's book is a valuable tool that offers concrete and insightful daily reflections to help keep the teacher focused on the bigger picture of living out and exemplifying his faith in his daily work."

Timothy O'Donnell
President of Christendom College

"The core of McClain's book lays out a path for all Catholic educators, and his style of daily reflections brings new insight and a depth of understanding to the role of Catholic teachers. Each daily reflection prompts us to understand more deeply our role as Catholic educators in the faith. The extent of the resources provided by the author is a gift to all Catholic teachers."

Br. Richard Kiniry, C.S.C.
Retired community mentor at Bishop McNamara High School
Forestville, Maryland

"Justin writes from a wealth of experience and deep meditation on Scripture and its application for the classroom and in life. This book will be a blessed gift to educators today, particularly beginners in the field."

Sr. Myra Gilbart, I.H.M.
Retired teacher at St. Mary of the Assumption Elementary School
Upper Marlboro, Maryland

"This book can help a teacher and others who work with students find the strength and fortitude needed to move forward in teaching without losing sight of their remarkable goal: to transform the lives of those they are called to teach. The Scriptural references and concise reflections should be able to find a place in any busy teacher's day or week."

Br. Donald Blauvelt, C.S.C.
Executive Director of the Holy Cross Institute
St. Edward's University

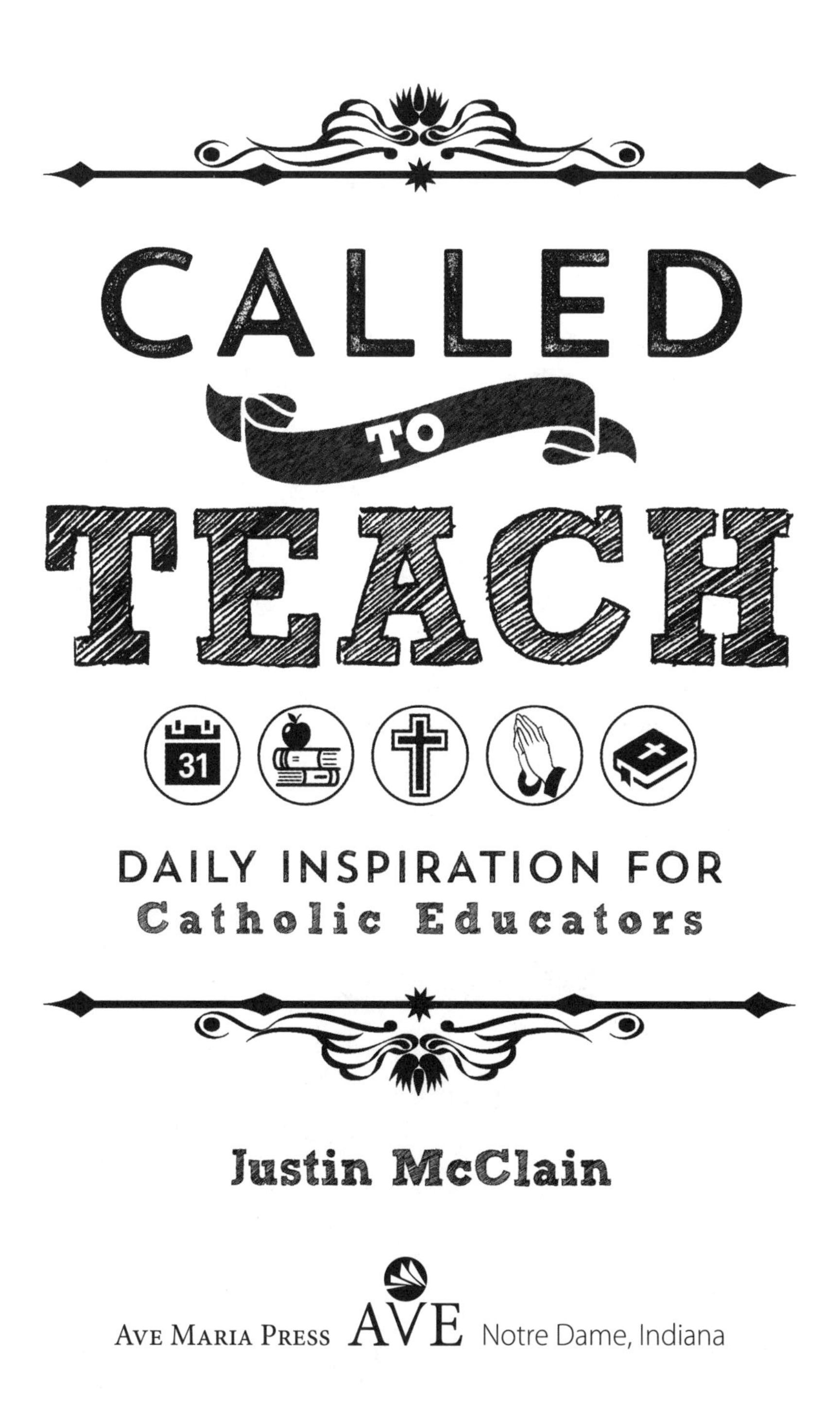

CALLED TO TEACH

DAILY INSPIRATION FOR Catholic Educators

Justin McClain

Ave Maria Press AVE Notre Dame, Indiana

Founded in 1865, Ave Maria Press is a ministry of the United States Province of Holy Cross.

www.avemariapress.com

Paperback: ISBN-13 978-1-59471-685-0

E-book: ISBN-13 978-1-59471-686-7

Cover and text design by Christopher D. Tobin.

Printed and bound in the United States of America.

Broadly, this book is dedicated to all of those educators who daily have the courageous commitment to teach in our Catholic schools. In a special way, I dedicate this to the Mustangs of Bishop McNamara High School—students, faculty, staff, administrators, the board of directors, volunteers, alumni, as well as everyone else affiliated with this unique Catholic familial community. (The 2015–2016 academic year marked my tenth year of teaching at McNamara, and I am privileged and blessed to be able to work alongside my colleagues . . . even when we are at our busiest.) This book is likewise dedicated to all of the staff at Ave Maria Press, along with the variety of other ministries of the Congregation of Holy Cross. *Our Lady, pray for us! Saint André Bessette, pray for us! Blessed Basil Moreau, pray for us! Ave Crux Spes Unica!*

Therefore, my beloved brothers, be firm, steadfast, always fully devoted to the work of the Lord, knowing that in the Lord your labor is not in vain.

—1 Corinthians 15:58

Our principal duty, after seeking the holiness of our own souls, is to bring the truths of religion to all by teaching and by example.

—Blessed Basil Moreau

INTRODUCTION

This set of daily reflections is intended to provide ongoing encouragement to anyone who teaches, or otherwise works, in a Catholic school. The reflections are primarily for my fellow high school teachers, although administrators and staff at all levels, including within a K–8 setting, will hopefully benefit as well, as will homeschooling parents, DREs, and RCIA or CCD instructors. Even the retired Catholic school teacher might appreciate this text as a method of being soporifically lulled to sleep while slumped in a comfortable armchair, enjoying a well-earned perpetual summer vacation!

BACKGROUND ON THE REFLECTIONS

The reflections themselves comprise opportunities to meditate profoundly on the vocation of teaching in a Catholic school. The reflections are not just for theology teachers, nor are they only for those of the Catholic faith. In fact, they may even be better received by those who are not theology teachers, since teachers in other fields and with other faith backgrounds sometimes wonder how they can contribute to the Catholic mission of the school even when the curriculum does not necessarily accommodate direct instruction on matters relating to faith. In essence, these reflections are for the Catholic school teacher who may be wondering: How can I invite the Lord into my classroom and into my teaching philosophy and framework? Hence, such is the beauty of being able to teach in a Catholic school, a community in which students are exposed to the complementary features of matters of Christian faith and the role of faith in society.

My goal in writing this book was to provide a very short reflection for each day of the year. Each reflection opens with a short scriptural passage. Every effort was made to provide exemplary passages from throughout all of scripture. Many well-known passages were referenced, although some lesser-known passages were as well. To accommodate lay readership in particular, all scriptural excerpts within the text are courtesy of the *New American Bible, Revised Edition*.

HOW TO USE THE REFLECTIONS

Even for slow, yet methodical, readers—such as yours truly—the reflections are designed to take no more than one minute to read, affording even the busiest teacher the time to read one per day. In fact, they are so short that you might even want to read the same reflection two or three times per day (or more, if you have some down time and need an infusion of spiritual strength prior to holding your parent-teacher report card conferences). You may choose to read a reflection whenever convenient—perhaps in the morning prior to leaving for school, upon arriving at school, during your lunch break, before leaving for home, before dinner, after putting the kids down to bed, while trying to procrastinate in order to avoid grading that stack of your sophomores' essays, before going to sleep, and so forth.

HOW THE REFLECTIONS ARE ORGANIZED

An important feature of these reflections is that they are not chronological, which means that you do not have to have read prior reflections in order to understand future ones. In other words, you can begin at any point in the year and not have "missed" anything. In fact, you can catch the overlooked dates when they come around the next year.

Similarly, if you grow tired of the textual soliloquy of an allegedly inspirational Catholic school teacher, you can put the book down for a few days and then return to this exercise in literary mortification later. Although the reflections, of course, have a markedly theological outlook, the only ones that coincide with a particular date on the liturgical calendar are those solemnities that are likewise holy days of obligation: January 1 (the Solemnity of the Blessed Virgin Mary, the Mother of God), August 15 (the Solemnity of the Assumption of the Blessed Virgin Mary), November 1 (the Solemnity of All Saints [All Saints' Day]), December 8 (the Solemnity of the Immaculate Conception of the Blessed Virgin Mary), and December 25 (the Nativity of the Lord [Christmas]).

Also, please note that there are two helpful indices in the back of the book. The subject index organizes the reflections around a variety of topics that include theological, scriptural, doctrinal, pedagogical, and educational themes. The scripture index organizes all the scripture passages used in this text for each day's reflection.

Ultimately, these reflections are meant to provide some measure of daily inspiration to my fellow Catholic school educators. On a personal note, with 2016 being my tenth year of teaching, I felt called to write down constructive reflections based on the experience that I have acquired within this time. Of course, we are all learning. Therefore, I would encourage you to supplement these reflections with reading the Bible more in depth, allowing yourself to be captivated by the Word of God. Thank you for your service to your students, to your Catholic school, to the Catholic Church, and ultimately to the Lord Jesus Christ through your fulfillment of your vocation as a Catholic school teacher. May God abundantly bless you and your Catholic school community. Teach on!

DAILY REFLECTIONS

JANUARY 1

> But when the fullness of time had come, God sent his Son, born of a woman, born under the law, to ransom those under the law, so that we might receive adoption.
>
> **—Galatians 4:4–5**

Today is the Solemnity of the Blessed Virgin Mary, the Mother of God. Mary, as Jesus' Mother, knew him better than anyone else with whom he interacted throughout the course of his time on earth. In fact, Mary is the only person to have remained unquestionably faithful to Jesus throughout his entire earthly life, from his conception by the power of the Holy Spirit (see Lk 1:31) through his passion and crucifixion (see Jn 19:25)—as well as during his resurrection and ascension, and then Pentecost and beyond. Although our students are not quite divine (even if some of them may think so), they are indeed children of God and therefore deserve our concern for their spiritual well-being. Your belief in your students' God-given worth, value, and dignity may be the only source of hope and encouragement that they receive on a given day. Mary's selfless support for Jesus has given us a model of constant fidelity to the Lord and of inviting others to follow him. Remain devoted to seeking opportunities to bring your students to know Jesus Christ.

JANUARY 2

> [Jesus] said in reply, "He who sows good seed is the Son of Man, the field is the world, the good seed the children of the kingdom."
>
> **—Matthew 13:37–38a**

The Catholic school teacher is constantly "planting seeds." However, we must recall that Jesus himself is the actual "sower," and we merely cooperate with him, through the power of the Holy Spirit, as he does his good work in our students. These spiritual seeds will not necessarily sprout while the student is in school. Make sure that you plant mustard seeds (see Mt 13:31–32), rather than poison ivy or nettles. Give students the spiritual foundation that they will need to flourish into adult men and women replete with spiritual wisdom. Make sure that your lessons are oriented toward the gospel in such a way that they allow your students to enhance their relationship with Jesus Christ. Corroborate the good lessons that they have received from other teachers, because students will reliably flourish from the spirit of professionalism and collegiality that is fostered within a Catholic school. Our youth are still learning and getting used to how to navigate life in a way that orients themselves to God's kingdom.

JANUARY 3

> Train the young in the way they should go; even when old, they will not swerve from it.
>
> **—Proverbs 22:6**

Lesson planning can be either one of the most difficult or one of the most rewarding of endeavors for the Catholic school teacher. On various occasions, it can be both. No matter your field of pedagogical expertise, you must aim to design good lessons. Make sure that your lessons provide an educational foundation for your students that will eventually enable them likewise to establish the framework for teaching others whenever they have the opportunity in the future. No matter what subject you teach, determine how your lesson is going to serve your students both now and decades from now, so that it provides for their ultimately enduring wisdom. Especially in terms of lessons in morality—which can, depending on the scope of your course, easily be intertwined into your curricular framework—always be on the lookout for those "teachable moments" that will show your students the lesson's broader implications for humanity. The more solid your students' training, the more they will appreciate your contribution.

JANUARY 4

> But whoever obeys and teaches these commandments will be called greatest in the kingdom of heaven.
>
> **—Matthew 5:19b**

Our students are looking for objective moral truth. Every teacher has been a teenager. For younger teachers, you may have been a teenager just a few years ago, while for older teachers, it has been . . . well, longer. However, no matter how long ago you were a teenager, you probably had your fair share of dire questions, doubts, uncertainties, preoccupations, and ponderings about how the world works, especially in terms of matters of faith. In the midst of modern times, society is often unwilling to provide anyone, let alone the youth, with semblances of certainty regarding living a life of faith. Therefore, look for ways to lead students to become familiar with God's commands—including, at a minimum, the Ten Commandments. Have your students know them, perhaps by reading the account of their first scriptural appearance via Moses in Exodus 20:1–17, or by reviewing the familiar "Traditional Catechetical Formula" (available for free on the Vatican's website). Draw your students to know and love the Lord's will.

JANUARY 5

> Always be ready to give an explanation to anyone who asks you for a reason for your hope.
>
> **—1 Peter 3:15b**

Absolutely, look for opportunities to provide your students with testimony of your faith in Jesus Christ. Wondering about questions of faith is a natural, normal, healthy curiosity that students may have, and this can serve as yet another opportunity for them to gain wisdom from an adult figure. What is your *story*? This does not mean that every class session has to feature an exercise in homiletics, but take advantage of chances to share your faith experience with your students. Many students are genuinely inquisitive about others' journeys with Christ, especially since they often have so many questions about matters of faith, whether those questions are general or specific. Sharing your own experience of faith allows your students to realize that you are a human being, rather than an automated production from the assembly line at the teacher factory. Allowing your students to see your rich faith in Christ will allow them, in turn, to have faith in your own genuineness.

JANUARY 6

> Since we have gifts that differ according to the grace given to us, let us exercise them.
>
> **—Romans 12:6**

Encourage your students to use their God-given gifts and talents. For the sake of clarity, *talent* here does not signify the ability to chew gum in class without getting caught, or the ability of a guy to devise a creative way to ask a girl out to prom. Gifts and talents that could glorify God include musical performance, intellectual pursuits, athletic abilities, and so forth. Remind your students that they do not have to wait until graduation to start using their gifts, but no gift should ever be self-serving. Help them to distinguish between gifts that will contribute to the kingdom of God and gifts that are not as noble. If you have students who are good writers, teach them that effective writing can be used to compose a treatise on the Church's teachings on the "four last things," rather than to post on social media an eloquent description of how the demands of their most difficult teacher are probably getting them time off Purgatory. Every student has a treasury of gifts to help serve the kingdom of God. Your students' souls will thank you in the end.

JANUARY 7

> Let the word of Christ dwell in you richly, as in all wisdom you teach and admonish one another.
>
> **—Colossians 3:16a**

There is a great store of spiritual richness that comes from being a positive influence within any institution. This is especially true within a Catholic school, in which the gospel should permeate every aspect of the school's educational framework in order to be effective. Any stranger walking into the school for the first time should know that it is a Catholic institution. Negativity reliably drains the life out of any community that could otherwise prosper in various ways, and a faith-based community is hardly immune. This negativity can come in various forms, whether manifested as cynicism, pessimism, resentment, acrimony, biting sarcasm, passive aggression, doctrinal dissent, or some other mindset that casts a dark cloud of despair over every avenue that the offender frequents. Alternatively, being a positive person leads others to see the light of Christ by your presence. If criticism (or better, *critique*) must ever be offered, ensure that this is carried out with joyful charity, so that it is ultimately constructive in its scope.

JANUARY 8

> [Show] yourself as a model of good deeds in every respect, with integrity in your teaching, dignity, and sound speech that cannot be criticized.
>
> **—Titus 2:7–8a**

One of the most vital lessons that a teacher can bestow is the need to acknowledge that no one knows it all. The totality of facts regarding all that has ever been, all that is, and all that will ever be is far too elusive for any one human being to obtain, even if a lifetime were allotted for such an initiative. Remind your students that life is not measured by how much we know, but by what we do with the time that God has given us. Of course, the teacher should be well versed in the content of his course. After all, a theology student would be lead astray to think that the names of the three Magi were Larry, Moe, and Curly, and a chemistry student would be disadvantaged to believe that the atomic number for platinum referred to how many albums his favorite singer has sold. If you were unclear in presenting material, or made a mistake when writing a test that coerced students into answering incorrectly, give them an opportunity to make up the points lost. Your example of Christian mercy could be an even more effective lesson in the end.

JANUARY 9

> Hold fast to instruction, never let it go; keep it, for it is your life.
>
> **—Proverbs 4:13**

The best teachers are the best students. It takes courage to pause and remember what life was like "on the other side of the desk." Teachers should always aim to continue learning. This learning can be of the formal variety, such as through professional development, continuing education, advanced degrees, seminars, and so on. This is true for learning about both course content and pedagogy. However, informal learning is similarly vital to the educator's growth. New teachers should seek, and be supported by, the wisdom of veteran teachers. Meanwhile, the veterans should allow themselves to be inspired by the imagination and energy of new teachers. Regarding faith, strive to continue learning about the Lord and Christian principles. You may never receive a gold star sticker for your efforts, but your overall effectiveness as a teacher will be strengthened, ultimately enriching your Catholic school community. Also, never be afraid to learn from students. Many have a deep, abiding faith that we ought to appreciate for our own inspiration.

JANUARY 10

> Therefore, my beloved brothers, be firm, steadfast, always fully devoted to the work of the Lord, knowing that in the Lord your labor is not in vain.
>
> **—1 Corinthians 15:58**

Make sure to understand the vast distinction between stubbornness and determination, whether in terms of yourself or your students. Stubbornness is essentially vanity, and it is often rife with the dreadful effects of pride, while determination will have positive results, particularly in matters of faith. Make sure that you are not somehow merely going through the motions when it comes to presenting your lessons to your students, stubbornly speeding through the material simply to cover it. Make sure that your students are ultimately grasping the lesson at hand. Determination equated with perseverance is what will lead to enduring comprehension. In terms of encouraging your students' faith, leading them to know Christ is of utmost importance, and this determination should underscore a Catholic school teacher's educational framework. Working for the kingdom of God will not necessarily be accompanied by a flashy career or temporal success, but determination in leading others to the gospel will truly "bear fruit that will remain" (Jn 15:16).

JANUARY 11

> But it shall not be so among you. Rather, whoever wishes to be great among you will be your servant.
>
> **—Mark 10:43**

The ideal Catholic community is one in which all stakeholders embody an attitude of service. From the student to the administrator, from the teacher to the custodian, from the parent volunteer to the coach on the field, a truly Christ-centered school must inherently, and necessarily, possess a framework that provides for acts of service—for chances to put others before oneself. The New Testament is rife with "servant" imagery. In fact, each of the gospels mentions the role of "servant" at least once. And it is hardly a coincidence that the more beloved heroes from national and world history were often powerful leaders who served others through deed and example. In the theology or history classroom, endeavor to highlight those saintly servants who happened to be royalty or nobility and used that status for good, such as Saint Elizabeth of Hungary, Saint Margaret of Scotland, Saint Wenceslaus, and so on. (Students wishing to receive bonus points might wish to point out to the right teacher that Saint Margaret was Scottish, or attempt to spell *Wenceslaus* for extra credit.)

JANUARY 12

> But seek first the kingdom [of God] and his righteousness, and all these things will be given you besides. Do not worry about tomorrow.
>
> **—Matthew 6:33–34a**

Before you leave school at the end of each day, think about at least one event that occurred that day for which you can smile. Especially aim to do this on days that did not go very well, for one reason or another. Perhaps a student let you down through his or her misbehavior. Perhaps you did not finish all of your grading, and now you have to take home a foot-tall stack of essays to read through. Perhaps the photocopier was malfunctioning, and you learned just how strong the temptation was to bestow upon it a variety of colorful epithets. No matter the trials that you face each day, at least one event or student's action should make you smile when you take the time for reflection. It could have been a colleague thanking you, a student holding the door open for you, or some other uplifting moment in the midst of adversity that will benefit your ultimate well-being as an educator. Make sure that your educational philosophy truly furthers the gospel, and you shall remain confident in your teaching role. God's gift of tomorrow is a new day to look forward to.

JANUARY 13

> Therefore, you shall love the Lord, your God, with your whole heart, and with your whole being, and with your whole strength.
>
> **—Deuteronomy 6:5**

Teaching is exhausting work. You plan lessons. You supervise extracurricular duties. You are on your feet for hours on end. Exhaustion is perhaps especially true for the novice teacher, who is still attempting to navigate the myriad day-to-day expectations of an educator's life. However, even veteran teachers can be fatigued by trying to keep up with the many demands of the teaching profession. When the Lord is at the forefront of our day, all other matters fall into place. This means loving God with the fullness of ourselves. Our hearts must be open to him in order to receive his mercy. We must make sure that other aspects of our lives (not merely our educational outlook) are oriented toward his will. We must use every ounce of our strength to bring him glory. If your body is exhausted from physical exertion, get rest. If your mind is exhausted from teaching for the fourth time that day that Saul did not ride a horse to Damascus, take a nap. However, if your *soul* is exhausted, you have a cause for concern and need to reorient your will to God's.

JANUARY 14

Come, children, listen to me; I will teach you fear of the LORD.

—Psalm 34:12

"Fear of the Lord," a gift of the Holy Spirit, does not imply *fear* in the sense of trepidation or frightfulness. Rather, a closer explanation might connect fear of the Lord with respect, or appreciation, for God's autonomy, sovereignty, authority, and providence. Make sure to remind your students that legitimate authority is far from being a bad thing; in fact, it is a very good thing. What athlete does not appreciate the guidance of a coach to improve his or her performance? What orchestral musician does not value the leadership of a conductor to keep the symphony at the right tempo? What student does not appreciate a wise theology teacher's exegetical explanation contrary to an Internet search's revelation that a misguided theologian has hypothesized that Jesus was married to Mary Magdalene? Although respect is instinctive and intuitive, it must still be fostered and cultivated within a Catholic school community. It is through leading our students to fear the Lord that we bring them to better understand his ultimate outpouring of sheer love for them.

JANUARY 15

Guide me by your fidelity and teach me, for you are God my savior.

—Psalm 25:5

As a teacher, remember to listen to God. This may seem to be a trite expectation, but we teachers must commit to this. Throughout the work day, do not try to go it alone, as a victim of the "Atlas Complex." After all, much less depends on us in life than we might realize. The glorification of God, rather than our productivity, is our goal. At the end of the day, the Catholic school teacher should be able to say that he or she built up the kingdom of God with his or her duties as an educator. Relying on God is especially true for prayer. Someone who claims that he or she is too busy to pray is someone who does not want to mature spiritually. Many times, people must recall that prayer is a wide two-way street, rather than a narrow side alley. Prayer is not just us talking to God as a shortcut, or a convenient pull-off, but it is listening to him abundantly, as well as sharing with him the fullness of our joys and sufferings. Jesus gave us the apt example of prayer by calling out to his Father in heaven during critical moments of his passion.

JANUARY 16

> Behold, you desire true sincerity; and secretly you teach me wisdom.
>
> **—Psalm 51:8**

Within schools run by the Congregation of Holy Cross, our educational charism focuses on educating both students' minds *and* their hearts, an important approach propounded by the founder of Holy Cross, Blessed Father Basil Moreau, C.S.C. It is fair to deduce that the possession of wisdom is a reality of both the mind and the heart. Someone can be an exceptionally bright person but not have a good heart. Someone can be a living saint and not have an impressive intellect. We should encourage our students to attain and retain wisdom, and we must have the same approach to our own edification. However, it is important to note that wisdom is acquired, rather than taught. Since the Latin verb *educare* means "to draw or lead out of," it is our responsibility as educators to tap into our students' God-given potential in a way that ultimately brings them to greater wisdom as they learn about the Lord's will. We teachers need to do more than simply instruct; we need to encourage our students to lead sincere lives, inspired by Jesus' true wisdom.

JANUARY 17

> I will teach the wicked your ways, that sinners may return to you.
>
> **—Psalm 51:15**

Do not get into the habit of denigrating students for their actions. Definitely do not get into the habit of referring to them as "wicked," lest you end up called to a meeting with your department chairperson or principal and a concerned parent. However, it is critical to recall that, within a Catholic school, we have the opportunity to discuss an action's virtue or lack thereof. It is one thing to ask a student why he did not do his homework, but it is potentially more meaningful to remind him that, in not completing his homework, he actually violated the fourth commandment: "Honor your father and your mother" (Ex 20:12; see Mt 15:4, Mt 19:19, and Mk 7:10). In this case, the commandment would also apply to respect for your authority, as his teacher. Do not "dumb down" the dilemma of sin. Students have consciences, and they need to know that God has given us the gift of free will in order to honor and glorify him through virtue, not to separate ourselves from him through sin. We must instill in our students an enduring desire for virtuous living. Leading our students to *want* to live virtuously is a true achievement.

JANUARY 18

> Teach me, LORD, your way that I may walk in your truth.
>
> **—Psalm 86:11**

Our students belong to the Lord. Before, during, and after the time that they are under our vigilance as their teachers, they are the Lord's.

Their parents, teachers, and other adults care for them, but they ultimately belong to the Father. Hence, the Catholic school teacher should strive to lead students to love the Lord's will. The youth, far from being the raucous, hormone-driven troglodytes that they are occasionally perceived to be, actually seek truth and goodness, perhaps even more fervently than jaded or world-weary adults. The teacher has already passed through the school years, but the student is in the midst of an educational voyage that is replete with opportunities to learn about life. If we do not strive to lead our students to an understanding of the truth of the gospel and God's abundant love for them, we are derelict of our key ministerial duties as Catholic school educators. Seek out various ways to underscore examples of the Lord's goodness to your students. They ardently yearn to recognize and receive his outpouring of love.

JANUARY 19

> Blessed the one whom you guide, LORD, whom you teach by your instruction.
>
> **—Psalm 94:12**

If a Catholic school is fulfilling its mission, Christ is the veritable teacher. We will not be teachers forever (which some students may readily celebrate). The classroom teacher is ideally merely the facilitator of his or her students' awareness of the Lord's call. Remind your students that Christ is calling each of them to greatness: "It was not you who chose me, but I who chose you and appointed you to go and bear fruit that will remain" (Jn 15:16). However, beyond worldly power, money, or other illusory goals, this "greatness" should be a life according to God's will. Saint Teresa of Calcutta, who accepted the Lord's will for her to live among the poor and dying, herself equipped with scant earthly possessions, hardly lived what society alleges to be "success"; rather, she is in heaven for all eternity because she obeyed the will of God. We are not left clueless or wayward in finding our way. Christ taught us by his example to follow the Father's will. Leading students to imitate Christ is asking the Lord to bless them.

JANUARY 20

> Teach me wisdom and knowledge, for in your commandments I trust.
>
> **—Psalm 119:66**

Our students should leave our Catholic educational institutions with the eager ability to comprehend both wisdom and knowledge. The two are complementary. A computer database is replete with more mere "knowledge" than any one person could ever possess, but "wisdom" implies the discernment to use that knowledge appropriately. History is full of examples of the misapplication of knowledge in order to further deviant desires, but wisdom endures in bettering the world around us. Regarding wisdom, the Lord always knows best. Therefore, teach your students concern for the poor and the homeless, in the midst of a society that promotes insularity and selfishness. Teach them the temporal and spiritual rewards of chastity and abstinence before marriage, in the midst of a society that mocks self-control and celebrates sexual immorality. Teach them the beauty of honesty, in the midst of a society that embraces deception. Teach them hope, in the midst of a society that deifies doubt. Teach them the manifold attributes of God's will.

JANUARY 21

> Instruct the wise, and they become still wiser; teach the just, and they advance in learning.
>
> **—Proverbs 9:9**

Wisdom begets wisdom, and from there justice is fostered in service of God's kingdom. Teach your students that the presence of justice should be the norm, not the exception. Recall that justice is one of the four cardinal virtues (along with fortitude, prudence, and temperance). People are naturally attracted to the prospect of true justice, and the youth are no exception. (If you do not believe this assertion, see what happens the next time you play a trivia game in class and, having told the students that they will have five seconds to respond before moving on, you only give a certain student 4.926 seconds. In the remaining 0.074 seconds, observe the rapidity with which the student's teammates summarily deliver a rousing cacophony of diatribes, battle cries, and incinerated effigies, calling for fairness.) Orient all of your students' "thirst for righteousness" (Mt 5:6) toward using their actual wisdom to spread Christ's gospel. As they step out into the world, they will appreciate your charitable instruction.

JANUARY 22

> Thus says the LORD, your redeemer, the Holy One of Israel: I am the LORD, your God, teaching you how to prevail, leading you on the way you should go.
>
> **—Isaiah 48:17**

A feature of the Catholic school teacher's educational philosophy should be the recurring theme that God knows what is best for humanity. In other words, God knows what he is doing. There is, too frequently, the false perception that the Catholic Church is the "Church of no," the curmudgeonly miser of an institution bent on nothing less than enacting a litany of rules and injunctions intended to wag a finger and shut down the party, heaping a burden of inconvenience upon humanity. However, the reality is that when the annals of the Church's moral teachings, whether as expounded within such texts as the *Catechism of the Catholic Church* or the *Code of Canon Law* or accurate biblical commentaries, are analyzed through a philosophical—that is, rhetorical—lens, the beauty of the Church's ultimate intentions is realized. No matter what subject you teach, gaining a foundational comprehension of the Church's wise doctrine will provide you with a deeper knowledge of the connectivity between faith, morality, and academe.

JANUARY 23

> Then Jesus said to his disciples, "Whoever wishes to come after me must deny himself, take up his cross, and follow me."
>
> **—Matthew 16:24**

It is important to teach students that suffering is a part of life. In fact, Jesus emphasized this often, explaining that the crosses that we bear are so frequent that we should even expect them "daily" (see Lk 9:23). Jesus elaborated: "Whoever does not carry his own cross and come after me cannot be my disciple" (Lk 14:27)—that is, "is not worthy of me" (Mt 10:38). Our crosses are more bearable when we recall that Jesus himself innocently bore *the* Cross for our own offenses. He knows our trials intimately, in the midst of all that we are dealing with. Outward trials might come in the form of physical ailments, temptations to sin, workloads, and so forth. However, we must remind our students that self-attributed suffering of the soul is unhealthy and requires a return to God. For example, the mental anguish of guilt after having cheated on a test (especially a theology one!) is the type of suffering that requires reconciliation with God. Remind your students that fidelity to the Lord is strength, and not weakness.

JANUARY 24

> You are the light of the world. A city set on a mountain cannot be hidden. Nor do they light a lamp and then put it under a bushel basket.
>
> **—Matthew 5:14–15a**

No matter what subject you teach, seek ways to link your content area with moral considerations. Particularly within a Catholic school, every academic subject can be connected to matters of faith. In the midst of rapid technological innovation typified by the "digital age," remind students that technological developments devoid of thorough ethical reflection have led to such diabolical contrivances as nuclear weaponry, the gas chamber, abortifacient materials, and too many other abominations that have resulted in the tragic obliteration of scores of human lives. Alternatively, responsible advancements in technology have given us such benefits as the transportation of food and life-saving medicines to indigent populations thousands of miles away, the complementary availability of the Bible online, the possibility of facilitating a video conference call between a displaced child refugee and his worried parents back in his home country, and multiple other resources that aid humanity in light of the gospel.

JANUARY 25

> If your brother sins, rebuke him; and if he repents, forgive him.
>
> **—Luke 17:3**

The Catholic school teacher must be prepared to forgive. Students are human beings. They, like we adults, will inevitably make mistakes and, worse, sin. Of course, students need to be charitably corrected, but the teacher must remember to extend forgiveness. You will note that Jesus subsequently asserts: "If he wrongs you seven times in one day and returns to you seven times saying, 'I am sorry,' you should forgive him" (Lk 17:4). Perhaps a student has forgotten to pick up his water bottle from the floor after class yet again. A constructive critique is due, but life goes on. Worse, you catch a student cheating on an exam. Notice that Jesus qualifies his expectation with "if he repents," indicating that it is acceptable for us to encourage a student to admit having done something wrong, because this is all part of the process of spiritual maturation that we must foster in our students. Students justifiably do not want to be coddled or belittled in their faith lives. A student who receives a teacher's forgiveness will ultimately observe a reflection of God's own mercy.

JANUARY 26

> Come to me, all you who labor and are burdened, and I will give you rest.
>
> **—Matthew 11:28**

With all due respect to our faithful Catholic school administrators, Jesus is really the world's easiest leader to learn from. In fact, following Jesus is actually rather easy as well. Although any number of earthly endeavors will be challenging for the follower of Christ, what greater reward can we enjoy than to look inwardly, deep into the inner recesses of our souls, and know that, at our core, we are children of the Father and brethren of the Son? Likewise, we must always remind our students to bring all that is in their hearts to the Lord. Our students are dealing with a variety of difficult circumstances, whether in their families or with their many commitments. Remind your students to bring their worries to the Lord, because they need to know that living in accord with Jesus' teachings will always bring them authentic freedom and peace of mind. Jesus avowed, "Take my yoke upon you and learn from me, for I am meek and humble of heart; and you will find rest for yourselves. For my yoke is easy, and my burden light" (Mt 11:29–30). Repose in the Lord!

JANUARY 27

> Hear and understand. It is not what enters one's mouth that defiles that person; but what comes out of the mouth is what defiles one.
>
> **—Matthew 15:10–11**

Remember to choose your words considerately when it comes to speaking with your students, in order to bring about a positive learning atmosphere. The timeless adage "It's not what you say; it's how you say it" always holds true. Address your students in a manner that fosters a more uplifting educational environment. Choose phrases that are ultimately constructive. To offer just a few examples, instead of inquiring, "Why are you late to class?" ask, "Did something happen?" Substitute "*Don't forget* to do your homework!" with "*Remember* to do your homework!" In place of "Stop talking!" say, "Welcome back to the discussion." Rather than "Tuck in your shirt!" try, "Wouldn't you prefer to look like Mr. McClain?" Slightly adjusting your speech in order to encourage Christian optimism is far from exercising some semblance of pedagogical hand-holding or condescension; rather, all of us, whether young or old, want to be around positive people. Sanctify all of your speech for God, for the ultimate well-being of your students.

JANUARY 28

> And so I say to you, you are Peter, and upon this rock I will build my church, and the gates of the netherworld shall not prevail against it.
>
> **—Matthew 16:18**

In order to facilitate cross-curricular discussions from within the theological framework inherent to a Catholic school, consider having your students read thematically relevant papal or episcopal documents, at least in excerpted form. Many of these magisterial documents—including pastoral letters, encyclicals, apostolic exhortations, and so on—are readily available online for free. They can provide students with the opportunity to understand the Church's teachings as they relate to a variety of fields, including ecology or environmental studies, health and well-being, history, law and government, the social sciences, the physical sciences, technology, and, of course, in-depth theology. There are plentiful topics that the Magisterium has addressed throughout the millennia, particularly within the last two centuries, and students can have the opportunity to examine a topic's broader implications for humanity in light of the gospel. The writings of our United States Conference of Catholic Bishops are reliably in line with the Church's clear doctrine.

JANUARY 29

> God is faithful and will not let you be tried beyond your strength; but with the trial he will also provide a way out, so that you may be able to bear it.
>
> **—1 Corinthians 10:13b**

Despair is a beleaguering spiritual scourge that attempts to claim too many victims who are otherwise unaware of just how much God wants his children to return to him so that he can bestow his providence and love upon us all. Despair encumbers both young and old alike. We must beware of it in our own lives, as well as help students who are dealing with unimaginably innumerable struggles that are imperiling their relationship with the Lord. Our trials will come from various sources, although we must recall that "no trial has come to [us] but what is human" (1 Cor 10:13a). In other words, the Lord is not only present with us as we undergo what is ailing us; he also reminds us that we should come to him in order to seek that refuge that the world is unable to provide. We will all endure a multitude of temporal difficulties throughout our time spent on earth. Not a day will pass during which we will not undergo a difficulty of some degree or type. However, Jesus showed us how to patiently suffer while remaining oriented toward God's will.

JANUARY 30

> Do to others whatever you would have them do to you.
>
> **—Matthew 7:12**

As a Catholic school teacher, you should always endeavor to maintain and foster an elevated degree of professionalism, decorum, and collegiality. The collective gifts and treasures that your school's faculty, staff, and administration can offer is exceedingly greater than any one employee could ever hope to muster, even over the course of an extensive career in education. A teacher's compassionate demeanor toward his or her coworkers not only positively enhances that individual teacher's outlook; it likewise furthers a more uplifting learning atmosphere for the entire school community, with students especially benefiting. In other words, our students enjoy seeing their teachers get along. Smiley Sally's supportive words to her class about a fellow teacher's recent achievement will bring more glory to the kingdom of God than Smug Stan's judgmental grimace when a colleague walks into the classroom to return a borrowed stapler. Our students are always watching us. Are we treating our colleagues in a Christian manner?

JANUARY 31

> But the handmade idol is accursed, and its maker as well: he for having produced it, and the corruptible thing, because it was termed a god.
>
> **—Wisdom 14:8**

Beware of false idols that can crop up around school. They may be difficult to notice initially, but they eventually manifest themselves. These may come in various, occasionally veiled, forms: athletic performance at the intentional exclusion of sportsmanship, teamwork, and cooperation; academic success without truly constructive learning; illusory fame and fortune; technological innovation devoid of enduring reflection; and so forth. God knows well the perils of worldly concerns clouding our vision of him as our only Lord, so much so that he ratified the very first commandment: "You shall not have other gods beside me. You shall not make for yourself an idol or a likeness of anything in the heavens above or on the earth below or in the waters beneath the earth; you shall not bow down before them or serve them" (Ex 20:3–5a). This is likewise the commandment that receives the most commentary as transmitted by Moses. Ensure that worship of the Lord God remains at the forefront of your educational philosophy and mission.

FEBRUARY 1

> Jesus, however, called the children to himself and said, "Let the children come to me and do not prevent them; for the kingdom of God belongs to such as these."
>
> **—Luke 18:16**

The Catholic school exists for the well-being of the student. More specifically, the goal is to bring students closer to the Lord. The passage of Luke 18:16, which is likewise recounted in Mark 10:13–16 and Matthew 19:13–15, shows how Jesus has a special place in his heart for the youth. Young people usually have a fresher perspective than adults, and they are often more open to recognizing the presence of the Almighty. Whatever course you teach, strive to bring out the best in your students. The *best* is their innate desire to know, love, and serve the Lord, who ultimately wants to welcome them into eternity with him one day. Look for ways to draw your students closer to the Lord. The biology teacher might show how DNA proves that each of us is a unique masterpiece of the Lord. The English teacher might show how various authors have used the written word to express God's magnificence throughout the centuries. The math or physics teacher might highlight the exquisite ordering of the universe. Let your students recognize God's love for each of us in all that they learn and in all that they do.

FEBRUARY 2

Pride goes before disaster, and a haughty spirit before a fall.

—Proverbs 16:18

Our students need to know that humility is a noble practice. Humility strengthens, while pride weakens. Hubris and selfishness have wrought much destruction throughout human history. Meanwhile, the saints' lives reveal how humility was vital to their sanctification. Saint Catherine of Siena exercised humility when she dedicated her life to the Lord at a young age, and then eventually followed his will in meeting with Pope Gregory XI to restore the papacy to Rome. Saint Joan of Arc was not seeking personal acclaim when she undertook military leadership; instead, she was humbly dedicated to restoring a national unity that was oriented toward serving the kingdom of God. Saint Juan Diego was humbly open to the Lord's will in his life, and he was subsequently chosen to bring the message of Our Lady of Guadalupe to the people of México. Ultimately, teaching students how to be humble is teaching them how to be open to God's will for their lives. (Just make sure not to encourage them to brag about how humility is their best virtue.)

FEBRUARY 3

Your word is a lamp for my feet, a light for my path.

—Psalm 119:105

Look for opportunities to foster in your students a love for sacred scripture. After all, the Bible is God's living Word, and it is one of the most readily accessible texts in existence. There are a variety of ways to incorporate readings from the Bible into your lessons. For theology teachers, this is an obvious and clear expectation, while teachers of other subjects might find it more of a challenge. You might consider beginning class by reading the gospel passage from the day's Mass readings, which are available for free through various Catholic websites. You might even consider the practice of *lectio divina* or another way of drawing your students into a deeper encounter with the Lord through meditating on his Word. Personally, you might also be interested in developing your own devotion to reading the Bible daily. You do not have to attempt to read all 176 verses of Psalm 119 (the longest chapter in the Bible) during your lunch break, but find a quiet space during the day to be fully open to the Lord's Word as "a light for [your] path."

FEBRUARY 4

> As for me, far be it from me to sin against the LORD by ceasing to pray for you and to teach you the good and right way.
>
> **—1 Samuel 12:23**

The most important thing that a Catholic school teacher can do during the school day is to pray. Prayer is more vital than mere action, than pragmatism, than busyness, than testing, than grading papers. Even a cursory reading of the gospels reveals how Jesus spent copious time in prayer, particularly in the midst of his most significant trials. There is power in the prayers offered by a Catholic school community. Specifically, ask yourself such questions as these: How often have I *really* prayed for my students by name? Are any of my students dealing with difficult situations that are impeding their overall well-being, situations that I can pray for? Have I stopped to thank God for the privilege of teaching his children, who are our future, not to mention fellow aspirers to the kingdom of God? These are just some of the numerous questions that the praying teacher might consider. Regarding the last question, recall that all Catholic school teachers have a "supernatural ability" to see the future (by teaching the future). Make sure that your students' futures are prayerfully bright.

FEBRUARY 5

I have the strength for everything through him who empowers me.

—Philippians 4:13

It is important for students to know that the Lord is willing to grant to them only that which is oriented toward the kingdom of God. You should do your part as a Catholic school teacher to ensure they know it is through the imitation of Jesus Christ that they will live a life that reflects the Lord's will for them. Therefore, seeking illusory goals or fleeting temporal comforts is spiritually counterproductive. Christ's strength is not a sort of force that will necessarily lead to worldly success or to fortune and fame; rather, the power of Jesus Christ is a power that provides us all with the opportunity for redemption and salvation through him. The Lord *empowers* us to use what he has given us to not only draw near to Christ ourselves, but to likewise draw others close to him. Therefore, provide your students with opportunities to reflect on who Christ is and how his strength is the only kind of strength that ultimately matters because it is the only kind that provides true grace. The Lord's outpouring of grace upon his disciples helps us to remain close to him.

FEBRUARY 6

So turn from youthful desires and pursue righteousness, faith, love, and peace, along with those who call on the Lord with purity of heart.

—2 Timothy 2:22

The youth deserve to know the beauty and truth of the Catholic Church's teachings on matters of abstinence and chastity. Unfortunately, lust, rather than chaste love, has become society's goal, admittedly so or otherwise. In the treacherous twenty-first-century world, there are plenty of misguiding messages that are being thrown at young people regarding topics related to the perception of status, to aspirations to popularity, to the denial of the possibility of self-discipline, and other misguided allegiances that quickly lead people away from God. Meanwhile, the human body becomes objectified in the process, leading to widespread disrespect and contempt for the reality of how God intended for a husband and wife to honor each other through their marital chastity. Since students have teachers across different courses within a curriculum, this does not mean that a zoology teacher has to deliver the "birds and the bees" talk. However, if the issue ever presents itself, refer students to Christian principles about the topic of human sexuality.

FEBRUARY 7

> Children's children are the crown of the elderly, and the glory of children is their parentage.
>
> **—Proverbs 17:6**

Make sure that you are in the habit of communicating extensively with the parents of your students. No one knows their child better than a mom or dad. Parents want to see their children succeed. (They are, of course, the ones paying the tuition for a worthwhile Catholic school education, which is both an irreplaceable resource and a priceless spiritual commodity.) Communication with parents should be simultaneously formative, productive, objective, and straightforward. Make sure that you do not only communicate with parents when their children are *not* performing well; rather, if a child is doing well, perhaps particularly in the case of a student who has greatly improved, make sure to honor that student with a phone call to his or her parents, or at least an e-mail (or a letter, for the fortunately old-fashioned). Your approval of a student to his or her parents will make the day of everyone involved. The opportunity to highlight students' achievements reminds them that they are children of the Most High.

FEBRUARY 8

> Go, therefore, and make disciples of all nations, baptizing them in the name of the Father, and of the Son, and of the holy Spirit.
>
> **—Matthew 28:19**

Thus we hear the last words that Jesus gave to his apostles—no longer merely "disciples," because they are no longer merely *following* but have been given the Great Commission and are now *sent out*—prior to his ascension. This command, likewise reflected in such passages as Mark 16:15–16, Luke 24:47, John 20:21, and Acts 1:8, provides us with what is essentially the ultimate command for all Christians: that of evangelization. Spreading the gospel comes in various forms, but it is a foundational expectation for every Christian. It is vital for the Catholic school teacher to instill in students an interest in the international sphere. Students should know about the world, particularly in an age so typified by globalization. In the midst of this setting, we have an opportunity to bring Christ into the world, even in ways as simple as a smile to a neighbor or some other recognition of others' human dignity. The Catholic Church is global in scope, and our students will reliably benefit from awareness of global realities.

FEBRUARY 9

> [Give] thanks always and for everything in the name of our Lord Jesus Christ to God the Father.
>
> **—Ephesians 5:20**

Enter into each school day with a grateful demeanor. Make sure that your attitude is reflective of your appreciation for all that you have. No matter your school's condition, situation, or circumstances, you nevertheless have a lot for which you are still very capable of giving thanks. Why complain about having to walk to the other side of school to use the copier when some schools elsewhere in the world do not even have paper? Why get frustrated with an otherwise scholarly student who has not done his reading homework on one occasion when the fact that you assigned him reading signifies that he is fortunately literate at all? Why get upset when you have a full e-mail inbox when it means that your school has both electricity and an Internet connection, which is a valuable educational resource? With all of the gifts that you have access to every day, make sure that you are profusely grateful for each opportunity to use these resources to show students how to serve all others in a Christian manner.

FEBRUARY 10

O God, a new song I will sing to you.

—Psalm 144:9

Why are you afraid to be joyful? What is holding you back from allowing the joy that comes from following Christ to envelop you? It is very easy to fall into an attitude of cynical negativity, as if this outlook were intended to be the status quo, but God wants us to delight in following him: "Shout with joy to the LORD, all the earth; break into song; sing praise" (Ps 98:4). This does not mean that you have to skip down the hallways belting out your best rendition of "Edelweiss" from *The Sound of Music* (after all, depending on your vocal pursuits, your attempted manifestation of your own joy may convert a colleague's into acute misery). Nonetheless, look for chances to share your joy. Do not expect an immediate return on your generous investment. A door held open for someone now may initially cause suspicion of an ulterior motive, but the recipient will hopefully realize that your gesture of joyful consideration did not implу an expectation of reciprocity, and he or she may replicate the action later. Plan to be a joyous teacher.

FEBRUARY 11

> Be still and know that I am God!
>
> —**Psalm 46:11a**

The life of a teacher is replete with many preoccupations. There are many things that can happen on a daily basis that can reliably disrupt your joy. These preoccupations can come in the form of worries, fears, frustrations, exhaustion, exasperation, and so many other concerns. If you ever feel beset by these conditions, stop and ask yourself: What is my role as a Catholic school teacher? Who is ultimately in control? We may be tempted to fall into the trap of believing that a situation is so bad that we could not possibly overcome it. When we feel challenged by any variety of difficult scenarios, whether or not they are within our control, we need to stop and remind ourselves that God is God. We are not, and never will be God, and that is alright, because he lovingly draws us to his presence. God has command over our lives and will see us through our day-to-day endeavors, as long as they are actually oriented toward serving his will. Close your eyes for as long as it takes to recall to whom you belong. When you remember that you belong to God, everything else falls into place.

FEBRUARY 12

> I give thanks to my God at every remembrance of you.
>
> —**Philippians 1:3**

Beyond being grateful for that which is merely material, the Catholic school teacher must, first and foremost, ensure that he or she appreciates everyone within the entire school community. Thank God for the colleague who is a few seconds late to cover your class, because it means that she was able to help a student who broke down in the hallway over a serious situation at home. Thank God for the student who does not get the best grades, but tries as hard as he can, because he reminds you that there are so many who legitimately care about their learning. Do not merely try to appreciate others for the more obvious reasons. It is easy to appreciate a student who is always attentive in class, but do you likewise appreciate the one who is doodling because it distracts him from worrying about his family member who is suffering from a terminal illness? All members in a Catholic school community must be valued for their inherent human worth and dignity. Reach out to those undergoing tribulations on the margins.

FEBRUARY 13

Bless the LORD, my soul; all my being, bless his holy name!

—Psalm 103:1

Look for ways to dedicate every aspect of your teaching framework to praising the Almighty. From the moment you wake until the moment you sleep, consider how you can make decisions about your day that will bring greater glory to the kingdom of God. There are numerous opportunities every day to praise the Lord for his goodness. On school days in particular, ask yourself how your lesson plans can lead students to serve the gospel, both during the time that they are in your school and, of course, beyond graduation. This hardly means acquiring a drastic demeanor in terms of what you say and what you do. Rather, your mindset must reliably be: "If I am *not* serving the Lord with all of my life, whom am I serving?" After all, as Jesus affirms, "No one can serve two masters. He will either hate one and love the other, or be devoted to one and despise the other" (Mt 6:24; meanwhile, Luke 16:13 asserts "No *servant* can serve two masters" [emphasis added]). Devote every day to lauding the Lord God for his awesome goodness.

FEBRUARY 14

> Blessed are the peacemakers, for they will be called children of God.
>
> **—Matthew 5:9**

At all costs, avoid drama (unless you happen to teach theater). Catholic school teachers are hardly exempt from the Christian expectation to avoid gossip and any other pervasive menaces to peace of heart and mind. Heed the strong and direct words of Sirach 19:6–7: "Whoever repeats gossip has no sense. Never repeat gossip, and no one will reproach you." Unfortunately, the temptation to gossip is so strong that we are likewise faced with this stark imagery: "Like an arrow stuck in a fool's thigh, so is gossip in the belly of a fool" (Sir 19:12). If you feel compelled to gossip, have you ever considered trying "positive" gossip? "Did you hear about what Sheila did? She just led an awesome lesson on cell mitosis!" "Dan sure is a piece of work. His joke about how Jesus probably hovered over the water at bath time when he was little was hilarious!" "How about that new teacher, Al? He really seems to be a hard worker." Affirmation is an indicator of personal security and spiritual maturity, while gossip is ultimately puerile.

FEBRUARY 15

> Whatever you do, do from the heart, as for the Lord and not for others, knowing that you will receive from the Lord the due payment of the inheritance.
>
> **—Colossians 3:23–24**

Students deserve to know that their Catholic school places the Lord at the forefront of its educational mission. It is in serving the Lord through various fruitful capacities that a faithful Catholic school community comes to acknowledge that Christ is the source of all grace and true goodness. Students can easily tell if teachers are just going through the motions, or if they are genuinely interested and invested in their students' spiritual well-being. Therefore, make sure that you let your students express themselves when it comes to learning more about their faith or sharing their faith. This could be as simple as a student wanting to read the scriptural reflection aloud at the start of class. Other times, students might want to ask their teachers for advice on how they can live holier lives. Just beware of students who routinely ask, "What would Jesus do?" when you inform them that they received a zero for not doing the homework. Persevere and invite your students to really know Jesus Christ. When the Lord is your school's focus, you can say that your best friend runs the school.

FEBRUARY 16

> It was not you who chose me, but I who chose you and appointed you to go and bear fruit that will remain.
>
> **—John 15:16**

There will be times when you question your vocation as a Catholic school teacher. While not necessarily a good thing, this is a rather frequent curiosity, because we always seek to receive confirmation that we are following the Lord's will. Various holy men and women, including such prominent figures as Saint John of the Cross and Saint Teresa of Calcutta, experienced "dark nights of the soul." In fact, the spiritual powerhouse Saint Teresa of Ávila anecdotally did not even begin to take her vocation seriously until she was middle-aged! Your perceived doubt about your vocation can come in the wake of a variety of circumstances: jadedness after years in the classroom, exhaustion after grading your hundredth essay of the quarter, and so forth. However, this doubt is not an occasion for despair as long as you remember to lead your students to the knowledge that God comes first in life. After all, in the midst of a tumultuous world, we must recall Christ's words, "I have chosen you out of the world" (Jn 15:19b).

FEBRUARY 17

Blessed are the meek, for they will inherit the land.

—Matthew 5:5

Jesus' Sermon on the Mount is recorded in chapters 5 to 7 in Matthew's gospel and includes the Beatitudes in Matthew 5:3–12. The Beatitudes are critical to anyone who is striving to live the Christian life. The first two Beatitudes in Matthew's gospel are "Blessed are the poor in spirit, for theirs is the kingdom of heaven" (Mt 5:3) and "Blessed are they who mourn, for they will be comforted" (Mt 5:4). These two declarations do not relate, either directly or indirectly, to matters of teachers' pay or the melancholy invariably experienced annually upon the return to school in late August. Meanwhile, the Beatitude that makes reference to meekness reminds the Catholic school teacher of the reality that our job entails stepping aside and letting the Holy Spirit do the work. A Catholic school thrives spiritually when meekness and humility are thus encouraged, because the Lord and his will shine forth.

FEBRUARY 18

Whoever does not accept the kingdom of God like a child will not enter it.

—Luke 18:17

Draw the youth with whom you are entrusted to the kingdom of God. It is critical for the Catholic school teacher to provide his or her students with an accurate portrayal of who Jesus is. Nothing should interfere with a student's bond with Christ. So special are children to Jesus that the synoptic gospels provide three accounts of Jesus' teaching on the youth in the midst of the kingdom of God (Lk 18:15–17; also Mt 19:13–15 and Mk 10:13–16). In fact, Jesus reserved some of his strongest condemnations for those who would lead children astray in terms of morality. (When you have a moment, read Matthew 18:6–7 and Luke 17:1–2.) Therefore, you are expected to fairly and accurately portray the faith when relating it to your students. We do not teach anarchy alongside government; we do not teach alchemy alongside chemistry; nor should we lead impressionable students away from Christ. Be familiar with Christ's teachings, so as to lead others to follow *his* ways, not the world's.

FEBRUARY 19

But many who are first will be last, and the last will be first.

—Matthew 19:30

Jesus' momentously humility-inducing words of Matthew 19:30 are addressed to us by way of Peter and the chosen disciples who would eventually be named apostles, and they follow his famous encounter with the rich young man (see Mt 19:16–22). We likewise see his affirmation reiterated at the conclusion of his parable of the workers in the vineyard (see Mt 20:1–16). Thankfully, Jesus was not referring to the teacher who arrives early enough to make it to the front of the buffet line at the faculty Christmas luncheon. The Catholic school teacher must place the gospel at the prime position within his or her educational perspective. This is good to remember when lesson planning, even for the next school year. Placing God first will help you to draw closer to his kingdom, because the Lord not only suggests his primacy—he exerts it. The more you allow the love for the Lord to come forward in your life, the more your students and your entire school community will benefit in the end. And that "end" will be the continuation of his glory.

FEBRUARY 20

For everyone who exalts himself will be humbled, but the one who humbles himself will be exalted.

—Luke 14:11

Matthew's version of this account is preceded with Jesus' affirmation that "the greatest among you must be your servant" (Mt 23:11). It takes less strength to step into the limelight than to step back from it. The Catholic school teacher must be accustomed to the latter relegation. In order to bring his or her students to adore the kingdom of God, the effective teacher must retract his or her ego and let the Holy Spirit do the real work. Many, if not most, teachers go through their entire career with one job title: "teacher." There are no elaborate designations, promotions, or office suites for those who stay on the front lines in the classroom, courageously imparting their wisdom on their students for decades upon decades. There is not a *simpler* job title than that applied to an educator—yet it is hardly "simplistic." A teacher who attempts to go it alone, with prideful pretention and unwillingness to acquiesce to the ultimately refreshing will of God, is a ship adrift on a clear night with no regard for any observable constellation.

FEBRUARY 21

He restores my soul. He guides me along right paths.

—Psalm 23:3

The well-known Psalm 23 opens with this idyllically iconic image: "The Lord is my shepherd; there is nothing I lack" (Ps 23:1). Notice that a shepherd not only protects, watches over, feeds, and nurtures his sheep; he also *guides*, as we read in Jesus' description of himself as the Good Shepherd: "The sheep hear his voice, as he calls his own sheep by name and leads them out" (Jn 10:3). God does not merely tell us what to do in terms of following his will. He also leads us and guides us throughout life. For the Catholic school teacher, this signifies that our desire to follow the Lord will build up the kingdom of God in such a way that our students will likewise benefit spiritually. Lead your students to a true restoration of their souls as well, by encouraging them to follow God's will for what he wants them to do with their lives. Make sure that this encouragement is for both their time as a student and beyond. In school and otherwise, drawing others to heed God will lead to fulfillment.

FEBRUARY 22

> Say to the Lord, "My refuge and fortress, my God in whom I trust."
>
> **—Psalm 91:2**

If your Catholic institution is blessed enough to have a chapel on-site, try to visit it as frequently as possible, especially when the Blessed Sacrament is present. This does not mean you have to go many times per day, or even every day, but try to go when your schedule permits it and when you particularly need a respite. Make a special effort to visit the chapel on days that have not gone very well. In order to avoid teacher burnout or other scourges that can wreak havoc upon your spiritual welfare, aim to keep the Lord in your sights as the protector of your soul. Teachers have numerous stakeholders, and there are various onslaughts from all sides throughout the school year, but we can rest assured that we are on solid ground when we are beholden to the Almighty himself for our ultimate well-being. Do not give in to the temptation to think that you can conquer difficult situations alone, because this spiritual hubris is caustically counterproductive. When you read the gospels, pay attention to how often Jesus makes haste to God the Father to bask in his very presence.

FEBRUARY 23

Then I heard the voice of the Lord saying, "Whom shall I send? Who will go for us?" "Here I am," I said; "send me!"

—Isaiah 6:8

Be a true leader within your classroom. In other words, make sure that you lead your students by your example. Be the one to step up to assist. When you see that a student is struggling, whether academically or spiritually, reach out to help him or her in some way. This charity will show your students that they can remain confident that you care about their ultimate well-being. Thus, you can have another opportunity to draw your students closer to Christ. Responding to the call of the Lord to serve as a Catholic school teacher does not mean only spreading the gospel with your words; it likewise means sharing Christ's love. The teaching profession can be tiring in various ways, but each ounce of effort that you give in terms of serving the Lord by way of bringing your students to Christ will be repaid based on your labors in building up the kingdom of God. When the Lord calls on you to serve him, opt to answer affirmatively. After all, when he calls you to follow him, he has a certain response from you in mind.

FEBRUARY 24

If you remain in my word, you will truly be my disciples, and you will know the truth, and the truth will set you free.

—John 8:31–32

One benefit (of many) of working in a Catholic school is that you have the opportunity of fellowship with colleagues in a gospel-oriented framework. This is but one of various ways to "remain in the Lord's word." There is certainly true freedom that accompanies sharing and spreading the gospel. Knowledge of the truth of Jesus Christ and his will for you implies an awareness of his love, a love that is so profound that he was willing to die on the Cross as an expression of the fullness of his resolve. Look for many opportunities to build up your entire Catholic school community collectively through means such as attending daily Mass if your school happens to offer it, participating in community-wide prayer services, organizing a public recitation of the Rosary after school, and so forth. Allow the truth of the gospel to fully pervade various avenues of your school community in thoughtful ways. Doing so will keep your community open to the full outpouring of God's grace and love that he reliably wishes to impart on all.

FEBRUARY 25

> Faith is the realization of what is hoped for and evidence of things not seen.
>
> **—Hebrews 11:1**

Students come in different ages, sizes, ethnic backgrounds, sexes, personalities, family structures, academic abilities, and so forth. However, the one factor that all students have in common is that none of them has graduated from your institution. In other words, they have not seen the world beyond being a student in your school. As a Catholic school teacher, the fact that you are teaching your students implies that you have faith in their inherent ability, not only to succeed academically, but also to be able to follow the gospel both during the remainder of their time in your school and beyond your school's walls. If you do not have faith in your students, then you must question why you teach at all. Having faith in your students is ultimately a manifestation of your faith in God, because it is through your faith in him that you better grasp the reward of sharing that precious gift of faith with others. Allow your students to see the measure of your faith, because they need the inspiration as they make their way through their own journeys.

FEBRUARY 26

> The one who sat on the throne said, "Behold, I make all things new."
>
> **—Revelation 21:5**

If every time you read a passage from the sacred scriptures, particularly from within the New Testament and especially from within the gospels, you do not read something in a new light, then there is something amiss in your spiritual life. Reading the words of scripture, no matter how many times you have seen a specific passage, should renew your spiritual vigor. As a Catholic school teacher, attempt to find at least one passage, or even multiple passages, to rely on when you encounter a difficult situation. (Difficult situations are not just a possibility, or even a probability; they are a certainty, sometimes daily.) Allow the gospel to permeate every realm in your life as a teacher, both within school and in your personal life. Likewise, lead your students to recognize how knowing Christ will enliven their resolve to serve the kingdom of God. The matters of the temporal world are dull, bland, cyclical trifles compared to the Word of God. Through his teachings, and especially through his paschal mystery ending in glory, Christ makes everything new.

FEBRUARY 27

> Amen, I say to you, whatever you did for one of these least brothers of mine, you did for me.
>
> **—Matthew 25:40**

Many students are dealing with particularly challenging situations. It may be difficult to discern what precisely is bothering a student, but you can rely on your intuition to tell that something is wrong. It is vital that you communicate with your student's guidance counselor if his or her demeanor is such that it warrants attention. Thereafter, make sure privately to pray for his or her ultimate spiritual well-being. It is worthwhile for a teacher to encourage students to reach out to their peers who are struggling, lonely, or dejected, because then they are comforting Christ himself. In having concern for your students' well-being and that of their souls, you are serving them in a truly Christian manner. By extension, you are thus serving the Lord. Be the face of Christ to others by serving those whose uniquely challenging situations make them the face of Christ to the world. Despite the world's myths, virtue is contagious—help to spread it far and wide.

FEBRUARY 28

> You are anxious and worried about many things. There is need of only one thing.
>
> **—Luke 10:41b–42a**

We find these peace-inspiring words of the Lord within the famous account of Jesus' interaction with Mary and Martha. (However, those inclined to *act* rather than to *be* might deem this an *infamous* account.) As Catholic school teachers, we can be tempted to get so busy in the course of attempting to complete our multitude of daily tasks that we end up losing sight of our ultimate expectation: serving God by way of serving his children, our students. Educating, especially in a Catholic institution, should never comprise merely checking off a list of tasks to be completed throughout the day. Although teachers are not taskmasters, we are admittedly expected to be multitaskers. Similarly, taking care of responsibilities throughout the day is a necessary reality of the teaching profession. Nonetheless, take a few moments throughout the school day to stop and deeply reflect on how you can be sure to choose “the better part” (Lk 10:42b) by spending time with the Lord.

FEBRUARY 29

> This is the day the LORD has made; let us rejoice in it and be glad.
>
> **—Psalm 118:24**

Take some time to thank God for yet another day . . . more than once every four years!

MARCH 1

They went forth and preached everywhere.

—Mark 16:20a

Immediately following Jesus' ascension, his apostles had the responsibility to share the gospel. In a similar way, the Catholic school teacher has apostolic opportunities to spread the gospel on a daily basis. Students are not only open to hearing the beautiful truth of God's Word; they are likewise eager to proclaim it as well. Bringing the gospel to your students gives them the opportunity to hear it, comprehend its meaning, and share it with others, both during their time as students and after graduating. There are daily negative messages spread throughout society's airwaves, and it is refreshing for anyone to hear the gospel's truth instead. There is no limit to where the gospel can be shared, as long as this endeavor is actually undertaken charitably. Hence, make sure to preach with your actions, lest we have a Pharisaical practice: "Therefore, do and observe all things whatsoever they tell you, but do not follow their example. For they preach but they do not practice" (Mt 23:3). Bringing the gospel into the world is bringing faith, hope, and love into the world.

MARCH 2

> May the eyes of [your] hearts be enlightened, that you may know what is the hope that belongs to his call.
>
> **—Ephesians 1:18**

The Catholic school teacher must be an advocate for the true hope that comes from following the Lord. Along with the other two theological virtues of faith and charity, there is hope attached to your ministry of spreading the gospel of Jesus Christ. If a community lacks love, which originates with God himself, then it is literally hopeless. Throughout the day, look out for opportunities to recognize the Lord's presence in such a way that you can thus respond to the call to continuously follow him. A community filled with gospel-oriented hope is a community that is prepared to benefit humanity on a broader scale. Make sure that the hope that you spread is truly hope in the Christian sense. For example, although hope does not necessarily refer to expecting that you will finish grading your stack of essays before tonight's episode of *Jeopardy!* or that your faculty yearbook photo did not turn out as badly as last year's, hope does mean drawing your students to know the reliably awesome attributes of the kingdom of God.

MARCH 3

> For God so loved the world that he gave his only Son, so that everyone who believes in him might not perish but might have eternal life.
>
> **—John 3:16**

John 3:16 is perhaps the most well-known of all biblical passages (at least within the New Testament broadly and the gospels specifically), and probably for good reason: the author thus provides us with the most foundational statement regarding why God came to us in human form. Within the Catholic school, the Lord must remain paramount in terms of the school's framework of providing its students with the knowledge that God wants them to achieve eternal life. After all, as we recall in the verse that immediately follows: "God did not send his Son into the world to condemn the world, but that the world might be saved through him" (Jn 3:17). The outlook of our students should be a promising one, based on their recognition of God's desire to draw everyone to himself. Imagine if students did not know that they were destined for greatness. Thank God for having revealed himself to us fully in the person of Jesus Christ. God's love thus enlivens the core of every Catholic school community.

MARCH 4

> Do you not know that your body is a temple of the holy Spirit within you, whom you have from God, and that you are not your own?
>
> **—1 Corinthians 6:19**

It is not a vain endeavor for the Catholic school teacher to care for his or her physical well-being. Not only does teaching require spiritual stamina and mental endurance—it also necessitates physical health. Taking such measures as remaining hydrated on warm days and eating a solid breakfast and lunch during the course of the school day is important to consider when it comes to being able to get through the day. Teachers are on our feet for much of the school day, use our voices constantly, and sometimes carry heavy loads of materials. God expects us to take care of our bodies, because they are essentially the corporeal vehicles to transport us during our earthly voyages. Taking care of your body does not mean that you have to enter a bodybuilding contest or other exemplification of exceptional physical performance. (Anything that is publicized, students will discover, and they will get on your case for such a "spectacle.") Do not get run into the ground languidly. Take care of your body in order to give greater glory to God.

MARCH 5

> I will put enmity between you and the woman, and between your offspring and hers; they will strike at your head, while you strike at their heel.
>
> **—Genesis 3:15**

This might seem to be an odd scriptural passage for a teacher to reflect on. However, for the theology teacher, this passage is easily recognizable: it is commonly referred to as the *Protoevangelium* or *Protoevangelion* (Latin and Greek terms signifying "the first gospel"). The *Protoevangelium* of Genesis 3:15 is essentially the first promise that we have of the coming of the Messiah. The Catholic school teacher must recall that the Messiah has already come, and we are not him. Nor are applications open for the position of "Savior of the World." In the midst of our innumerably pressing daily concerns, we may be tempted to think that the totality of our students' well-being depends entirely on us. Such an outlook, particularly when it comes to your spiritual life, will lead to nothing less than exhaustion, depletion of energy, and ultimately burnout. Alternatively, rely on the Lord Jesus to be who he is: the Christ ("Anointed One") and the Messiah ("Chosen One"). He is both the exemplary leader and the ultimate Savior in all of our schools.

MARCH 6

> I am the bread of life; whoever comes to me will never hunger, and whoever believes in me will never thirst.
>
> **—John 6:35**

It is with this well-known passage within Jesus' "Bread of Life Discourse" (see Jn 6:22–59) that we are better able to reinforce our awareness of the profound sanctity of the Holy Eucharist. In essence, the Holy Eucharist is the sacrament that is qualified as "the source and summit of the Christian life" (*CCC* 1324). The Eucharist's special designation therefore stems from the reality that it is "the body, blood . . . soul and divinity of our Lord Jesus Christ" (*CCC* 1374). The Real Presence of the sacrament of the Holy Eucharist, within the context of the Mass, is the most important reality that any Catholic school community can celebrate. Whether you teach theology or another academic subject, look for opportunities to remind students of the special opportunity that your community has to celebrate the Eucharist together. Even for those who are not of the Catholic faith, mentioning the Eucharist is a supremely cogent opportunity to discuss Christ's crucial position in salvation history.

MARCH 7

> God created mankind in his image; in the image of God he created them.
>
> **—Genesis 1:27**

Every student is a reflection of God's glory. (Sometimes, they even enjoy reminding us of this!) When teaching a student, particularly a student who might be a real challenge behaviorally, academically, socially, or otherwise, remember that you are teaching a child of God. Our students' parents and their other family members love them very much, and they justifiably want what is ultimately best for them. God, as the Father of us all, loves us even more than our families, with a truly supreme love, as we recall from his words in Jeremiah 31:3: "With age-old love I have loved you." Students do not always act in a God-fearing way, and that must be addressed appropriately, depending on their demeanor and mannerisms. In fact, even the most well-meaning of students might sometimes let us down. Nevertheless, take a proverbial step back and remind yourself that you have an opportunity to share with them knowledge of their Creator, who wants them to model his creativity. To live a life reflective of his glory is what he asks of us.

MARCH 8

> Then he told them a parable about the necessity for them to pray always without becoming weary.
>
> **—Luke 18:1**

Jesus did not merely tell us to pray constantly; he gave us an example in the multiple times that he prayed to God the Father throughout the gospels, particularly in the midst of trying situations. The teacher is beset with an endless array of multitudinous challenges throughout the academic year, and must therefore ensure that prayer figures prominently into his or her daily schedule. When someone is stressed, busy, run-down, exasperated, or otherwise beleaguered by an overwhelmingly challenging set of circumstances, prayer might seem to be the farthest thing from his or her mind; but note that Jesus declares that prayer is a "necessity" and is intended to prevent us from "becoming weary." Of course, beginning every class session with a prayer, even on a day with an otherwise busy schedule, will likewise provide your students with an opportunity to refocus their attention on what matters most in life. Whatever your dilemma, offer it to the Lord in sincere prayer. He will answer it in his appropriate way.

MARCH 9

> I am the way and the truth and the life. No one comes to the Father except through me.
>
> **—John 14:6**

John 14:6 is one of those foundational scriptural passages that every Christian should be able to meditate on continuously. Notice Jesus' use of the definite article *the* (rather than the indefinite article *a*). Effectively, he does not provide any semblance of options in the midst of his sovereignty. As true God, Jesus is the supreme teacher who provides the model for all teachers in a Catholic school. In other words, Jesus' lessons are divine. Look for opportunities to inspire students to know better the divine person of Jesus Christ, which is an achievement that far exceeds the outcome of any mere academic exercise. Catholic schools have the chance (or, better said, *prerogative*) to draw students to know Christ's love and his desire for forming true disciples. When we orient our students' focus on the Lord, we are giving them the epitome of a lesson, because we are giving them the opportunity to look for ways to support the kingdom of God, no matter their ultimate pursuits beyond school walls. Let the example of Christ's life enrich all of your lessons.

MARCH 10

> But the LORD was not in the fire; after the fire, a light, silent sound.
>
> **—1 Kings 19:12**

When the prophet Elijah was waiting for God to manifest himself by passing by on Mount Horeb, the Lord did not appear in the grandiose, thunderous form of a strong wind, nor an earthquake, nor even a fire (see 1 Kgs 19:11–12). Rather, God revealed himself to Elijah in the diminutive form of barely a whisper. A school community is hardly the place where one might expect to encounter "a light, silent sound." You may be more likely to encounter peace and quiet in the cacophonous, jackhammer-filled atmosphere of a downtown construction zone or at the threshold of a major runway at Chicago's O'Hare Airport at rush hour than in the preteen- and adolescent-filled corridors of a school building. Nonetheless, the Catholic school teacher must find some semblance of solitude at a certain time during the school day. This solitude, spending time with the Lord in prayerful reflection, will physically energize and, more importantly, spiritually revitalize the teacher. It is in this stillness of the heart that we can hear the Lord's voice.

MARCH 11

> For as in one body we have many parts, and all the parts do not have the same function, so we, though many, are one body in Christ and individually parts of one another.
>
> **—Romans 12:4–5**

This passage from Romans is correlated to 1 Corinthians 12:12: "As a body is one though it has many parts, and all the parts of the body, though many, are one body, so also Christ." Each Catholic school teacher has unique gifts that he or she can share with the community. Teachers, especially those who recognize the special role that they fill as ministers, can celebrate the example that Saint Paul provides: "Since we have gifts that differ according to the grace given to us, let us exercise them: if prophecy, in proportion to the faith; if ministry, in ministering; if one is a teacher, in teaching" (Rom 12:6–7). One gift that every Catholic school teacher should make sure to embrace is the opportunity to likewise encourage students to use their own gifts to bring God into the world and to others. Every member of a Catholic school community has gifts to share to the benefit of others. Even if they may occasionally seem unenthused, students actually appreciate their school's mission and want to live it out.

MARCH 12

> Standing by the cross of Jesus were his mother and his mother's sister, Mary the wife of Clopas, and Mary of Magdala.
>
> **—John 19:25**

All of Jesus' other followers were afraid, scattered, in denial, doubtful. John's gospel provides us with the knowledge of who was there at Jesus' feet during his most trying ordeal imaginable: his crucifixion.

Only a few had the courage to stand by the Lord, without fear of reprisal or of a similar condemnation from the religious authorities in collaboration with the Roman officials. The Catholic school teacher must be similarly courageous when it comes to defending the principles of Catholic education, since they are rooted in the gospel and, therefore, necessarily stem from Jesus and all that is entailed in his paschal mystery. Any Catholic institution would do well to have a crucifix, even if just a small one, in each room, as a visual reminder of the sacrifice of Christ that bought our redemption and salvation. Also, the Catholic school community should be committed to serving humanity in accord with how Jesus serves humanity—by offering true hope to a world that looks forward to Easter joy.

MARCH 13

> [Jesus] said in reply, "It is written: 'One does not live by bread alone, but by every word that comes forth from the mouth of God.'"
>
> **—Matthew 4:4**

Jesus provides us with a reminder of this Old Testament passage, which also appears in Luke 4:4, within the context of his temptation in the desert for forty days (see Mt 4:1–11; Mk 1:12–13; Lk 4:1–13). The passage is from Deuteronomy 8:3, and it recalls how God provided food in the form of manna (see Ex 16:4–36) for his Chosen People, the Hebrews, while they were wandering in the desert for forty years after gaining freedom from Pharaoh and his forces. God knows that we require far more than mere earthly comforts in order to be spiritually fulfilled. Therefore, the Catholic school teacher should endeavor to achieve a deep, prayerful comfort with the words of sacred scripture. In other words, become familiar with the Bible—its key passages, its origin, its many implications, and more. The Bible is replete with passages to enliven our resolve, particularly on challenging days. In addition to sacred scripture, there are numerous spiritual classics that can provide you with reflection so that you can be better able to fix your gaze upon the Lord.

MARCH 14

> This is how you are to pray: "Our Father in heaven, hallowed be your name, your kingdom come, your will be done, on earth as in heaven."
>
> **—Matthew 6:9–10**

The Our Father is the archetype of all vocal prayers, provided by the Lord himself. The Catholic school teacher can only benefit from gaining a strong devotion to the words of the Lord's Prayer, by focusing and concentrating on every single word, perhaps using *lectio divina* as a prayer format. The Gospel of Matthew's version concludes the above passage with these words: "Give us today our daily bread; and forgive us our debts, as we forgive our debtors; and do not subject us to the final test, but deliver us from the evil one" (Mt 6:11–13). Meanwhile, the version in the Gospel of Luke (11:1–4) is more succinct. Try to pray the Lord's Prayer at least once per day (or more if you pray the Rosary), perhaps even opening your class sessions with it. Do go slowly, methodically, and meditatively. (However, when reading it from Matthew's gospel, remind your students that, not only do they still have to take your "final test," but you are also not whom Jesus was referring to as "the evil one.")

MARCH 15

> We love because he first loved us.
>
> **—1 John 4:19**

God is the source of all goodness, of all that is truly good. Love is the goal, the highest good, and God is the fount of true love. In case we ever waver in our understanding of what God's love truly entails, we have the Cross as our reliably emblematic reminder. What distinguishes a Catholic school community is its inherent love. A love for Christ should permeate every Catholic educational community, and this love should be manifested in how we interact with our neighbors. The gospel is thus readily shared and received. It is important to underscore that real love is not the fleeting, superficial, replaceable sentiment that is too often defined as love in modern times. Rather, the love that ideally flourishes in a Catholic school community allows all community members, whether faculty, staff, administration, volunteers, alumni, parents, or especially students themselves, to focus their energies on working in accord with the Lord's will. God loved us first, and thus our love for him must be our primary objective.

MARCH 16

> So faith, hope, love remain, these three; but the greatest of these is love.
>
> **—1 Corinthians 13:13**

Faith, hope, and love (charity) are the three theological virtues. Saint Paul's First Letter to the Corinthians expands on the primacy of these virtues within the Christian life by teaching that, although they are complementary, love is "the greatest of these." In addition to having faith in the Lord, have faith in your students' abilities to approach him; adolescents' desire to follow God is stronger than one might suspect. Trust and believe that they will use their personal gifts and knowledge, reinforced by their Catholic education, to bring Christ into the world. Along with hoping for the kingdom of God, look forward to the many ways in which your students will glorify God with their lives through their impact on the world because of the reinforcement of Christian values that they have acquired within their Catholic educational institution. Above all, invite your students to accept the remarkably joyful gift of God's love, which surpasses any measure of love that a mere human is capable of. God's love is supreme.

MARCH 17

> But those with insight shall shine brightly like the splendor of the firmament, and those who lead the many to justice shall be like the stars forever.
>
> **—Daniel 12:3**

The theology teacher (or any other interested teacher, for that matter) would do well to remind his or her students that the portrayal of God in the Old Testament is not entirely one of a God of justice devoid of mercy, and likewise, the portrayal of God in the New Testament is not entirely one of a God of mercy devoid of justice. The sooner the scriptural scholar in particular realizes this, the more he or she will be able to appreciate better the complementary nature of the three divine persons of the Trinity. Nonetheless, it is critical to recall that justice is ultimately the Lord's to exact. However, discussions of justice with youth should transcend bickering over who took whose pencil, or why the cafeteria's French fries are not sufficiently crunchy, into topics of justice that truly matter in life. There are numerous injustices in the world, whether against the poor, the unborn, the immigrant, the infirm, or other marginalized populations. Inspire your students to correct wrongs in the right way—charitably, with Jesus as our true model.

MARCH 18

> Before I formed you in the womb I knew you, before you were born I dedicated you.
>
> **—Jeremiah 1:5**

The life of every single student was planned by God. No person ever just happened upon the scene, and our students are no exception.

God gave each of us our very life, our very soul. The teacher does not ultimately instruct in an academic field; instead, the teacher speaks to souls that God fashioned. In the desks in front of us, we do not have such lifeless figures as automatons, cyborgs, golems, or mid-June beach-bound teachers; we have fellow people. Catholic school teachers must recall their unique mission to orient these students back to the God who made us all. Although everyone has free will, students should be reminded that free will is not a spiritual endowment to be disregarded; rather, God wants us to use our free will to follow him. Look for opportunities to remind your students that God made each one of them to follow him and glorify him with their lives. Ask them to reflect on what they will do with their lives after this semester and beyond, after graduating. Likewise, lead them to remember that God has always known them and will care for them eternally.

MARCH 19

Draw near to God, and he will draw near to you.

—James 4:8a

In these polemical modern times, one of the most significant challenges in society is convincing the world of the reality that God has abundant mercy and wants us to come to him to repent and ask forgiveness of our sins. If we ever feel far from God, we moved, not him. Returning to the Lord is made that much easier by his constant desire to keep us close to him and his will. God is always overwhelmingly willing to draw us back to himself. What does this have to do with the Catholic school teacher? Effectively, the closer that a teacher is to the Lord, the more his or her students will ultimately benefit within their own spiritual lives. Students are very perceptive, and they can easily sniff out both the richness of sincerity and the poverty of insincerity. Therefore, to reiterate, the nearer that a teacher is to the

Lord, the nearer that he or she will likewise draw his or her students to him. Reflect on the array of Jesus' parables by which he calls us to return home. Practice virtue in order not to drift away. God is as close as our ego is far.

MARCH 20

> Get wisdom, get understanding!
>
> **—Proverbs 4:5a**

The best teacher is the best learner. Think back to your own youth and educational journey. No matter what level of schooling you achieved, every teacher was once a student. Of course, many teachers are still students, including those pursuing an advanced degree, those enrolled in a variety of professional-development courses, and even those undertaking critical studies in a vain attempt to quantifiably determine how much attitude can fit in a classroom full of adolescents. The Catholic school teacher must endeavor not merely to strive for expertise in his or her academic content area or in the latest trends in pedagogy; rather, in the interest of the gospel, the teacher's goal should be to achieve true wisdom. This continual quest for veritably enduring wisdom, which is a hallmark of the Christian's journey, is easily facilitated in the midst of the classroom. Acquire wisdom by remaining open to the Lord's loving affirmations and to knowing his will, through sacred scripture and the Church's social teaching especially.

MARCH 21

> Indeed we call blessed those who have persevered.
>
> **—James 5:11a**

The third academic quarter can be a challenging time for any teacher. Depending on where you live, the weather might be particularly dreary and overcast, the energy level for both students and teachers is at a minimum, and still there is a significant amount of the school year remaining. Additionally, all of the school community's stakeholders, particularly students, are interested in beginning to critique the overall results of the school year. During this time, we teachers are drawn to inquire of ourselves: Was it a good academic year, and if not, what did we learn from it? For the Catholic school teacher, the set of circumstances that comprises the third academic quarter coincides with at least part of the liturgical season of Lent. Look for opportunities to offer up your rather diminutive suffering to the Lord, recalling in a special way that he understands our suffering. Likewise, encourage your students to use this time to grow still closer to the Lord. Increase your commitment to prayer during this time. Persevere!

MARCH 22

> The words of one's mouth are deep waters, the spring of wisdom, a running brook.
>
> **—Proverbs 18:4**

Be careful with everything that you say to your students. Watch every word and every nuance, ensuring that you speak in such a way that you lead them to know your intention and that you have their best interest at heart. The adage "It's not what you say; it's how you say it" is mostly accurate, but the terminology that you use is also of significant pedagogical importance. Many students, particularly the younger ones, will not necessarily understand manifestations of sarcasm or irony, let alone satire. Be sure to use language that builds up your students, and do not be afraid of clarifying or rephrasing an earlier affirmation, regarding content or anything else, if it was not presented well the first time. Also, be sure that whatever you publicize, whether on social media, in printed form, or otherwise, is ultimately supportive of both your institution and the broader community. Ask yourself: Would I be willing to display these words on my school's announcements board? In all, be prudently wise!

MARCH 23

> There is an appointed time for everything, and a time for every affair under the heavens.
>
> —**Ecclesiastes 3:1**

Ecclesiastes 3:1–8 has much greater value than having provided the basis for the Byrds' iconic 1965 classic "Turn! Turn! Turn!" (as catchy of a tune as it is). Time is a great asset for teachers. No matter what subject we teach, we have an overwhelmingly daunting quantity of material to cover adequately in just under a nine-month span, and admittedly a lot depends on us. Our lessons will have a sizeable impact on our students' futures. Our teaching will hardly be the most critical factor, but this is a noteworthy consideration nonetheless. We all have to meet numerous expectations and achieve countless goals in the process of helping our students to achieve their own. Although mired in the third quarter, the "desert of the school year," we must recall that the school year will eventually end. In the remaining weeks, focus on lasting lessons that you would like your students to keep with them. If you are an especially challenging teacher, reassure them that there is both "a time to weep, and a time to laugh" (Eccl 3:4).

MARCH 24

> Let your "Yes" mean "Yes," and your "No" mean "No."
>
> —**Matthew 5:37a**

Be straightforward with your students when it comes to explaining your expectations. Furthermore, beyond your own expectations within a course, be sure that your students are supremely aware of God's own expectations. We cannot be duplicitous in matters that require decision and commitment. For example, when taking a course, it is vital for students to be able to understand well the requirements beforehand, so that both true learning and resultant academic success are ultimately possible. Make sure that you encourage students to be honest and forthright in all that they do. Honesty should be the norm, not the exception. This is something that the youth, perhaps particularly adolescents, could benefit from recognizing. Here is a case in point: when assigning an essay, provide students with a rubric outlining what must be done to meet the standards, rather than waiting to see if they just happen to do it right. When it comes to Christian ethical principles, students should know the rewards of truthfulness. Use clear speech.

MARCH 25

> He it is who shall build a house for my name.
>
> **—2 Samuel 7:13a**

These words from 2 Samuel 7 are from the prophet Nathan, who was to deliver them to King David. Within Old Testament typology, this is, of course, a foreshadowing of Christ and his divinely eternal kingship, because the passage continues: "And I will establish his royal throne forever" (2 Sm 7:13). In indirect, but hopefully still faintly relevant, relation to this passage, the Catholic school teacher can reliably envision his or her school building as an abode under the Lord's auspices. When you step onto the campus of your Catholic institution, you are on holy ground. Therefore, make every effort to embrace the charism of the religious order (e.g., Benedictines, Dominicans, Franciscans, Jesuits), congregation (e.g., Holy Cross), patron saint (e.g., Saint Anthony, Saint Rita), or diocese or archdiocese (e.g., Fairbanks, Washington) that sponsors your school. Furthermore, be sure to instill this devotion within your students as well. With these special gifts, let your Catholic school community thus serve as a "house for [his] name."

MARCH 26

> I will thank you forever for what you have done.
>
> **—Psalm 52:11a**

How often do you take the time actually to thank God for the gift of your students? Particularly toward the end of the school year, when students can be tired of their homework, studying, and so forth, and teachers can likewise be tired of grading essays, refereeing classroom drama, and so on, we all must step back and allow the Lord to reveal to us the great work that he has done in our students. Sitting before us is the future. We do not merely need to "believe," but we can *celebrate* that our students are going to flourish in the world beyond our walls. They are going to have the opportunity to use the breadth of their Christ-oriented learning as they go into the world to make a difference that will highlight the kingdom of God. Reflect on ways to share with your students your appreciation for them (without stroking their egos or watering down the lesson). For example, you might invite them to lead a discussion on a relevant topic of interest. Cultivate their faith through their specific learning styles. Tell them that God has great plans for them, for which we can all be especially grateful.

MARCH 27

> Who among you is wise and understanding? Let him show his works by a good life in the humility that comes from wisdom.
>
> **—James 3:13**

There will never be a point in time in which the Catholic school teacher has amassed the totality of knowledge, let alone wisdom. As the saying goes, the more that we know, the more that we realize how much there is that we still do not know. True wisdom is a quest that is endless, and thankfully so, because seeking wisdom for the good of humanity is an endeavor that keeps us both informed and humble. Education and knowledge for their own sake hardly ever lead to sainthood. The humility that comes with true wisdom is the humility that allows the Catholic school teacher to be an effective minister to his or her students. Pompousness and self-centeredness have no place in the classroom, lest the focus shift from the student to the teacher. The selfless nature of teaching in ultimate accord with Christ's gospel ensures that knowing the Lord himself is the true objective, instead of some illusory alternative.

MARCH 28

> Do not be saddened this day, for rejoicing in the Lord is your strength!
>
> **—Nehemiah 8:10b**

The tenet must be reinforced, time and again, that being a positive person enlivens not only the individual but likewise others with whom that person comes into contact. Instead of simply saying, "Be happy," it is better to say, "Be good," because actual happiness and fulfillment can only stem from being a holy person. Look for ways to praise the Lord throughout the day. This does not necessarily mean having to walk around with a perpetual smile upon your face, because such an endeavor might lead others to recommend your enrollment in an asylum. Ultimately, make sure that different features of your demeanor allow others to see the person of Christ shining through. For example, make sure that your words, whether to students, colleagues, or others, are uplifting. Make sure to extend kind gestures, such as opening the door for someone with full hands, lending an ear to a fellow teacher who is having a bad day, and so forth. Allow your Christian joy to lift up the spirits of others in your community.

MARCH 29

> Straight are the paths of the LORD, the just walk in them.
>
> **—Hosea 14:10b**

Sacred scripture reveals God's infinitely divine plan, and how he wants us to follow him in all that we do. We are called to be disciples of the LORD who is in control of our individual destinies. The Lord knows what he is doing. The Catholic school teacher must consistently bear in mind that God is the supreme teacher for us all, and he wants to keep us on the path that will ultimately lead us to him. Reflecting on the Lord's Prayer and other passages within the gospels, including Jesus' parables, shows us that God does not merely expect us to follow him in a mechanical, robotic sort of way. Rather, the Lord "guides [us] along right paths for the sake of his name" (Ps 23:3). Jesus provided us with the perfect example of how to follow the Lord's wonderful will through the exemplary (in the truest sense of the term) ministry that his very life comprised. Just as the Lord leads us along the path to him, so too can we help our students along his path of redemptive righteousness, thus benefitting the kingdom of God.

MARCH 30

> You recall, brothers, our toil and drudgery. Working night and day in order not to burden any of you, we proclaimed to you the gospel of God.
>
> **—1 Thessalonians 2:9**

Teachers, particularly in the midst of transitioning from the third quarter to the fourth quarter (the proverbial "home stretch" of the academic year), easily understand the demands that are placed upon those who strive to be professional educators. These challenges are both physical and mental. It often becomes evident that great endurance is required just to get through the day, let alone the week or the month. There are late nights spent grading papers, planning engaging lessons, and pondering how we can develop a remedy for students who are chronically allergic to punctuality. Then, for the Catholic school teacher who takes his or her faith seriously, it hits you: thank God for this time. Thank God for the time spent working for the gospel. Who has ever spent an extended amount of time contributing to that which is good, only to regret that this time was not spent on more selfish pursuits? No aspiring saint in his or her right mind would dare. Your time will be returned to you in the breadth of eternity.

MARCH 31

> Try to learn what is pleasing to the Lord. Take no part in the fruitless works of darkness; rather expose them.
>
> **—Ephesians 5:10–11**

Catholic school teachers are called to expose students to the gospel. Especially if you teach a subject other than theology, this does not have to come in the form of direct instruction. Rather, make sure that both what you say and what you do contribute to moral clarity. The youth, particularly adolescents, are especially mentally disposed to incessant inquisitiveness, legitimate curiosity, and profound reflection—actually far beyond that for which they are usually given credit. If something is objectively right, explain why. If something is objectively wrong, explain why. For example, in biology or anatomy class, you might briefly mention why adult stem-cell research is morally acceptable, while embryonic stem-cell research is immoral. In government class, you might use history to teach about the overwhelming benefits of God's covenantal bond between a husband

and a wife in marriage as a good for society. Expand your students' minds in ways that will build up who they are as God's own children.

APRIL 1

The LORD is gracious and merciful, slow to anger and abounding in mercy.

—Psalm 145:8

As we strive to imitate the Lord, we must recall that a significant character trait of the Catholic school teacher must be patience. In dealing with students, we are interacting with human beings. It is important for students to witness their teachers exercising mercy. If a student has suffered a family loss, or has been away from school for an extended period of time (such as with a severe illness), or encounters any sort of other challenging set of circumstances, be certain to approach the situation with patience, mercy, and understanding. Do not interrogate the student when he or she returns, or otherwise show a lack of concern. On another side of the spectrum, if you suspect a student of having committed an infraction, make sure that you make the effort to talk to him or her before issuing any semblance of a penalty. There may be the temptation to be angry or otherwise unsettled, but it is crucial to listen to the other side of the equation before passing judgment. In essence, provide an example of self-composure.

APRIL 2

Jesus said to him, "If you can! Everything is possible to one who has faith."

—Mark 9:23

Every teacher must always believe in his or her students. For the Catholic school teacher in particular, this belief must translate into recognizing that all students are capable of using their lives to glorify God, both while in school and after graduation. That which is possible because of faith is that which is inherently oriented toward the full flourishing of the kingdom of God, not that which is for our own glory. This is an important distinction to make for students. For example, a student should not expect to get a good grade on a test for which he or she has not prepared, merely anticipating academic success because such an endeavor is allegedly possible. Meanwhile, a student *should* expect that offering his or her academic preparation to the Lord for his use will ultimately lead to the student's witnessing how the Lord will open up various paths for that academic preparation ultimately to bring him his due honor. In other words, students must know that faith should be accompanied by acts according to God's will. Pray for greater faith!

APRIL 3

Give and gifts will be given to you.

—Luke 6:38a

The Catholic school teacher is required to give a great deal, whether in the form of time, energy, classroom space, resources, sanity, or some combination thereof. However, this generosity will always be returned to you as long as it is ultimately oriented toward the Lord. This return will not necessarily be substantively equal, but it will be in the form of an outpouring of grace that the Lord grants to those who give in a Christian manner. Look for opportunities to give within your school community, whether to a student fundraiser, a campus clean-up effort, or a similar endeavor. Give of yourself to the Lord by way of the unique abilities that he has bestowed upon you. Within your teaching career, you will probably likewise receive gifts from students at various points, perhaps before Christmas or at the end of the school year. Make sure that they know how much you appreciate their thoughtfulness through a thank-you note or a phone call. Have an attitude of generosity *and* gratitude, because such an approach to teaching will serve to build up your community.

APRIL 4

> I have told you this so that you might have peace in me. In the world you will have trouble, but take courage, I have conquered the world.
>
> **—John 16:33**

There will come a point, or probably many points, within your career as an educator in which you will have to address a heartbreaking and challenging situation. Perhaps a student will tragically lose a loved one. Maybe a student will be dealing with a severely difficult home life. If the matter requires prudence, sensitivity, and confidentiality, which it invariably will, make sure to stay in touch with the student's guidance counselor. When the time is right, the rest of your students should be reminded, perhaps in broad terms, that life is filled with numerous categories of difficulties. Jesus promised us that these would come. However, we should likewise remind our students that we can always come to the Lord with all that we are facing. The peace that the Lord offers is not some sort of temporal, fleeting peace; rather, it is the peace of knowing that we are children of God, and he wants us to live according to his will. Students, especially carefree and fearless adolescents, can benefit from recalling that the present life will one day vanish. Remain in the Lord.

APRIL 5

> Be satisfied with your wages.
>
> **—Luke 3:14b**

Those in any career field should strive to live frugally. This simplicity is a way to remain closer to the Lord and not to allow worldly concerns to cloud our spiritual vision about what ultimately matters. Finances, of course, do have implications for economic justice, such as those that Pope Leo XIII discussed within the framework of workers' rights according to Catholic social teaching in his 1891 encyclical *Rerum Novarum*. However, such is not the scope of this consideration. Rather, Catholic school teachers should recall that we must ensure that we live modestly, in order to provide an effective example for impressionable students. No one will necessarily become monetarily wealthy by serving as a Catholic school teacher, but the lasting rewards of faithful ministry are truly priceless, particularly in terms of the opportunity to witness students growing closer to the Lord. Do not hesitate to shop at the thrift store. Read a book rather than splurge on a cable television package. Store food carefully so as not to waste it. Watch your colleagues teaching if you want free and educational entertainment!

APRIL 6

> For this momentary light affliction is producing for us an eternal weight of glory beyond all comparison.
>
> **—2 Corinthians 4:17**

Notice that Saint Paul used the phrase "light affliction" to describe the situation of the Christian living in difficult circumstances. No, Saint Paul was not using euphemistic language to belittle those who are struggling to live out the gospel. The Catholic school teacher may be dealing with significant dilemmas, perhaps even on a daily basis.

However, there is no trial imaginable that is ultimately insurmountable or otherwise unable to be resolved. The same is clearly true for students, and teachers must remind them of this, lest they tread upon some dire path of despair. Saint Paul knew that the Church in Corinth needed extensive guidance, and the "Apostle to the Gentiles" was always striving to be prayerfully patient, but likewise charitably stern. So too, the Catholic school teacher must make sure that he or she is supportive of his or her students in a way that keeps the students on the right path, filled with hope. Help others through their afflictions, and allow them to thus see a person who loves the Lord.

APRIL 7

> My God will fully supply whatever you need, in accord with his glorious riches in Christ Jesus.
>
> **—Philippians 4:19**

An unfortunate myth about prayer, which likely contributes to shaking many believers' faith, is that God does not answer our prayers. In fact, God answers every single prayer. However, his response to our prayers is according to his will, because he knows what is best for our souls and for his kingdom. When it comes to prayerful petitions, do not expect God to answer prayers that are not ultimately oriented toward his glory. Have you ever asked yourself why you are praying for a specific thing? Change the focus of your prayer to what will truly build up the kingdom of God, instead of praying for that which will inevitably lead to merely temporal consolation and eventual desolation. Do not pray for the success of your school's fundraiser so that you can get a raise and be able to afford 533,000 cable channels (at least unless one of them is EWTN). Instead, pray for a successful fundraiser so that your school can have more funds to increase its financial aid package for struggling families.

APRIL 8

> Enter, let us bow down in worship; let us kneel before the LORD who made us.
>
> **—Psalm 95:6**

The most important event in which a Catholic school community can participate is not graduation. Nor is it senior prom (let alone one of Mr. McClain's pre-prom bowtie-tying training sessions). The most important event possible is a school-wide Mass. The Eucharist is the heart of the faithful Catholic institution. This sacrament provides the occasion for a school to gather in a prayerful celebration focusing on the remarkable nature of Jesus Christ as portrayed in bread and wine, which the priest consecrates into Christ's precious body and precious blood. Although not every student in a Catholic school is of the Catholic faith, all of us are children of God in one human family and are therefore invited to behold the Lord's goodness at the eucharistic altar—even if not receiving Communion, which is reserved for Catholics in a state of grace. Invite your students to be open to God's blessings and to meditate on the vast beauty of the eucharistic liturgy, during which we unite with the whole Church to worship and thus adore "the Lord who made us."

APRIL 9

> Trust in the LORD with all your heart, on your own intelligence do not rely.
>
> **—Proverbs 3:5**

Intelligence is a good thing. Being exceedingly intelligent, coupled with possessing free will and a redeemable nature, is what makes our human species stand out within the animal kingdom. However, the acquisition or maintenance of a keen intellect is not a guarantee that God is being served and honored. Those of us who are historians are readily aware of a myriad assortment of historical personalities who boasted the epitome of a sharp mind, but who unfortunately ended up using it to carry out a slew of woefully dastardly deeds against their fellow man. Any Catholic school teacher would do well to ensure that your extracurricular personal reading includes reputable spiritual material, in order to supplement your additional academic pursuits. This does not mean that you have to read from Saint Thomas Aquinas's *Summa Theologica* daily. You should, however, read about the saints' journeys to Christ and be humbled by their gospel-centeredness.

APRIL 10

> We do not cease praying for you and asking that you may be filled with the knowledge of his will through all spiritual wisdom and understanding.
>
> **—Colossians 1:9**

Students need the prayers of their teachers. This does not mean prayers of exorcism are needed in response to the occasional seemingly demonic oscillations of a student whose grade in theology class has plummeted from an A to the "bad" grade of a B. In the fullness of fittingness, make sure to pray for your students. Thank God in accompaniment to your students' joys. Ask the Lord to bestow his grace upon a student's family as they deal with a difficulty. Some teachers are brave enough to invite drama-imbued adolescents to share their prayer intentions at the beginning of class. An alternative to this desire for two dozen vocalized requests to the Almighty that he convince the teacher to cancel the unit test would be to tell students to offer their intentions in the silence of their hearts. If their intentions are sincere, the Lord will respond accordingly, based on his prerogative. Infuse your classroom with prayer in various forms. Your entire school community will benefit from prayerful envelopment.

APRIL 11

All the earth falls in worship before you; they sing of you, sing of your name!

—Psalm 66:4

We spend too much time indoors. We do not go outside enough, to spend time in the midst of God's glorious creation. Teachers should use the outdoors for various reasons. For instance, the Catholic school teacher would do well to take his or her students outside occasionally for a class session. Encouraging students to marvel at the beauty of the natural world is an opportunity to lead them to appreciate God's gifts. We do have "dominion" over the earth (see Gn 1:26, 28), but make sure to remind students that the Church teaches that the environment must be respected and protected, not abused or taken for granted. Take the time to read Pope Francis's 2015 encyclical *Laudato Si' (On Care for Our Common Home)*. Ultimately, the earth is merely our temporary home: "They do not belong to the world any more than I belong to the world" (Jn 17:16), Jesus said. For further amazement, observe the rapidity of the students' realization that there is a direct correlation between a pop quiz being distributed and your being a "tree killer."

APRIL 12

[Jesus] is the image of the invisible God, the firstborn of all creation.

—Colossians 1:15

This may come off as trite, but always remember to remind students of Jesus' shared nature: he is *fully* God and *fully* man. Theology teachers are readily familiar with the term *hypostatic union* to refer to this Christological reality of the person of Jesus Christ within salvation history. There are hardly any new heresies, and those that often manifest themselves tend simply to be repackages of prior errors that dispute either Jesus' humanity or Jesus' divinity. This point may seem rather deeply theological for an otherwise easily digestible set of reflections, but it is cogent inasmuch as it leads us to remember that Jesus was far more than simply a really good guy, an itinerant sage, a part-time carpenter, or a food distributor. He is God incarnate. Lead students to reflect deeply on the implications of this reality that God loved us so much that he stepped down from eternal glory in order to humble himself, roll up his sleeves, and show us how to live truly moral, God-fearing lives. Emphasize to your students that Jesus is not merely a model; he is also the goal. Let Jesus be himself.

APRIL 13

> For the Son of Man did not come to be served but to serve and to give his life as a ransom for many.
>
> **—Mark 10:45**

Being a servant does not mean being a doormat. Nor does it mean being *servile*. Being a servant ultimately requires making various sacrifices for the benefit of others—particularly in Jesus' case for the *spiritual* benefit of others. Jesus was the archetype of this understanding of what true sacrifice entails. The Catholic school teacher should likewise endeavor not only to serve in various capacities but also to encourage his or her students to seek ways to serve. The world has far too many incidences of self-serving activities throughout various parts of society, and it is therefore in great need of the courageous witness of people willing to cooperate with Christ's expectation (not recommendation) of us to serve like him. Being courageous by taking on the role of a servant is so considerably countercultural that only the morally strong are capable of serving others at the probable risk of being suspected of having some ulterior motive. In spite of whatever challenges may come your way, persevere in your service. Be Christ to others. Encourage your students to do the same.

APRIL 14

> What profit is there for one to gain the whole world and forfeit his life?
>
> **—Mark 8:36**

Catholic schools do not exist merely to be "good" or high-performing schools, as far as academics go. They often happen to be so because they allow students not only to accomplish resource-laden exercises in cognitive synthesis, but also to view the broader picture of the present human condition in light of eternal truths. Therefore, any practices aligned with such temporal dilemmas as careerism, prestigious aspirations, unbridled ambition, consumerist branding, or otherwise illusory factors should be tempered by our remembrance of the role of Catholic schools in serving the Lord's interests. Take some time to learn about the contributions of such prominent figures in the American Catholic educational legacy as Saint Frances Xavier Cabrini, Saint Katharine Drexel, Saint Philippine Rose Duchesne, Saint John Neumann, Saint Elizabeth Ann Seton, Servant of God Mother Mary Lange, and Archbishop John Carroll, among various others—all Christian heroes!

APRIL 15

> Unless the LORD build the house, they labor in vain who build.
>
> **—Psalm 127:1a**

The role of an educator is to build up the student. The teacher who tears down the student, whether with his or her words or actions (or inactions), is the teacher who is on a destructive path, bent on imperiling students' God-fashioned souls. The best way to build up students is to remind them that they are children of God. If a teacher can win over his or her students by leading them to acknowledge that they are made for the kingdom of God, then this teacher is practicing sanctification. The Lord must be reliably present within the framework of a Catholic school, both in its mission and its day-to-day operations; in that way, both students and all community members are quickly aware that anything qualitatively (or quantitatively) admirable has God as both its origin and goal. If a Catholic school muddles its mission by committing the folly of either rhetorically or practically relegating the Lord to the position of an aside, as some sort of an asterisk within the breadth of its legacy, a tale of disillusionment is underway. Labor in truth!

APRIL 16

> The heart of the intelligent acquires knowledge, and the ear of the wise seeks knowledge.
>
> **—Proverbs 18:15**

Intelligence is a gift. As with any gift, intelligence can either be appreciated and used or be taken for granted, cast aside, or otherwise neglected. In the Catholic school, teachers must look for various opportunities to remind students that the gift of intelligence, if it is ultimately acquired and put into practice, is best accompanied by the necessity of attaining knowledge. Many teachers are familiar with, and disheartened by, students who are very bright but whose energy and drive are mostly lacking. Just as intelligence is a gift and a considerably good thing, so too is knowledge an obviously beneficial feature within the assorted goals of education. However, the ability and inspiration to use this knowledge to better serve humanity and, therefore, the kingdom of God must not be conceived as an addendum to any other educational goal. In other words, bringing students to verily know the Lord Jesus Christ should be prized, adored, and acclaimed.

APRIL 17

And the victory that conquers the world is our faith.

—1 John 5:4b

The Catholic school teacher should not ever be dismayed by factors that are knowingly fleeting. In the midst of the Easter season, we recall the saying, "After every Good Friday comes an Easter Sunday." If a set of circumstances is ultimately ordered toward the kingdom of God, then it will turn out satisfactorily, at least in terms of reflecting the ultimate will of God. Hence, remaining stalwart in your striving to live out the Lord's commands as the underpinnings of your ministerial efforts within the classroom is what will lead to "success" regarding the things that matter to God. Would you still teach a class full of thirty students if just one of them came to know how to orient his or her life toward following the will of God? If the answer is an unqualified yes, then you care, and you should continue to strive to embrace an attitude of service. However, be sure to aim to reach all students, of course. Stay on the course to spread the gospel with joy, conviction, accuracy, and sincerity, always grateful to God for his victory and our faith.

APRIL 18

All scripture is inspired by God and is useful for teaching, for refutation, for correction, and for training in righteousness.

—2 Timothy 3:16

Although Lent is a time of spiritual renewal, it is vital for the Catholic school teacher to recall that the zeal for this preparatory renewal to celebrate the Lord's resurrection at Easter does not somehow imply that a penitential practice should be abandoned once Lent is over. Giving up ice cream during Lent does not mean that, following the Triduum, the aspiring disciple of Christ must hightail it to Häagen-Dazs to load up on three tubs of tiramisù gelato (especially since the classic strawberry is much more desirable). What penitential practice can you adopt in this Easter season to further strengthen your relationship with the Lord? (After all, your own spiritual fortitude will thus heighten your students' attentiveness to the Lord's call in their own lives.) A reliably worthwhile practice could be to devote more time to studying and praying with scripture. Perhaps you might just read a chapter of the Old Testament in the evening and a chapter of the New Testament in the morning. You might join, or begin, a Bible study group. Remain receptive to the Word.

APRIL 19

> Know this, my dear brothers: everyone should be quick to hear, slow to speak, slow to wrath, for the wrath of a man does not accomplish the righteousness of God.
>
> **—James 1:19–20**

Has being angry, or angrily embittered, ever improved your life at all? Think deeply on this question, because it ultimately determines the trajectory of your mindset. Is anger productive? In essence, that which makes you angry wields mighty power over you. Frequently, the peripheral source of potential anger will come in the form of an inanimate object—a photocopier that keeps jamming, or a computer system that seems as slow as molasses in January, only to log you off faster than a photon landing on a cheetah. Peripheral sources of anger are inevitable, but it is the response that matters. It is also wise to think about deeper causes of anger. In all cases, it is vital for the Catholic school teacher to be exceptionally wary of becoming angry, particularly toward a student. A lot can happen within an eight-hour school day, but we must begin our day with a certain peace of mind, looking forward to the growth that can occur. A teacher's calmness and coolness will put out a fire more effectively than fanning the flames of wrath, even if efforts appear to invoke justice. Calm responses spread peace.

APRIL 20

> And his commandment is this: we should believe in the name of his Son, Jesus Christ, and love one another just as he commanded us.
>
> **—1 John 3:23**

Love for neighbor must permeate the environment of any Catholic school in order to fulfill such a school's ultimate mission to spread the gospel. Teachers must exhibit this selfless interest in each student's well-being by showing every student great care when it comes to the formation of the entire person, and particularly the soul, of course. When we plan a lesson, grade an essay, or instruct students on the intricacies of particular mathematical formulae, we have an opportunity to deliver to our students the message that God wants to draw all of them to himself, in order to lead them ultimately to reflect and repeat that same Christian love in their own service to humanity, whether during their time as a student or upon graduation. Notice that we are "commanded" to love one another, rather than "recommended" or "suggested." Our love for our neighbor is an elemental Christian expectation. Reflect on teachers who made an impact on your own education, and think about how they loved within their own communities. Love to the end.

APRIL 21

> I came into the world as light, so that everyone who believes in me might not remain in darkness.
>
> **—John 12:46**

The Catholic school teacher must avoid the possibility of leading any student into spiritual darkness. In a similar vein, no matter what subject you teach, make sure that you do not keep your students in intellectual darkness, which could impede them from using the totality of their ideally plentiful scholarly resources to respond to

God's call to serve him by serving humanity broadly. Encouraging a student to use all of his or her intellect is always in the ultimate interest of the kingdom of God. It must be stressed to the students *ad infinitum* that knowledge or learning devoid of morality-imbued intentionality is intellectually counterproductive and ultimately rhetorically wayward. Here is a case in point: a quick Web search can readily inform us of how many drops of water there are in the Indian Ocean, or how many world leaders of the eighteenth century were left-handed, but a Web search would turn out to be inconclusive if an inquiry were made as to the meaning of life. (Hint: it is to serve God.) Let his light shine, so that we can be inspired to remain close to him.

APRIL 22

> Whoever despises the hungry comes up short, but happy the one who is kind to the poor!
>
> **—Proverbs 14:21**

The gospels are replete with Jesus' call for us to serve those living in poverty. Perhaps Matthew 25:31–46 (commonly referred to as the "parable of the judgment of nations") in particular leads us to fathom more concretely what ultimately awaits those who serve people who are suffering, along with the dire consequences for those who do not. Poverty comes in various forms, including material poverty or spiritual poverty: "Blessed are the poor in spirit, for theirs is the kingdom of heaven" (Mt 5:3). Catholic schools have both the possibility and the expectation to lead students to serve the poor among us. Practically any academic field can invite students to consider possibilities for serving those living in poverty. In a computer course, students could learn how to use digital imagery to produce a poster for a canned-food drive. In a political science course, students could learn how to enact public policy to serve the homeless or jobless. Always teach students to understand that, no matter one's socioeconomic status, God bestows equal human dignity.

APRIL 23

> Not everyone who says to me, "Lord, Lord," will enter the kingdom of heaven, but only the one who does the will of my Father in heaven.
>
> **—Matthew 7:21**

It is important for the Catholic school teacher to encourage students to honor God's name. Pay close attention to how God is referenced in modern times—the unfortunate reality is that God is mentioned less and less, while rather objectionable language is elevated to the level of tolerability. In other words, God's name is hardly afforded the degree of respect that it ought to be given. The Christian position is that references to God are sacred, as are the name and titles of Jesus. This is, admittedly, not the Lord's specific trajectory in this particular passage of Matthew 7:21, but it is a worthwhile consideration in terms of how we must encourage students to speak respectfully, especially when using language that refers to God. Of course, make sure that students know that they are expected to reinforce their words with actions, in order to foster a greater degree of actual servant leadership. Students should know that the world will evaluate them on their speech and deeds, so they ought to use sanctified language and witness to their faith in the way they live.

APRIL 24

> But the tax collector stood off at a distance and would not even raise his eyes to heaven but beat his breast and prayed, "O God, be merciful to me a sinner."
>
> **—Luke 18:13**

The Catholic school teacher should encourage students to admit it when they have done something wrong. An explanation is due, in order to avoid a punitive outlook. Veteran teachers are probably able to recall at least one episode, or perhaps even more than one, in which a student did something wrong and came to you and admitted it, rather than trying to cover it up somehow or making excuses as to why it happened. There is a reason that you probably came to hold that student in high repute—because his or her courage, honesty, and other values came to light. Students must realize that we are all sinners. We equivocate. Of course, we should not plan to commit sin, because we have to answer for it, but we must admit our shortcomings so that fellow members of our community are not tempted to take the sanctimonious approach of the Pharisee (see Lk 18:11–12). In sum, recall that the youth, including adolescents, are far more aware of virtue and vice than we might realize. Help them to choose the former, to please God.

APRIL 25

> I came so that they might have life and have it more abundantly.
>
> **—John 10:10b**

Catholic school communities should provide students with an awareness of pro-life principles. Indeed, this is a cause that youth tend to fathom and support. However, these issues are predictably sensitive when it comes to addressing them, but they must be adequately discussed if our students are expected to be able to promote them once they step into the world. Discussions on pro-life principles including opposition to abortion, euthanasia, and capital punishment, along with various other offenses against the sanctity of human life, may be covered more in depth within the content of a text on Catholic social teaching. Depending on the scope of your course, at a minimum, encourage students to reflect on such life-affirming scriptural passages as Deuteronomy 30:19, Jeremiah 1:5, and various others. The right to life is the first of all rights. It forms both the foundation and the core of all other human rights, since everything else stems from the right to exist at all. Human life is a truly sacred gift.

APRIL 26

> Be free, yet without using freedom as a pretext for evil, but as slaves of God.
>
> **—1 Peter 2:16**

The concept of freedom can be a challenge to teach students about. Many people, students included of course, are reliably certain that they know the meaning of freedom beyond a reasonable doubt—which actually leads to eventual ensnarement by that which has been alleged to be freedom. Informing someone that what he or she has long held to be freedom is actually illusory at best or deceptive at worst can lead to an erosion of trust if the conversation is not carefully developed. Ultimately, the classical understanding of freedom, as propounded by the prominent Greek philosophers, is probably best understood to be, succinctly, "the ability to do that which is good." Essentially, freedom is having ready access to the practice of virtue. It is vital for students to know that God wants all of us to use our freedom to serve him unreservedly. As an example, freedom does not mean spending a study hall socializing with friends; it means using the study hall to prepare academically, in order to use the knowledge gained to help in the world, ultimately for the honor of the kingdom of God.

APRIL 27

> The LORD is good to those who wait for him, a refuge on the day of distress, taking care of those who look to him for protection.
>
> **—Nahum 1:7**

Remember that there is not a thing that we cannot offer to the Lord in prayer. We must come to him with our gratitude, lest we boast or otherwise forget him. Likewise, we must come to him with our sorrow, lest we despair or otherwise distrust him. We should not dare neglect the Lord in the midst of our well-being; nor should we accuse him in the midst of our tribulations. The most effective teacher is the prayerful teacher, since we teach who we are, and we want our students to be at peace. Striving to educate in a morally formative manner without being prayerful is like attempting to build an igloo in the Sahara at noon. Do not be dismayed if you feel that the Lord has not responded to your prayer; he will, but in his time and in the fashion that best befits his kingdom. Make sure to remind your students of the ultimate benefits of their shared reliance on the Lord, bringing to him all the cares, worries, anxieties, joys, delights, thanksgivings, or other situations of the heart. God wants us all to come to him in prayer.

APRIL 28

> Hear, my son, your father's instruction, and reject not your mother's teaching.
>
> **—Proverbs 1:8**

Although hopefully our students will not often need a reminder, make sure occasionally to emphasize the teaching of the fourth commandment: "Honor your father and your mother" (Ex 20:12). When we as teachers encourage and inspire our students to honor, respect, and appreciate their parents, it means more to our students than it does when they hear this perspective from other sources. The role of the teacher, perhaps especially the Catholic school teacher, is one that is quasi-parental but also obviously quite distinct. For example, if Lackadaisical Lenny stops doing his homework, we cannot withhold his allowance, ground him, or keep him from attending that post–Vatican II theologically discursive panel lecture that we just know he has been yearning to attend. In the same vein, make sure to keep parents informed of how their children are doing, not only in terms of their academics, but also regarding their bearing. Supporting both our students and their parents is a Christian compulsion.

APRIL 29

> Cast all your worries upon him because he cares for you.
>
> **—1 Peter 5:7**

The teacher is beset with worries daily. If we are not careful, those worries can engulf our demeanor, overtake our energy, and otherwise lead to burnout. Make sure to dispose of your worries, particularly by offering them up to the Lord in sincerely devout prayer. Ensure that your concerns and preoccupations have to do with that which you can control. After all, we cannot justifiably—let alone productively—worry about that which we cannot impact. If something is bothering you so profoundly that it is drastically affecting your ability to carry out your apostolate of teaching with a charitable and ministerial outlook, increase your prayer and take a more concentrated approach in it by both paying attention to what you are saying to God *and to what he is saying to you!* Rare is the person who has ever complained about praying more extensively or otherwise spending more time with the Lord. Make sure that you dedicate a great deal of your prayer regimen to imploring the Lord to facilitate your students' real well-being.

APRIL 30

> The wise by hearing them will advance in learning, the intelligent will gain sound guidance.
>
> **—Proverbs 1:5**

A foolish person is someone who has decided that he is wise enough and needs to know no more. We will never reach such repletion of either intelligence or its affiliate, wisdom. This is particularly applicable to the Christian, who recognizes that any secularly engendered wisdom that supersedes the true wisdom of the matters of God is illusorily conceived, fleeting, and bankrupt of ultimate substantial benefit. Not only should the Catholic school teacher be open to true wisdom within his or her academic field of study, but we must also seek opportunities to grow in this wisdom, particularly in terms of inspiring others to learn about the Lord and his goodness. The more that we learn and strive to grow in the wisdom of God, the more that we truly look forward to learning more, to knowing more, to understanding more, and to serving the Lord more. Every factor that eventually leads to true wisdom has God as its actual origin. A hunger for enduring wisdom will be accompanied by a yearning for Jesus Christ, along with truly charitable generosity.

MAY 1

> Mary said, "Behold, I am the handmaid of the Lord. May it be done to me according to your word."
>
> **—Luke 1:38**

The month of May is "Mary's month," a time devoted to taking time to honor, love, and reflect on the courageous Christian witness of the Blessed Virgin Mary. Mary, the first Christian, focuses her gaze upon the Lord and invites us to do likewise. The closer that we are to Mary, the closer that she brings us to her Son, Jesus Christ. Pay close attention to Mary's response to the archangel Gabriel in the Annunciation (see Lk 1:26–38; in fact, make sure to read the entire account prior to proceeding further with this reflection). Mary identifies herself as "the handmaid of the Lord." She is already serving Jesus even before he grows to encourage us all to serve others in the context of spreading his gospel (see Mt 23:11). In other words, Jesus' Mother, Mary, was essentially oriented toward understanding this expectation of Christ that calls us all to his service. Now, she readily implores her Son to draw us to himself. Mary's intercession is powerful. Challenging days at school may tempt us to scream, "Mayday!" but we should offer up a Hail Mary instead.

MAY 2

Amen, amen, I say to you, whoever believes has eternal life.

—John 6:47

It is important for the Catholic school teacher to have students consider the significance of eternity. What does this imply? Eternity is not that which can be conceived as "a really long time." Eternity is beyond measurable time and space; it is incalculable. Why is this important for the student? They may be led to think that they are invincible and are going to live forever here on earth. The older ones among us, particularly those who have gained a vast array of valuable life experiences, know how life is both short and delicate. It is pitiably fleeting. This set of theological circumstances does not somehow imply that we must place an effigy of the grim reaper on our classroom wall as a prop, nor that we have to proclaim the gospel with a "fire and brimstone" approach. Rather, we must bring our students to meditate on eternity gently, patiently, and charitably, thus inviting them to a spiritual maturity to inspire them to aim for heaven, attempting to better conceive of "what God has prepared for those who love him" (1 Cor 2:9c).

MAY 3

Before me no god was formed, and after me there shall be none.

—Isaiah 43:10c

The stark reality is that, one day, God forbid, your Catholic school could close. Whether you teach in a well-to-do Catholic school with a hefty endowment or in an acutely struggling inner-city Catholic school that is just trying to hang on, your school could eventually come to an end. The question, therefore, remains: What would your school's enduring legacy be in terms of how significantly it contributed to its mission of spreading the gospel and supporting the kingdom of God? How many souls (of both students as well as various other community stakeholders) would your school have made aware of God's love? This should not imply that a Catholic school's effectiveness can be ascertained quantitatively, numerically, or otherwise objectively to a particular degree, as if its evaluative assessment were determined by some calculable formulae. However, it does imply the expectation of openness to living the tenets of the gospel. Otherwise, how is a Catholic school distinct from other schools? God was, is, and will be. Catholic schools operate by his good grace.

MAY 4

> Each must do as already determined, without sadness or compulsion, for God loves a cheerful giver.
>
> **—2 Corinthians 9:7**

The effective Catholic school teacher is the teacher who gives to others. This generosity comes in the form of time, talent, treasure, or some combination thereof. When Sonorous Sara approaches you asking for a five-dollar donation for her choir trip fundraiser, she is not conjuring material for a comedy act by assuming that a Catholic school teacher has any more than eight cents in savings at any point in time. Make sure that your generosity is equitable. For example, some teachers have a policy of pledging a donation only to the first student to ask for a donation for a fundraiser within which many students are participating. If you are particularly well known by the student body as a teacher who frequently donates, observe how they descend upon you like faithful Catholics upon a free Friday fish dinner. Giving in terms of time and talent is similarly crucial. Giving in the vein of a Christian mindset does not seek a reward, an accolade, or a semblance of recognition—it simply selflessly seeks the real building up of the kingdom of God.

MAY 5

Better to be poor and walk in integrity than rich and crooked in one's ways.

—Proverbs 19:1

How much time do you spend encouraging your students to be *good* people? *Good* in this case does not refer to their grades, athleticism, popularity, or any other temporal factor. Rather, *good* as presented here in the ultimately more accurate sense of the term signifies possessing a framework of morality to draw oneself closer to the Lord. Students are pulled in all different directions in terms of others' expectations regarding their performance, probably in order to meet avowedly worldly standards of achievement. This does not mean, in the slightest, that a student should go home and tell Mom and Dad that grades do not matter, sports are overrated, and being a recluse is the way to live. Quite the opposite, simply make sure that all activities are oriented toward Christ. Support students' efforts to have good hearts. Those who have a clean heart and a clean conscience (which go hand in hand) will be "successful" in God's eyes, and that is what matters in the end: "Blessed are the clean of heart, for they will see God" (Mt 5:8).

MAY 6

By hard work of that sort we must help the weak.

—Acts 20:35a

Worldly thought (if that which is reliably deemed "thought" ever actually enters into the equation) encourages looking beyond the weak, downtrodden, and less fortunate in order to arrive at personal achievement. The false perception is that those who are suffering in life must have done something to arrive at this unfortunate set of circumstances. This fallacious argument is the very point that Jesus clarified in his addresses to those who were suffering, whether from illness, ailment, social standing, or other semblance of incapacitation that would have led to societal disrepute in the first-century Holy Land. Reading through the gospels, particularly the Gospel of Luke, gives the reader an idea of the special place that the marginalized have in Christ's heart. The Catholic school teacher must reach out to those students who need help to feel close to God and be virtuous. Likewise, we must encourage our students to use their God-given abilities to serve the weak: the unborn, the hungry, the infirm, and our other brethren in need.

MAY 7

> The LORD's acts of mercy are not exhausted, his compassion is not spent.
>
> **—Lamentations 3:22**

The Catholic school teacher should always remember to exercise true mercy to his or her students, whenever appropriate. Mercy must be distinguished from charity (the latter being a goal as well, but that is a topic for a different day). Mercy is distinct from charity because charity is done when the recipient gains that which he or she could have received by himself or herself, whereas mercy is done when the recipient gains that which he or she could not have otherwise attained. God bestows his mercy upon us in abundance. Likewise, the Catholic school teacher, in fitting consideration of Christian expectations, ought to practice mercy. In fact, merciful acts are such an expectation that they are not a suggestion, but a requirement: "Be merciful, just as [also] your Father is merciful" (Lk 6:36). Mercy is hardly some indication or manifestation of weakness; as with all sanctifying considerations, it is accompanied by the four cardinal virtues of fortitude, justice, prudence, and temperance. As a teacher, exercise Christian mercy.

MAY 8

> Do not fear: I am with you; do not be anxious: I am your God. I will strengthen you, I will help you, I will uphold you with my victorious right hand.
>
> **—Isaiah 41:10**

The Catholic school teacher may face various fears throughout the course of the school year: Will my students succeed? Will the struggling students learn this material? Will I get through all of the curriculum? With just weeks remaining in the school year, do I have a sufficient store of sanity to allow me to make it to the end, or will Billy ask to sharpen his pencil for the third time this class period? The Christian fears little, if at all, because the Christian knows of the Lord's ultimate providence. The Lord's providence is not some semblance of material providence (other than that which is oriented toward the kingdom of God); rather, the Lord's providence is his truly divine providence that allows us Catholic school teachers to be fearless as we carry out our role in sharing the gospel with our students. Our role is uniquely rewarding in that we do not have to rely on our own resolve by any incapable measure of our imagination. At various points throughout the school day, stop and meditate on the great work you have been called to undertake fearlessly.

MAY 9

> If you lavish your food on the hungry and satisfy the afflicted; Then your light shall rise in the darkness, and your gloom shall become like midday.
>
> **—Isaiah 58:10**

The world's "developed" countries are unfortunately reliably laden with consumerism, materialism, and a culture of waste that seeks the next commodity. The youth are often the targets of this destructive mindset, as we see in advertisements that attempt to sway them with the lie that they must have the latest phone, clothing, and other status symbols in order to be happy. This deceptive mentality is the antithesis of the Lord's will. Reading through both the Old Testament (as in Isaiah 58:10) and the New Testament (particularly the Gospel of Luke), we find reminders of how we are expected to serve the less fortunate. Look for opportunities to support initiatives in your Catholic school such as food drives, clothing collections, and other efforts that allow the entire school community, particularly students, to recall that the Lord requires us to serve others. After all, it is in our giving to others that we are met with ultimate fulfillment by acting according to his will. Teach your students to give.

MAY 10

> Then I will proclaim your name to my brethren; in the assembly I will praise you: "You who fear the LORD, give praise!"
>
> **—Psalm 22:23–24a**

Never fear an opportunity to legitimately share your faith with others in your Catholic school community, whether (or perhaps *particularly*) with students, colleagues, parents, and so forth. Your sharing of your faith does not have to be like that of the judgmental Pharisee in Luke 18:11–12, nor like that of the "hypocrites" or the "pagans" who want others to behold every display of their superficial faith (see Mt 6:1–8). Rather, allow your actions to draw others to Christ. Something as minute as making the Sign of the Cross prior to eating a meal in the faculty lounge, or telling someone, "God bless you," instead of, "Good luck," will invite others to consider ways in which they can similarly invite the Lord into every aspect of their own lives. You do not have to turn every trip through your school's hallways into a pilgrim's journey along the Via Dolorosa; nor do you have to commandeer the school's public announcements system to recite passages from Saint Ignatius of Loyola's *Spiritual Exercises*. Simply praise God outwardly, but truly humbly.

MAY 11

> Cast your care upon the LORD, who will give you support.
> He will never allow the righteous to stumble.
>
> **—Psalm 55:23**

There are times when the Catholic school teacher may feel alone. Maybe your students have been struggling to understand what life was like before Internet search engines, and they refuse to concede that people used to actually have to check out printed books in order to conduct research. Perhaps you are forced to stay at school well after the end of the school day to finish grading a stack of essays on the Council of Trent, only to be dismayed by one student's response that the Counter-Reformation required free samples of granite and marble. You might be feeling badly because a student asked you in front of the class what the twelve-thousandth word in the first edition of the Douay-Rheims Bible was, and you were unaware, so now your entire class has decided that you clearly do not know anything. In the midst of your starkly beleaguering sentiments, recognize that God is always in control. All that he asks in return is that you orient your will to his and that you strive to bring him to your students; this is your ultimate educational priority.

MAY 12

> I consider that the sufferings of this present time are as nothing compared with the glory to be revealed for us.
>
> **—Romans 8:18**

Suffering comes to all who are alive. You do not have to be a Thomistic philosopher in order to discern the fact that, because Catholic school teachers are alive (possibly to the chagrin of the students of more challenging teachers), suffering is inherent to teaching. However, suffering does not have to be in vain. Likewise, there is a grand distinction between self-imposed suffering and inadvertent suffering. For example, a teacher cannot wonder why he or she is "suffering" because those assignments did not get graded, when the teacher stayed up late watching old reruns of *Murder, She Wrote* and meditating on the risks of living in Cabot Cove, let alone why so many crimes occurred only when Jessica Fletcher was around. On the other hand, teaching while tired after having to stay up late with a sick child is a measure of suffering that we must accept and offer to God. Orienting your mindset toward serving the Lord within the broader framework of your educational philosophy will be rewarding. Stay close to the Lord (and far from Jessica Fletcher).

MAY 13

For whom the Lord loves, he disciplines.

—Hebrews 12:6a

Encourage your students to recall that discipline, particularly self-discipline, is a good thing. No matter one's pursuit, whether academic success, athletic performance, or some other goal, self-discipline is vital. This is perhaps particularly true regarding the spiritual life. Self-discipline entails mastering one's own resolve in order to be able to postpone instant gratification for a reward that is ultimately long-lasting and better. In modern times, instant gratification—typified by the expected receipt of that which is construed as a right (but is often actually merely a privilege) with a minimum of effort—is too often the goal. Heeding the dictum "God disciplines" reminds us that his discipline is a reliable indicator that he is ultimately the one in control, the one who knows what is best for us and for the ultimate benefit of his kingdom. Of course, to be fair, "discipline" in the school setting does not merely mean issuing a student a disciplinary referral or otherwise recommending some type of sanction; rather, it means inviting him or her to be a refined scholar and a child of God.

MAY 14

> Children, obey your parents in everything, for this is pleasing to the Lord.
>
> **—Colossians 3:20**

A Catholic school teacher should look for every opportunity to lead his or her students to love, value, and appreciate their parents. Parents send their children to a Catholic school for some good reason or a variety thereof. There are probably numerous intersecting rationales for why they want a Catholic school education for their child. Look for ways to lead your students to reflect on why their parents sent them to your school. Surely, it is not because they enjoy doling out thousands of dollars per year in order to have no desired impact. When a student's mother and father decide to send their child to a Catholic school, they have made a courageous decision to engage with a faith-filled community that will ideally infuse them with gospel values. The more supportive Catholic school teachers are with parents, and vice versa, the more the community will thrive. Leading your students to honor their parents will encourage them toward greater spiritual maturity, enabling them to better accept God as Father.

MAY 15

> And this is the testimony: God gave us eternal life, and this life is in his Son. Whoever possesses the Son has life; whoever does not possess the Son of God does not have life.
>
> **—1 John 5:11–12**

Have you ever thought about what Jesus would be like as a modern teacher, perhaps employed at your school? This question is a fair consideration, no matter the academic field. What type of grades would he give? (Actually, considering that Jesus was rarely impressed by his followers' responses, perhaps it would be best if he did not give grades after all.) Another question to consider is this: Do your students exhibit an undue preoccupation with their grades, to the exclusion of true learning? Although this worrisome mindset is human nature, it is vital to lead students to appreciate the knowledge that they gain, rather than the grade that they receive (although we veteran teachers must concede that this is far easier said than done). The goal is for students to acquire an education that will not only last a lifetime but also be used to serve humanity. Such is the expected outcome of a Catholic school education. Inspire your students to know that they have the unique opportunity to use their education to teach others about Christ, in the hopes of gaining eternal life.

MAY 16

For we walk by faith, not by sight.

—2 Corinthians 5:7

Until we witness our students walking across the stage at their graduation, it is entirely impossible to know if their time in our Catholic educational institution will meet this marker of success. No matter what type of Catholic school you teach in, and no matter whether a student is a transfer or has been there from the beginning, a lot can take place between when students come into our school and when they depart. This reality is a fair one to reflect on because it is safe to deduce that we must have faith in how they are going to use their time. Ultimately, however, our faith in them must translate into the faith that truly matters, which is our faith in God. Our students' status as children of God must inspire us to recall whose they are, in order to draw them to serve the Lord. Hence, we have faith in God in order to ask him prayerfully to bring our students to follow him, both during their time in our school and beyond. Courageously look forward to watching how your students can improve our world for God's greater glory.

MAY 17

They claim to know God, but by their deeds they deny him.

—Titus 1:16a

It is critical for the Catholic school teacher to watch his or her conduct, both in school and out of school. Our students are always watching and observing our comportment, and like it or not, it is rightfully their prerogative to do so. Anyone with good sense would be upset by the prospect of an environmental scientist promoting deforestation, or confused by a dietician giving away fast-food coupons, or bothered by a librarian claiming that literacy is overrated. Similarly, the Catholic school teacher, no matter the field that he or she teaches, must take seriously the impressionable nature of our students' psyches. These young people are looking for models for right living, and the stark reality is that adequate exemplification of good behavior in broader society is rather scant. What is on television often does not aid us. What is on the radio is replete with messages counter to the gospel. What is found on the Internet is too often devoid of any uplifting moral standards. Be courageous, and help your students on the path of virtue.

MAY 18

Let us hold unwaveringly to our confession that gives us hope,
for he who made the promise is trustworthy.

—Hebrews 10:23

Have you ever taken the time to think about what Jesus sounded like? By this, we are not concerned with his spoken language, because we know it to be Aramaic. Rather, what intonation, nuance, and turn of phrase did he use when addressing others, whether followers whom he was teaching, demons whom he was expelling, or specific figures with whom he was speaking one-on-one, such as the Blessed Mother, Simon Peter, God the Father, or even Judas Iscariot? It is difficult to imagine Jesus being unsure of himself, or appearing uncertain in his speech. He knew precisely what he was saying, and he never feared talking about difficult matters. So too the Catholic school teacher is called to have confidence when teaching principles to the youth. No one respects a duplicitous rhetoric, particularly concerning the important matters of life, which are invariably present in the spectrum of Catholic social teaching. When we have confidence in our abilities as educators, we trust in God's promises.

MAY 19

> Therefore, we ought to support such persons, so that we may be co-workers in the truth.
>
> **—3 John 1:8**

Seek out opportunities for fellowship with your colleagues. Just because you teach in a Catholic school hardly means that Christian sentiments abound so frequently that dialogue between two employees on a theological topic as simple as God's goodness can be taken for granted. Discussing the Lord and his goodness with colleagues places the broader picture into perspective, and it provides a buffer against an insular, cynical, or jaded outlook, all of which can creep into an individual teacher's life if his or her specific outlook is virtually whitewashed of any supernatural underpinnings. This position hardly implies that teachers should adopt a practically Pharisaical or otherwise showy or flashy philosophical demeanor when addressing Christological topics. Instead, ensure that all conversation regarding such topics has love for the Lord as both its root and its goal. Pray for all of your colleagues, as well as for their ultimate peace of mind (especially if it is their first year)! Help others to grow.

MAY 20

> They shall beat their swords into plowshares and their spears into pruning hooks.
>
> **—Isaiah 2:4b**

No matter what field you teach, look for opportunities to encourage your students to be people of peace, both during their time in your school and after graduation. The world is often unwilling to be the safe haven that a Catholic school ideally provides, and one need simply turn on the evening news in order to notice that there is severe discontent, turmoil, and violence throughout the world. Taking the time within your classes to pray for lands and nations torn by armed conflict, terrorism, gang warfare, abject poverty, and other semblances of civil discord is vital. Unrest can result from social ills that violate virtue, as seen in an erosion of norms of sexual morality, a warped consumerist ideology that captivates the citizenry, an acutely pervasive secularism that seeks to dominate truly free thought, and so on. This is the world that students will enter, and they must be aware. Lead students to rely on the peace of Christ, who is ultimately the peace that the world cannot give (see Jn 14:27).

MAY 21

> Son of man, he said to me, feed your stomach and fill your belly with this scroll I am giving you. I ate it, and it was as sweet as honey in my mouth.
>
> **—Ezekiel 3:3**

This is a curious passage within scripture. Its context, intention, and scope are worthwhile considerations. However, that is the topic of hermeneutics and exegesis. A point to emphasize here is that the

Catholic school teacher would be wise to seek opportunities to incorporate scripture into his or her course. While students will likely not leave your Catholic institution as experts in biblical studies, they can at the very least attain a budding love for the Word of God. Basic—or hopefully, eventually more advanced—knowledge of scriptural references will provide students with a vitally critical skill when it comes to dialoguing with the world regarding the Bible's seventy-three books (forty-six in the Old Testament and twenty-seven in the New Testament), from Genesis to Revelation. No matter your academic subject, teaching at a Catholic school affords you the opportunity to use the Bible for prayer during class time. Consume and know scripture!

MAY 22

> And [Zacchaeus] came down quickly and received [Jesus] with great joy.
>
> **—Luke 19:6**

The story of Zacchaeus is a thought-provoking one. Although Zacchaeus "was a chief tax collector and also a wealthy man" (Lk 19:2), he "was seeking to see who Jesus was" (Lk 19:3). In other words, Zacchaeus was a man of civil power, and he was short. Zacchaeus realized that Jesus was something (i.e., some*one*) new, and he was eager to see him and experience him. We are unaware of the totality of what was in Zacchaeus's heart as he sought the Lord, but we can suspect that he was open to following Jesus, since he even went to the extent of selling many of his possessions and converting himself to the Lord (see Lk 19:8). Zacchaeus can serve as a model for teachers and students alike, because Jesus wants us to follow him, and he is willing to meet us halfway when we orient our lives toward him. (Note that Zacchaeus came down quickly from the tree to meet the Lord when Jesus commanded him to [see Lk 19:5].) No matter our social condition, Jesus calls us to leave our self behind to follow his will.

MAY 23

> Those who offer praise as a sacrifice honor me; I will let him whose way is steadfast look upon the salvation of God.
>
> **—Psalm 50:23**

In a considerable way, every school year has its own legacy. This does not refer to a particular graduating class (especially since, after all, the Bishop McNamara High School Class of 2000 has been widely recognized as the best throughout educational history [see author biographical note]). At this point in the academic year, everything has quickly drawn to a close, leading the more contemplatively imbued teacher to reflect on what this school year has meant. There are still various uncertainties, on the part of students, parents, teachers, administrators, staff, and other stakeholders. It is during this reflective period that the Catholic school teacher has the worthwhile opportunity to become reoriented toward what the ultimate legacy of this school year and these current students will shape up to be. Likewise, it is never too early to meditate on how the next school year will go. What successes might be repeated? What mistakes might be corrected? In the midst of any school year, no matter other considerations, continue to praise the Lord with the fullness of your very being.

MAY 24

> At once [Jesus] spoke to them, "Take courage, it is I; do not be afraid."
>
> **—Matthew 14:27**

Have you ever noticed that it is easier to tell someone *else* not to be afraid than it is to abide by the same request of someone who tells *you* to give up your fear? In other words, it is easier for us to expect others' fearlessness than it is to exude our own. When Jesus spoke in the gospels, many (not most) people paid attention, but some listened to Jesus without *hearing*. A dilemma that humanity continues to face nearly two millennia later is the fear to commit to Christ's expectations for how we should model our lives after him. When Jesus tells us not to be afraid, his confidence is even greater than a math teacher's awareness that 2 + 2 = 4, or a band conductor's recognition that a timpani is part of the percussion session, or a theology teacher's knowledge that having a bible is always a good thing but having an edition of Saint Jerome's *Vulgate Bible* in the original Latin is an even better thing. Do not ever be afraid to remain with Jesus, and encourage your students to do likewise. Profoundly recall: Do you know anyone who has ever regretted following him?

MAY 25

> Desire without knowledge is not good; and whoever acts hastily, blunders.
>
> **—Proverbs 19:2**

It is critical for the Catholic school teacher to remind his or her students not to act hastily, carelessly, recklessly, or otherwise imprudently. Rely on the timeless adage "Haste makes waste." The tendency in modern times is often to want to get things done and get them out of the way as quickly as possible. This is true in terms of both schoolwork and a myriad of other life experiences as well. However, bear in mind that, perhaps quite unfortunately, it is much easier to *encourage* people to take their time than to be able to effectively *explain* to them why it is so important to slow down. Some analogies might serve you well when sharing with students why, both now and in their future careers, taking the time to do things *well* is vital. Ask them if they would want to fly on an airliner piloted by someone who hurried through flight school, or be operated on by a surgeon who rushed through medical school. Slowing down provides for deeper discernment in terms of listening to how God wants us to live, according to his will.

MAY 26

> For I am not ashamed of the gospel. It is the power of God for the salvation of everyone who believes.
>
> **—Romans 1:16**

As your students prepare to depart your course, take a moment to testify once again that Jesus Christ is our best friend, our brother, our Savior, our all. This may be a challenge for students to fathom, but remind them, especially as they continue on their respective paths in life, that God loves them more than do their families, than do their friends, and than Johnny loves his brand new high school sweetheart whose name he swears he will get tattooed on his arm when he turns eighteen in four years. Whether your students are planning to be the next great scientist, musician, artist, linguist, mathematician, teacher, author, philosopher, theologian, or any combination thereof, remind them of what their Catholic education has hopefully reinforced for them: the gospel has power for their lives. Make sure to encourage them truly to recognize that their enriching faith-based education is exceptionally precious in a world that so yearns for God's love. (Also, make sure to give an extra nod to those who want to be teachers, authors, philosophers, and theologians.)

MAY 27

> For you were called for freedom, brothers.
>
> **—Galatians 5:13a**

The Catholic school teacher must consider it crucial to remind students of the necessity of understanding the meaning of liberty—what liberty ultimately entails and demands. True freedom hardly means that we live our lives based on whatever whim or fancy comes our way, or that we rely on feelings or fleeting sentiments rather than reason, prudence, and sound judgment. No matter your academic field, draw students to note examples of historically prominent figures, about whom they have learned over the years, who have chosen to use their abilities to better serve humanity—whereas they could have used their free will incorrectly by carrying out self-serving pursuits (but fortunately did not). Students, no matter their grade level, will probably be able to amass a variety of examples of people both familiar to all and familiar only to a few who have used the gift of freedom wisely. Follow up by having the students share how they are going to use their own free will to serve the Lord.

MAY 28

> The revelation of your words sheds light, gives understanding to the simple.
>
> **—Psalm 119:130**

Never refer to a student as "simple" in nature or academic skills; nor should you ever use *any* deprecating remark, whether when speaking directly to the student, about the student, or otherwise. However, for the sake of this reflection, it is worthwhile to understand what is meant by *simple* in the passage above. We all have different intellectual gifts, abilities, talents, predispositions, and preparation; however, what we all have in common is that we will never know it all. Encourage your students to be their best. A long time ago, there was a little boy who was beset by difficulties in mathematics, and he has been trying to figure out that whole "Trinity as three in one" thing ever since. Thank God for having given us the ability not to give in to the temptation of hubris or egotistical enterprise, falling into the mistaken belief that we have the fullness of understanding of any concept, idea, circumstance, or notion. That having been said, we must lead our students to view the rich store of spiritual renewal that we can find in the Lord's revelation of himself in sacred scripture.

MAY 29

Whoever cares for the poor lends to the LORD, who will pay back the sum in full.

—Proverbs 19:17

One of the most enduring lessons that a Catholic school teacher can impart on his or her students is providing them with a keen awareness of their privileged call to serve those in less fortunate situations than themselves. It is typically easy to care only about our own needs, but the Christian is called to place the needs of others first. Along that same trajectory of reality, the Christian is called to labor for the Lord in such a way that our service to others satisfies not only their temporal needs but more importantly, their enduring spiritual needs, through which their souls will receive the fullness of satisfaction by drawing closer to the Lord. Students must realize and celebrate that there is no good that they can perform during their time on earth that will not contribute to the building up of the kingdom of God; thus, no good deed escapes the notice of the Lord, who has asked us to follow him and has simultaneously provided us with the epitome of righteousness in the life of Christ.

MAY 30

Enter through the narrow gate; for the gate is wide and the road broad that leads to destruction, and those who enter through it are many.

—Matthew 7:13

In this passage, Jesus continues by reminding us: "How narrow the gate and constricted the road that leads to life. And those who find it are few" (Mt 7:14). Students must know that none of us, in an attempt to follow Christ, can blaze our own trail by deciding that our own will supersedes the Lord's. This destructive mentality will lead to dissatisfaction, misery, and despair. Hence, it is critical that we take the time to study Christian principles in order to do our best to follow God's will. There are many temptations that can lead us astray, distracting us from following the Lord, but we must recall that living as a Christian, whether in the twenty-first century or otherwise, has never been without challenges and difficulties. Yet, the Christian life has likewise never been without the promise of grace and ultimate spiritual delight by living as a disciple of Christ. The closer that we stay to the Lord, the happier and more satisfied we will be. The farther that we stray from the Lord, the more our hearts will ache until we return to him again.

MAY 31

> For the Lord sets a father in honor over his children and confirms a mother's authority over her sons.
>
> **—Sirach 3:2**

Do not allow your students to close the school year without their extending some gesture of gratitude to their parents for all that they have done to nurture them, both in their support of their child's academic path and even more in the loving care they have provided. Students would do well always to remember the innumerable ways in which their parents have supported them. In leading students to reflect on what their own parents have done for them, they are thus drawn to reflect further upon the manifold ways in which our ultimate parent, God the Father, has poured out his love for us in order to show us how seriously he wants us to follow him and stay close to him. We hope thus to draw others to him in the process of evangelization. The fullness of God's love, of course, was manifested by Christ's paschal mystery. As we close May, the month of Mary, invite your students to reflect further on the eternal rewards that await those who follow her Son, the Lord Jesus Christ. Thank God for his gifts upon humanity, including the example of Mary's faith.

JUNE 1

> You are my shelter; you guard me from distress; with joyful shouts of deliverance you surround me.
>
> **—Psalm 32:7**

The beginning of June ubiquitously means the same thing to all teachers: you have arrived at the home stretch, and the school year is either over or nearly over. Whether you are a novice teacher or a veteran educator, you have "made it." However, before you prepare to put away your last green grading pen (or red grading pen, if you are the type who likes to inspire more intimidation in your students), make sure that you take some time to reflect on the many ways that the Lord has blessed you this year. These blessings will undoubtedly include the times when the Lord provided you with rest, respite, and protection from despair, in order to allow you to be as effective as possible in serving his kingdom. No matter whether the shouts that surrounded you this school year comprised shouts of deliverance or screeches of discontent from students who feared that they could take no more from their teacher, one reality remains: you shall learn from this school year. Plan to listen to what God has to say to you about the past school year, and promise to listen to him even more in the coming school year.

JUNE 2

> Even to your old age I am he, even when your hair is gray I will carry you; I have done this, and I will lift you up, I will carry you to safety.
>
> **—Isaiah 46:4**

One of the most enduring lessons that a Catholic school teacher can instill in his or her students is the particular awareness that God will never change. God's faithfulness to us is unwavering. In the Old Testament, we see God's constant fidelity through his covenants with the figures of Adam and Noah in sacred myth, as well as Abraham, Moses, and David in history. In the New Testament, God offered his covenant *par excellence* with humanity by coming to us in the person of his Son, Jesus Christ. In this passage from the prophet Isaiah, we are reminded of how God always abides with us. If we ever feel far from him, it is never because he moved away from us, because he will not; it is because we moved away from him! Invite your students to meditate upon this reality. Any seasoned teacher can show you the gray hairs earned from students who have been, to use a judicious term, "mischievous." No matter any student's disposition, it is the priority of the Catholic school teacher to draw students to God and also to encourage them to remain with him.

JUNE 3

> God is faithful, and by him you were called to fellowship with his Son, Jesus Christ our Lord.
>
> **—1 Corinthians 1:9**

Fellowship does not always have to take place within the context of a prayer meeting, a Bible study, a conference, a retreat, or another setting that is specifically organized around discussing faith matters with fellow disciples. After all, fellowship, sometimes even the most formative fellowship, can occur in an unplanned scenario. Be open to opportunities for fellowship with colleagues in your Catholic school. These opportunities can take place at the lunch table, in the hallway between classes, at the copier while one of you is removing a paper jam caused by a rookie teacher who tried to photocopy the *Summa Theologica*, and so forth. Similarly, when former students come back to visit you at school, be sure to ask them how their faith life is doing. This is supremely important for students who are currently in college, where their faith experience can either be enhanced by ministerial involvement or stifled by forces of secularism. Indeed, no saint in heaven loved God *too* much!

JUNE 4

> If I speak in human and angelic tongues, but do not have love,
> I am a resounding gong or a clashing cymbal.
>
> **—1 Corinthians 13:1**

Do not fill your students' ears with useless noise. In other words, do not waste your time or theirs by providing them with anything less than an education underscored by the knowledge that they are children of the Father. A student may be unaware of (or unmoved by) how many degrees you have, or how many years of teaching experience you have, or how many professional-development conferences you have attended. However, what a student does know is whether you are teaching from the heart, with a deep love for the Lord, passion for your content area, and appreciation for him or her as a person journeying to God. It is crucial to allow students to see our faith lives insofar as they are uplifting and oriented toward serving the Lord. Never miss an opportunity to pray for your students by name, especially those who are suffering. Students can tell if you care about their well-being. Just as a catchy tune gets stuck in your head, make the gracious melody of Christ's love get stuck in the *hearts* of your students.

JUNE 5

As for me and my household, we will serve the Lord.

—Joshua 24:15b

A teacher's service to the Lord is enhanced by the support of his or her school community, such as administrators, faculty, staff, students, and parents. Living a life in service to Christ (and thus the kingdom of God) will constantly be fraught with challenges, and the world is infrequently open to the notion of the actually transcendent, let alone Christian principles, even in a broad sense. Let us recall the dictum with which Jesus closed his Beatitudes in Matthew's gospel: "Blessed are they who are persecuted for the sake of righteousness, for theirs is the kingdom of heaven. Blessed are you when they insult you and persecute you and utter every kind of evil against you [falsely] because of me. Rejoice and be glad, for your reward will be great in heaven. Thus they persecuted the prophets who were before you" (Mt 5:10–12). Remind your students that—as they will find out sooner rather than later in their futures—following God does not promise temporal rewards, but eternal ones. Serve the Lord!

JUNE 6

You are the salt of the earth.

—Matthew 5:13a

It is not conventional to reflect on the significance of the element of salt. The good chemistry student is familiar with NaCl—sodium chloride—but what is it really? Salt can actually often have rather negative connotations, such as its being unhealthy or bland. However, Christ uses the imagery of salt nonetheless, and we are reminded that salt both preserves and enhances. The preservation of the gospel, passing it along to future generations, is a gem of an opportunity in which Christians have the chance to evangelize and spread God's

Word. Likewise, Christians should enhance the world by living a life in accord with God's will. These two factors relate to the Catholic school teacher because he or she is able to rejoice as, at the close of each school year, students prepare to depart the classroom or school community with the renewed ability, the distinct *treasure* of an opportunity, to dedicate themselves to serving humanity broadly.

JUNE 7

Yet in your great mercy you did not forsake them in the desert.

—Nehemiah 9:19a

Around the conclusion of each school year, teachers may feel as if they are going to collapse. With the weight of the year upon your shoulders, do not despair. Remember that the students are similarly exhausted. We must recall that the Lord offers us repose. However, this repose is not some semblance of a temporal rest. Jesus is not interested in providing us with a programmable bed, flannel sheets, or a contoured mattress (as worthwhile as these may be, especially after being on your feet teaching all day, only to go home and read a student's opinion essay about how he is going to be a teacher when he grows up because teachers have it "easy"). God gives us what we need in serving him, and he is always drawing us to persevere during the difficulties of our spiritual journey. His store of inspiration for his followers, especially when beset by spiritual challenges, is superabundant: "My cup overflows" (Ps 23:5b). Just as God watched over the Hebrews in the desert, he likewise guides and invigorates his faithful.

JUNE 8

Seek me, that you may live.

—Amos 5:4b

Far from a suggestion or a recommendation, God has given us the *command* to "seek" him. However, we must recall that our *seeking* him never implies that *he* is somehow the one who went astray—it was *us* who wandered away, through our sin. Seeking God does not require a GPS or Internet directions that end up having you make seventy-four turns in the process of driving 0.2 miles down a straight street. Let us recall Jesus' teachings on how he pursues those who have neglected his offer of salvation. For example, this idea is illustrated in three parables that are successively nestled within chapter 15 of Luke's gospel: the parable of the lost sheep (see Lk 15:1–7), the parable of the lost coin (see Lk 15:8–10), and the parable of the prodigal son (see Lk 15:11–32). Read and deeply reflect on these. If we as Catholic school teachers take our role seriously, and are thus called to imitate Christ, then we too must go after those "lost" students who feel far from God's presence. Similarly, we should encourage our students to use their futures to bring others "back home," inviting them to the font of eternal life.

JUNE 9

> Do not fear, for I have redeemed you; I have called you by name: you are mine.
>
> **—Isaiah 43:1b**

One of the best practices for the Catholic school teacher to adopt, whether at the close of one school year or at the beginning of a new school year, is to (1) remind yourself that your students are merely passing through your school, and (2) remind your students that they are merely passing through your school. In other words, both you *and* they need such a reminder because education is a process—and Catholic education is even more so, since it is a journey whose goal is eternal life. If we are the Lord's, then we must live as if we are. God wants us to remain close to him, because we are his. Because your students are, of course, also the Lord's, remember always to hold them to that standard of discipleship. In other words, encourage them to take their status as children of God seriously. Some students will naturally listen to your instruction, whereas others will be more interested in advancing adolescent pursuits. No matter your students' dispositions, always pray for them to be open to God's calling.

JUNE 10

> Welcome anyone who is weak in faith, but not for disputes over opinions.
>
> **—Romans 14:1**

People have their own strong opinions. No one is more keenly aware of this than the teacher. Students are opinionated. Adults are also opinionated. Admit it, we all are. However, the key factor to remember is that, while matters of opinion are of import, clear thinking is vital to your teaching. A mere opinion is ultimately inconsequential. For example, Tommy may opine that blue ink is more appealing than black ink. He may even have the opinion that writing "Mr. McClain is ugly" in black ink is unacceptable whereas using blue ink to write such a statement (the veracity or speciousness of which we must set aside for the time being) is somehow regarded as tolerable. Look for opportunities to emphasize to students the vast importance of recognizing objectivity and truth. We live in an age of moral relativism, in which anyone's opinion is held to be worthy of ethical deliberation. Strengthen others' faith by sharing the Lord's goodness with them.

JUNE 11

> The LORD is king, the peoples tremble.
>
> **—Psalm 99:1a**

Fear of the Lord is a good thing. We are reminded of this when we read and profoundly reflect upon various scriptural passages, particularly in the Old Testament. However, we must recall that fearing God does not mean "being afraid" of God; it means devoting our utmost respect to him as the Almighty. Similarly, it is better for the Catholic school teacher to be *respected* than *feared.* This is because respect *forms*, while fear *controls*. Respect is manifested by such a gesture as students listening attentively to a geometry teacher discussing the Pythagorean theorem because they recognize the teacher's expertise and desire for them to learn and succeed. Meanwhile, down the hallway, students are in frightful agony because Mr. Todd the Tyrant is berating them for not understanding what "they should know by now." The good Catholic school teacher effectively educates by both living and teaching with virtue. We should remind our students that we manifest our fear of the Lord through our love and respect for one another.

JUNE 12

> Who will not fear you, LORD, or glorify your name? For you alone are holy.
>
> **—Revelation 15:4**

Jesus Christ, as God incarnate, serves as our model of unobstructed virtue, of the fullness of divinity, of moral perfection. In the anecdotal words of a wise priest, "The Church already has a Messiah, and we are not him." Nevertheless, we must recall the high standard to which Jesus holds us: "So be perfect, just as your heavenly Father is perfect" (Mt 5:48). Lest the reader be more confused than a theology teacher grading an essay on how the authorship of the three synoptic gospels was a concerted effort by myopic ophthalmologists, is Jesus implying here that we too can somehow achieve divinity? No. Will we reach spiritual perfection? No. Nonetheless, it is in our striving that we are the most open to God's grace. The Catholic school teacher must bear in mind that we should be thankful that God came to us in human form, in order to provide us once and for all with "the image of the invisible God" (Col 1:15). By reflecting on God's supreme sanctity, both we, as teachers, and our students can grow in humility.

JUNE 13

> For I know well the plans I have in mind for you . . . plans for your welfare and not for woe, so as to give you a future of hope.
>
> **—Jeremiah 29:11**

Seek out various opportunities to remind your students that they are made for veritable greatness. However, this does not mean they should expect success in worldly matters, such as riches, popularity, or power. Rather, this *greatness* refers to saintliness, holiness, and virtue. The most fulfilling hope that we can have, based on the plans that God has for us, is to participate one day in the kingdom of God. The ultimate destination of our souls is, of course, for the Lord to decide, based on his own determination. There is no "celestial supreme court" to whom we could appeal. Therefore, we must live our lives in accordance with his will, because using our free will to honor and serve him is what constitutes abiding by his plans. Provide your students with an ongoing awareness that the future is something to look forward to, and a future replete with hope in Christ is the type of future that we must aim for. Students have the right to know that their teachers support them in the midst of their striving for God's kingdom.

JUNE 14

> Do not wear yourself out to gain wealth, cease to be worried about it.
>
> **—Proverbs 23:4**

A Catholic school teacher attempting to gain wealth is like an astronomer attempting to find another sun in our solar system—it just will not happen. But we do not teach for the money. On a related note, the person who has had even a modicum of life experience can attest that people who are good and virtuous are happy people. People who are consumed by things, by stuff, by foolish pursuits, are not satisfied by what they have. Is it not true that those who *have* more are those who still *want* more? They suffer from an insatiable desire. If you are having difficulty following this logic, think of the many fallen CEOs, political rulers, and entertainers who were met with ruin because they wanted "just a little more"—more money, more power, more influence. The point is that we must remind our students that wealth is not wrong in and of itself (reflecting on the many saints who came from nobility, but were selflessly generous with all of their resources). Hence, any aspiration must be accompanied by discernment of how to serve God in the process.

JUNE 15

> I raise my eyes toward the mountains. From whence shall come my help? My help comes from the LORD, the maker of heaven and earth.
>
> **—Psalm 121:1–2**

At this point in the calendar year, you have either definitively finished the school year, or had so many school snow days to make up that you might as well get ready to watch the fireworks from the faculty lounge on Independence Day. If you are in the latter category, do not despair, because your students are probably suffering even more than you are right now. In all seriousness, pray for them to persevere. No matter the time of year, the Catholic school teacher should periodically take some time, whether daily, weekly, or monthly, to reflect on the future and regain some refreshing perspective on various considerations: What am I doing well as a teacher? How effective am I in the classroom? In what ways can I improve as a teacher? Are my students *learning*, or am I just going through the motions? The most important personal inquiry that a teacher can make is whether his or her students are drawing closer to God. The Lord offers to help us draw nearer to him, and he favors those teachers who readily help guide his young disciples to him.

JUNE 16

> For your might is the source of righteousness; your mastery over all things makes you lenient to all.
>
> **—Wisdom 12:16**

Any semblance of might, righteousness, or mastery that the Catholic school teacher allegedly has comes from God. Furthermore, we necessarily recall that, while we will never reach God's magnanimity (and thank him for that, because we would have no capacity, let alone ability, to function with such authority), we are still called to imitate him in all that we do. When it comes to our students, we must always bear in mind that any power that we possess as teachers must be used wisely, judiciously, prudently, and in ultimate accord with God's will, rather than wielded recklessly based on pretentious human pursuits. Think of how many times the Lord has been lenient with you during your own lifetime, how frequently he has forgiven you or extended his mercy. Should we not similarly be sure to extend truly Christian mercy toward our students in need? Many of them have deep-seated personal pain and trials that are impeding their school performance. Attending to these students will help to remind them that they are God's children.

JUNE 17

> I tell you, unless your righteousness surpasses that of the scribes and Pharisees, you will not enter into the kingdom of heaven.
>
> **—Matthew 5:20**

The scribes and the Pharisees were well versed in the Mosaic Law, but they ended up so blinded by what essentially amounted to crippling litigiousness that they did not see the "big picture"; that is, they did not comprehend Jesus' true identity or the essentials of his loving message. On an interesting note, the scribes and the Pharisees were not necessarily very divergent from Jesus in terms of their teachings; rather, they had a somewhat shortsighted view of the *why* of their teachings, which comprised loving God. In other words, the scribes and the Pharisees would have done well simply to recognize and accept God's love. Similarly, the Catholic school teacher should endeavor to lead his or her students to understand the *why* of learning about God. It is not just to "get a good grade." No matter what subject you teach, if your students are just going through the academic motions, rather than realizing the wonder of the Lord's presence in their lives, then consider changing your approach. Look for chances to remind them that we follow the Lord's will because we ultimately love him.

JUNE 18

How long, O Lord, must I cry for help and you do not listen?

—Habakkuk 1:2a

God answers every prayer. There is no prayer that he does not, or would not, answer. However, what we must concede and accept is that we need to distinguish between a legitimate prayer request and a whim. Furthermore, God responds to prayer in the manner that he deems fit, not in the manner that we believe to be the best. The Catholic teacher must meditate on this reality and likewise remind his or her students of this. For example, do not expect that God will respond to your request for brand new classroom materials simply because the teacher at your neighboring school has them. Rather, pray that you receive new classroom materials because they will help all of your students to gain a better comprehension of the course's content and thus more effectively serve their fellow man for the greater glory of the kingdom of God. Do not yell out in despair that your order of jumbo-sized paper clips did not arrive on time, claiming that you have it so hard and that God ignores you. Open your heart to the Lord's blessings, which are truly plentiful.

JUNE 19

> Better are the God-fearing who have little understanding than those of great intelligence who violate the Law.
>
> **—Sirach 19:24**

Anyone who has ever studied the way humans interact with one another, whether in a school setting or otherwise, should be familiar with someone who may not appear at first glance to be the most intellectually prepared, but who is a still the quintessence of a good person. When we stand before the Almighty for judgment one day, there is no indication that we will have to give an accounting of our degrees, our societal status, our income, our school report card, or another fleeting entity. If anything, God is interested in how we use what we have, and the hope is that we do not misuse or otherwise neglect that which we have been given: "Much will be required of the person entrusted with much, and still more will be demanded of the person entrusted with more" (Lk 12:48b). It is difficult to sufficiently emphasize this, but make sure that you look for every opportunity to remind your students that mere intelligence without virtue is akin to a whitewashed sailboat on a dried lake bed: inutile, deceptive, hopeless, and crumbling.

JUNE 20

> I always strive to keep my conscience clear before God and man.
>
> **—Acts 24:16**

These words of Saint Paul, proclaimed during his trial before Felix (see Acts 24:1–27), remind us of an important reality about why

Saint Paul is such a model Christian: he opted to follow God's law, rather than try to impress his associates. Let us recall that, prior to Saul's conversion (see Acts 9:1–19), he had been one of the harshest persecutors of Christians (see Acts 7:58–8:1), but Jesus had special plans for him. The Catholic school teacher should thus remind his or her students of Saint Paul's heroic conversion, in order to lead them to reflect on how God is similarly calling them to a change in life in order to better follow him. We are all in need of an ongoing conversion. At no point during our earthly journey to Christ do we decide that our magnitude of virtue is irreproachably elevated, or that we are as inspired as we could possibly be. Negative peer pressure is nothing new in human history, and we must encourage our students to choose the correct path of righteously following the Lord. When morality thus reigns, everyone truly benefits.

JUNE 21

> Not to us, LORD, not to us but to your name give glory
> because of your mercy and faithfulness.
>
> **—Psalm 115:1**

It is in our very human nature to worship something other than ourselves. This does not mean we worship something *in addition* to ourselves; rather, we worship something that *is not* us, and that "something" is actually a *Someone*: God. Throughout the course of salvation history, there have been numerous other "gods" that have distracted humans from the one true God. For the Catholic school teacher, it is our duty to dissuade our students from being lured away from the Lord and his eternal promises. If that hundredth pair of shoes did not fulfill you, neither will that one-hundred-and-first pair. If you just want to be "rich" when you grow up, but have no plans to serve your fellow man in order to help build up the kingdom of God, then what will your wealth lead to? Money will ultimately not give us the fulfillment that we yearn for, which is found in God alone. The Lord's mercy and faithfulness to us are abundant. He offers them to us limitlessly, and we, praising him, have the opportunity to imitate him by being faithful and merciful to all our neighbors.

JUNE 22

> Indeed I shall continue to rejoice, for I know that this will result in deliverance for me through your prayers and support from the Spirit of Jesus Christ.
>
> **—Philippians 1:18b–19**

Saint Paul's Letter to the Philippians is one of which we refer to as his "captivity letters" because he wrote it while imprisoned. Note that even Saint Paul, the courageous "Apostle to the Gentiles" himself, readily asked his fellow Christians to pray for him. As teachers, with all that we have to deal with, we must rely on the prayers of others. Of course, we can pray to God directly for ourselves and our intentions, and he hears every prayer, but others (our family, friends, priests, etc.) can pray for us when we are unable to—for example, when we are distracted, asleep, mentally or emotionally distraught, or otherwise incapable of focused prayer. The prayers of others can help us greatly. Of course, it is in our distress that we ourselves should pray the most and also be sure to ask for the prayers of others. Imagine the power of multiplied prayers. Speaking of which, that is why, for around two thousand years, the Catholic Church has celebrated the role of the saints in helping us while we are earthbound; they are in God's presence, in constant, unimpeded prayer, giving God his honor and praying that we may one day be where they now are.

JUNE 23

For God did not give us a spirit of cowardice but rather of power and love and self-control.

—2 Timothy 1:7

God has given us the spiritual tools that we need to follow him and thus to live in accordance with his divine will. The *power* and the *self-control* with which he has endowed us, not to mention the *love* that typifies our Christian demeanor, must be used not only to rest comfortably within our personal Christian convictions but also to draw others to him. The Catholic school teacher has the opportunity to remind students that they too are recipients of God's graceful gifts. Therefore, never miss an opportunity to remind students of the numerous saints who died relatively young (in their childhood, adolescence, or twenties) but were already spiritually mature enough to embrace the Lord's call to discipleship. Some of these saints include Saint Agatha, Saint Agnes, Saint Charles Lwanga and Companions, Saint Joan of Arc, Saint Maria Goretti, Blessed José Luis Sánchez del Río, and many others. No matter what subject you happen to teach, tell your students that you believe in their ability to be saints in this world and with the Lord in heaven.

JUNE 24

Bear one another's burdens, and so you will fulfill the law of Christ.

—Galatians 6:2

Believe it or not, occasionally, the teacher has to tell students *how* to help each other. Effectively, what constitutes "help" has a varying conceptualization based on whom you might ask. Here are a few examples. You might have to break it to Generous George that lending his homework answers to another student is not "helping"; it is academic dishonesty. You might have to remind your students that an eighteen-year-old senior is not helping a seventeen-year-old junior by buying cigarettes for him. This is not camaraderie; it is sinful (and illegal). There are numerous other examples that could be examined, but ultimately, make sure that you share with your students that the only way truly to help someone else is by aiding him or her to do what is oriented toward the kingdom of God. Emphasize to them that bearing others' burdens lets those being helped recall their God-given human dignity, and this service humbles us by reminding us that we can do nothing alone, let alone achieve our salvation through our own merits.

JUNE 25

> Can you find out the depths of God? or find out the perfection of the Almighty?
>
> **—Job 11:7**

Instill in your students an inquisitive pondering about God. A healthy inquisitiveness, a worthwhile curiosity that can be fostered through intellectual engagement, can invite students to fathom God's goodness, including the abundance of his mercy and his desire to draw us ever nearer to him. This attempt to instill curiosity in students should not border on leading them to doubt their faith, because Jesus reserved some of his strongest language for those who would lead his most impressionable disciples away from him (see Lk 17:1–2). One of the numerous benefits of educating in a Catholic school is that you can operate in a truly cross-curricular environment by encouraging students to tap into what they have learned in other courses to better reflect on God's goodness. Consider the beauties of the universe that astronomy exhibits, or reflect on the wonders of the human mind that psychology, anatomy, and physiology readily reveal in plenitude, and so forth. Be in awe of it all!

JUNE 26

Let another praise you, not your own mouth; a stranger, not your own lips.

—Proverbs 27:2

One of the beneficial features of a Catholic school community is that there are so many opportunities to celebrate others' achievements. Primarily, teachers can celebrate their students' successes. Likewise, students can celebrate achievements by their teachers, teachers can celebrate achievements by their colleagues, administrators can celebrate their staff, the entire community can rally to celebrate parents, and so forth. In essence, there is hardly any shortage of opportunities to highlight what others have accomplished. Meanwhile, as an exercise in ensuring that God remains at the forefront of any Catholic school's mission, the supportive employee of a Catholic school will not seek out chances to identify his or her own accolades. Otherwise, the employee's ministerial initiatives may transition from being mission-driven to self-focused. Though you may believe that you do enough to deserve your own gold-encrusted desk chair, door-to-door limousine, and concierge service at school, you do not. Reflect on Mark 10:43–45.

JUNE 27

I have competed well; I have finished the race; I have kept the faith.

—2 Timothy 4:7

Do not hesitate to use athletic references in the classroom. Many students benefit from explanations of material that include such effective analogous discussions. For example, the theology teacher could mention the lesson in humility acquired by being the last one picked to be on a team for dodgeball during physical-education class in elementary school (surely a hypothetical scenario). With all due gravity of intent, Saint Paul provided us with a personal witness of how to persevere to the very end in terms of faith. While athletic success will eventually come to a conclusion (whether through the weakening of the body over time or through an ailment contracted in youth at the earliest or as an elder at the latest), and while even the mind will decline in time, we must remind our students of the need to hold on to faith. With God-fearing virtue and the support of the kingdom of God as our true goals, tell your students to compete well in life (better than some did in dodgeball).

JUNE 28

> He must increase; I must decrease.
>
> **—John 3:30**

The words of this passage, spoken by Saint John the Baptist regarding Jesus, show us how to be humble. One of the realities of being a teacher is that you have the opportunity to be the center of attention. You are in front of your students, spouting knowledge, whether they would like to hear it or not. This is one of the most perilous dynamics conceivable, insomuch as it could lead to the individual teacher's personality becoming the focal point, rather than the content of the lesson itself. Although it may come off as challenging, look for ways to remain humble as a teacher. Pray for God to give you the strength to clarify your lessons in order to make them as relevant, enriching, applicable, and uplifting as possible for your students. In the same vein, make sure to check students' humility through a charitable and cautious approach. Loudspeaker Lloyd does not have to take away from class by disruptively leading others astray. Pull such students aside and gently remind them that God is the focus, not us. They will thank you in the long run.

JUNE 29

May mercy, peace, and love be yours in abundance.

—Jude 1:2

The author of the Letter of Jude, a short one-chapter book of the New Testament, includes the words from this passage in the opening of his letter. These are words that the Catholic school teacher would do well to have in mind whenever he or she approaches not only his or her overall pedagogical and ministerial approach but also his or her daily practices in the classroom. In other words, the Catholic school teacher should seek opportunities to spread "mercy, peace, and love" within every facet of the school community. Who would ever want less of one of these three gifts? What would you think of someone who proclaimed, "I want less mercy," "I want less peace," or "I want less love"? If you were to hear a colleague say such a thing, you would be inclined to check whether this poor soul's vintage faculty polo is so tight that it is cutting off circulation to his head. Your community will thrive from an outpouring of benevolence, because the more that virtue is practiced and celebrated, the more it proliferates.

JUNE 30

Bring us back to you, LORD, that we may return: renew our days as of old.

—Lamentations 5:21

These words appear in the conclusion of the last chapter of the Book of Lamentations. This request made to the Almighty leads us to reflect on what we can look forward to in terms of both following the Lord and inviting others to do likewise. With June having now come to a close, in mere hours it will be July and you will be able to declare: "School starts next month!" Although it may feel as if the previous academic year just ended, the realization that the upcoming school year is nearby should not strike fear in the rueful teacher as you grimace while conjuring images of adolescents inhabiting your school's thoroughfares. Ask the Lord to "renew [your] days as of old" and to lead you to reflect on the wisdom that you have acquired in your educational field to help bring your future students to him. Being with God is the desire of all of humanity, whether or not we realize it. As you enjoy the remainder of your summer, start thinking of the joys that come at the start of every new school year.

JULY 1

> Yet even now—oracle of the LORD—return to me with your whole heart, with fasting, weeping, and mourning.
>
> **—Joel 2:12**

The reader of this passage cannot help but recall the beautiful words of Deuteronomy 6:5: "Therefore, you shall love the LORD, your God, with your whole heart, and with your whole being, and with your whole strength." The Lord wants us to return to him and abide in him with the entirety of our being. Bear in mind that our "weeping and mourning" do not have to come as the result of realizing that, with today being the first day of July, the new school year will start next month. After all, the Catholic school teacher must remember to remain close to the Lord the whole year through. Our desire to follow him cannot be a spiritual orientation that we turn on and off based on a season or period of the year. The Catholic school teacher ought to have a missionary heart that should accompany the Lord's call to follow him. What are little sacrifices that we can make daily that allow us to remember to rely on God and live according to his will? The more that we strive to imitate Christ, the more our students will likewise imitate him.

JULY 2

> Ask the Lord for rain in the spring season, the Lord who brings storm clouds, and heavy rains, who gives to everyone grain in the fields.
>
> **—Zechariah 10:1**

In many parts of the country, summertime brings torrential rain, occurring with thunderstorms and accompanied by crashing thunder and illuminating, if not dangerous, lightning. The following statement may seem trite, but when it rains, we get wet. In other words, people sometimes get surprised when they get rained upon (especially when an umbrella has been left at home or in the car). However, when an event seems inconvenient, is it not true that the Christian has the opportunity to view it positively? For example, if you were suffering from the effects of drought, you would actually welcome a storm, not scorn it. If you were blind, you would welcome being able to look at an ugly painting. If you were beset by spiritual struggles, you would yearn for the opportunity to return to the Lord. (Fortunately, he yearns for the same thing, so go back to him.) Catholic school teachers have the opportunity to view things in a new light, and by doing so we spread hope that benefits our students and our entire community.

JULY 3

> With length of days I will satisfy him, and fill him with my saving power.
>
> **—Psalm 91:16**

We are given relatively few days to have the privilege of serving as Catholic school teachers. If you are a new teacher at the beginning of your career in Catholic education, you will realize how quickly this time goes. If you are an experienced veteran teacher with years or even decades of experience, you might be surprised at how quickly these years have passed. (If you are in the latter category, your years have probably gone by faster if you acquired the skills necessary to grade papers efficiently and deal with temperamental photocopiers, thereby sparing yourself a lot of stress.) With the time that you have remaining as a teacher, dedicate yourself to your primary mission as a Catholic school educator: bringing our students to the Lord. In reality, God has given us ample time, but we cannot let it dissipate. One day, we will stand before the Almighty for judgment, and the Lord will survey how we spent our fleeting time here. If only we can say that we used our brief life to lead others to his merciful redemption and love!

JULY 4

> Thus says the Lord who made you, your help, who formed you from the womb.
>
> **—Isaiah 44:2a**

How often do you take the time to meditate on what a gift and a privilege we have to be able to teach God's fellow children? Our students belong to the Lord. He knew who you were before he made you and, in the same way, our students. We can appreciate the Lord's providence and love for our students even on those difficult days when they return from lunch unfocused and more hyper than a gnat that has ingested caffeine. Those teachers who have celebrated the gift of their own children will readily realize how special our students are to their own parents, with our ultimate parent being God himself, who drives away our pretentions of incertitude in order better to draw us to him: "For you did not receive a spirit of slavery to fall back into fear, but you received a spirit of adoption, through which we cry, 'Abba, Father!'" (Rom 8:15). Along with appreciating how your students are so valued, be sure to remind *them* of the God who loves and parents them. Just do not pamper their egos, because being spoiled could make their spiritual outlook go amiss. Thank God for your students, literally.

JULY 5

> A limited number of days he gave them, but granted them authority over everything on earth.
>
> **—Sirach 17:2**

Experience has shown, at least anecdotally, that there is a direct correlation between how often a particular student complains that a certain teacher uses a lot of paper and how much that student resents doing paperwork. Ask such students how they get to school each day, because if it is by car, they should not be patronizing the roadways, for which forests often had to be cleared in order to facilitate their construction. Any tangential considerations aside, the point is that we still must remind students of ways to be stewards of the environment, which is a gift from the Lord, without abusing or misusing its resources. Look for opportunities to hold class outside so that your students can appreciate being outdoors. Review the Church's social teaching as it relates to caring for the earth. In addition, have students reflect on ways, in our few days as inhabitants of the earth, to prepare ourselves for how we will spend time on the other side of eternity. This world is not our home, but it is on loan for us to respect.

JULY 6

> I have told you this so that you may not fall away.
>
> **—John 16:1**

Although God realizes that we will occasionally stray from him, he does not want us to. Thus, Jesus came to us as God in human form so that he could roll up his sleeves and give us a model of perfection in terms of how to follow God's will. Even if we do fall away, his desire is for reunion (in the truest sense of the term). Take a moment to recall from Luke 15 the parables of the lost sheep, the lost coin, and the prodigal son, among others, and realize that Jesus wants us to be near to him. It is particularly fitting to meditate on this during the summer, because the summer vacation can be a period of rest and renewal, but unfortunately, it can also be a period of temptation to slip from being *relaxed* to *lax* in matters of faith. It is up to us to seek opportunities to reinvigorate our spiritual lives during the summer, including through observance of the sacraments, through deeper reading of scripture, through being more serious about prayer, through occasions for fellowship, and so forth. The students whom you will meet in a few weeks deserve an uplifting teacher.

JULY 7

> Thus says the Lord: Do what is right and just. Rescue the victims from the hand of their oppressors.
>
> **—Jeremiah 22:3**

Lest someone has become familiar with the scriptures and Christian morality and still does not comprehend how God wants us to follow him, God sometimes has to remind us: "Do what is right and just." We should live every day as if God wants us to follow him and be like him, because he does! Whether or not we immediately realize it, part of our role as Catholic school teachers is that of "rescuer," because God has given us the expectation and the responsibility to do our part to protect our students from anything that would get between them and the Lord. As teachers, this will most frequently come in the form of encouraging our students to use the knowledge that they gain through their education to turn away from sin and make the world a better place. This is our duty no matter our specific subject area (and, in fact, it would be especially meaningful for students to hear this from different teachers). We must give them multiple tools to serve.

JULY 8

> But the noble plan noble deeds, and in noble deeds they persist.
>
> **—Isaiah 32:8**

Encourage your students to be uplifting people. This is only possible when you likewise encourage them to be *good* people, because the world can never have too many good people. The sooner (rather than later) they work toward being more virtuous, the easier it will be for them to continue being virtuous as they enter into adulthood. Being virtuous implies resorting to a deep reliance on the Lord to guide us. Attempting to be truly good without being a God-fearing person is akin to attempting to assemble an intricate puzzle in total darkness, unable to see how the pieces fit together and unsure of whether or not it is put together correctly. It is one thing to tell someone about the importance of being righteous, but it is more challenging to provide the means. So, rely on the Holy Spirit to provide the means by fostering a strong prayer life.

JULY 9

> But thanks be to God who gives us the victory through our Lord Jesus Christ.
>
> **—1 Corinthians 15:57**

Do not merely thank God one or two times during the day by rote. Having a healthy prayer regimen is vital for your spiritual well-being if you expect to be an ultimately effective Catholic school teacher. Therefore, again, thank God beyond set points in the day. Of course, this is not just for school days. After all, even when we are not "on the clock" at school, our psyche is still oriented toward the teaching profession, and our mindset is geared toward our role as pedagogues and educators. Essentially, make sure to thank God as frequently as possible, throughout the entire day, at every occurrence and every opportunity. You do not have to recite the Litany of the Saints when you want to express your gratitude to the Almighty. Simply say a silent prayer: "Thank you, God, for the privilege of sharing your gospel"; "Thank you, Lord, for this warm classroom on a cold winter day"; "We praise you, God, for letting us glorify you within our school community"; and so forth. The grateful teacher is an effective and inspirational teacher.

JULY 10

And the apostles said to the Lord, "Increase our faith."

—Luke 17:5

Never fear asking God to give you more faith. Faith is not some sort of spiritual sponge that can become saturated. Rather, our faith can be exponentially increased throughout our earthly life, and the more that we have, the more that we are open to receive, and the more significant it will become on our journey of spreading the gospel. "The Lord replied, 'If you have faith the size of a mustard seed, you would say to [this] mulberry tree, "Be uprooted and planted in the sea," and it would obey you'" (Lk 17:6). The more faith we have in the Lord, the more graceful our teaching experience will be. If we did not have faith in the Lord to inspire our students to be capable of glorifying him with their lives, both during and after they are in our school community, then why would we teach? Thorny Thelma might bother you with her need to question all that you affirm, but use her curiosity to display the rewards of faith. Tell your students about the saints; they lived their lives as ordinary people like you and I, but their faith endured.

JULY 11

Better the meagerness of the righteous one than the plenty of the wicked.

—Psalm 37:16

As you know, students are impatient. However, lest we forget, we adults are also impatient. In our modern times, instant gratification is often recognized by society as a desirable thing. This is unfortunate, because instant gratification is to virtue what a loose thread is to a cardigan: if left uninhibited, it gives way and unravels. Hence, the Catholic school teacher has a special responsibility to reinforce to his or her students that being a *good* person is much more desirable in God's eyes than being what broader society might consider a *successful* person. This assertion finds particular relevance when we consider the importance of instilling academic honesty in our students. Once they get to a college setting, there is likely a zero-tolerance policy against academic dishonesty. In addition, students must know that it is favorable to be honest (and therefore righteous), as opposed to deceptive and therefore morally adrift. Steer students toward righteousness!

JULY 12

Beloved, if God so loved us, we also must love one another.

—1 John 4:11

One privilege (of numerous) of being a Catholic school teacher is that we have the opportunity to explain to students what is meant by the Christian conceptualization of "love." There are so many misconceptions about love in modern times that confusion abounds when it comes to trying to discern its veritable characteristics. The word has lost its true meaning: I *love* French fries! I *love* that show! I *love* this song! I love writing long essays for Mr. McClain's class! Instead, the best exemplification of love is God's love for us—his complete outpouring of love, which he exhibited to us by dying for our sins on the Cross. This act of love indicates that he seriously wants us to follow him and to lead others to him, because it is in orienting ourselves to his will that we better sense his love. Once we experience God's love, we are drawn to better understand what it means to love our neighbor and thus bring greater glory to God. Catholic school teachers show our love within the community by serving others and drawing others to better know the Lord.

JULY 13

> The light of the just gives joy, but the lamp of the wicked goes out.
>
> **—Proverbs 13:9**

Have you ever known anyone to celebrate when the power goes out? Teachers loathe the occasion of the power going out, but students reliably relish it. Inevitably, at the onset of such a power outage, students' heads begin to swivel maniacally as they await the Apocalypse, only to be dismayed that Mr. McClain has survived the incident. Some of them may believe that the school day will thus end and students will be sent home, since humanity can apparently not subsist without the presence of electronic technology for eight nanoseconds. Lest students wither away at such a prospect, remind them that technology is merely a tool, not an idol. Regarding the analogy of light, make sure that your students are equipped to bring the light of Christ into a darkened world that is significantly bereft of the reality of his love, and subsequently lacking in true hope. Students must be encouraged to be good people, and thus to allow Christ's light to shine in them: "Your light must shine before others" (Mt 5:16a). Illuminate us, Lord!

JULY 14

Peace I leave with you; my peace I give to you. Not as the world gives do I give it to you. Do not let your hearts be troubled or afraid.

—John 14:27

Notice that Jesus emphasizes to us that his peace is not merely a worldly peace. Peace, as in the absence of armed conflict, is an ideal aspiration. However, the Christian understanding of peace goes far beyond a mere lack of violence. True peace has to do with the presence of the correct ordering of things within the universe. For this reason, we speak of such matters as *peace* of mind and *peace* of heart. In the Catholic school classroom, the peace of Christ must permeate the learning environment if our goal is to support our students in such a way that they too are drawn to the peace of Christ. If a student's aspect or demeanor does not appear at ease, it could be a matter of his or her need to find resolution for an internal struggle. At a minimum, ask the student how he or she is doing. If the student is dealing with a serious situation, be sure to reach out to a counselor or administrator. No matter the disposition of the circumstance, offer up prayers for the student, so that he or she can ultimately experience the beauty of Christ's peace.

JULY 15

As the shining sun is clear to all, so the glory of the LORD fills all his works.

—Sirach 42:16

Depending on the climate where you live, there is nothing quite like the mid-July sun. If you are outside during this time of the year, you are exceedingly aware of the impact of the sun on you. The awareness that we are called to have of God's presence in our lives should be similar to our awareness of the primacy of the July sun. We must look for those numerous opportunities to appreciate all that he has given to us. It may seem trite, but we Catholic school teachers should give thanks to God for the summer vacation—no, not in order to work on that tan or to see how many baked crabs you can devour in one sitting—but rather, because we have this time to reflect on God's glory and to meditate on ways that we can share lessons on his goodness with our students in the coming school year. No matter what subject you teach, look for ways to supplement your lessons by reminding your students of how readily "the glory of the Lord fills all his works." Make God's presence clear to them, because it is in drawing our students to the Lord that we fulfill our vocation as teachers.

JULY 16

> As for yourself, you must say what is consistent with sound doctrine.
>
> **—Titus 2:1**

The Catholic school teacher should endeavor to present matters of faith as accurately as possible. This is reasonably most pertinent to the lessons of theology teachers, but teachers of all different academic disciplines can appreciate this expectation. This has been justifiably repeated often in these reflections: make sure that you give students the opportunity to reflect on God's glory within your respective field of expertise. This, of course, does not mean that if you teach philosophy or mathematics, you have to dedicate every class period to dissecting the particular idiosyncratic permutations of Pascal's wager. If you teach music, you do not have to open every class session with an excerpt from Bach's beautiful *Mass in B Minor* or his captivating *St. Matthew Passion* (although Beethoven's *Missa Solemnis* would be quite the fascinating opportunity). Just make sure that all that you present to your students, in consideration of its overlap with matters of faith, is truthful and provides your students with an opportunity to grasp the grand scheme.

JULY 17

> I urge you therefore, brothers, by the mercies of God, to offer your bodies as a living sacrifice, holy and pleasing to God, your spiritual worship.
>
> **—Romans 12:1**

Anecdotally, some teachers who have worn pedometers during the school day have found that teachers can easily walk a total distance of more than three miles throughout the corridors of a school building each day. Teaching is corporeally demanding work. Make sure that you take sufficient time during the summer months to rest your body. Once the new school year arrives in a few short weeks, you will have to be back in action, prepared to stand on your feet for hours per day, speak to classes for extended periods of time, lug around boxes of copy paper, practice drawing your smiley face on the occasional student's "A" paper without getting a cramp in your hand, and so forth. The better we are doing physically, the better equipped we will be to cope with the physical demands that are placed upon us as teachers. The physical challenges that we deal with daily coincide with our broader ministerial efforts. Be sure to find a pair of comfortable dress shoes (of which there are many for sale on the clearance rack or at the thrift store).

JULY 18

> Do not be afraid; just have faith.
>
> **—Mark 5:36b**

Within the gospels, we read that Jesus asked all of his followers to tap into their faith on multiple occasions. A treatment of these plentiful episodes could not be suitably effected here, and the topic could be reflected upon in books of thousands of pages or more. However, take note of the term Jesus uses in this passage from the Gospel of Mark: *just.* As Catholic school teachers, of course, our faith must be reinforced by our actions. After all, if a student is failing your English class, you could not honestly say to him or her, "*Just* have faith that you will do better," without mapping out a plan for enhancing the student's study habits or for taking another approach. If two students are having a disruptive spat of teenage drama, you could not rightly tell them, "*Just* have faith that you will resolve your dispute." Instead, you would ask them to step aside and would work with them to find a way for them to reconcile. There is much that is out of our control as teachers, and we ultimately need to have faith that the Holy Spirit knows what is best for us. The more we are open to him, the more our faith will mature.

JULY 19

You must not distort justice: you shall not show partiality.

—Deuteronomy 16:19a

It is in our nature, and written upon our hearts, to be people of justice. People are driven to be just. There is a naturally ascribed visceral revulsion when a severe injustice has taken place. Since human beings seek justice, and students are human beings (yes, they are, you have to admit, even when it is the period before lunchtime and some of them are so famished that they appear on the verge of sprouting more heads than Cerberus), then it logically figures that students pursue justice. There are two significant factors to consider here. First, the teacher must ensure that he or she is impartial, fair, and unbiased with students; they can sniff out injustice readily, quickly, and enthusiastically. Second, make sure to steer your students toward being justice-driven people, both during their time in your school and after they have graduated and found themselves in "the real world." Inspire them to be champions of actual justice, rather than supporters of fleeting social fads that are actually not gospel-oriented. Students truly respect teachers who are fair.

JULY 20

Hear my cry, O God, listen to my prayer!

—Psalm 61:2

God hears our every prayer. Whether we are praying to give him thanks, praying for the well-being of a sick loved one, praying for the repose of someone's soul, praying for the guidance of the Holy Spirit, or praying that the start of the new school year does not come too quickly, God hears us. However, what he does with our prayers is his prerogative. It is up to him how to respond to our supplications. We can thus rest assured knowing that he will address all of our prayers in the way that most benefits the kingdom of God, rather than our mere ego. Our prayer regimen, particularly during the school day, does not have to become so regimented that we end up inclined to feel that we can only pray at certain times. Christ asks us to "pray always without becoming weary" (Lk 18:1). Do not wait until the first week of school to start offering prayers for your school community. If you have a full load and a challenging curriculum ahead, you may want to go ahead and start praying in earnest.

JULY 21

Those who walk uprightly fear the LORD, but those who are devious in their ways spurn him.

—Proverbs 14:2

All teachers were once adolescents. No matter how cultured, collected, and respect-inducing we may now appear, all of us were once teenagers and questioned authority in some way. Even if simply at a subconscious level, we know what it is like to be an adolescent. Nevertheless, we must remind our students that being young is hardly an excuse for not being as holy as possible. By reflecting on the numerous saints who died at a young age (many of them willingly, through martyrdom), our students can be led to discern that God is calling them to be holy here and now. Delaying holiness is to the spiritual life what delaying medication is to the body: even if you think you do not need it, not having it will only make things harsher and more uncomfortable in the long run. Be sure to be positive when it comes to encouraging students to "walk uprightly." Students want to be good people. Praise them when they make noble decisions; after all, you may be the only person that day to affirm their innate goodness and worth.

JULY 22

> The people who walked in darkness have seen a great light;
> Upon those who lived in a land of gloom a light has shone.
>
> **—Isaiah 9:1**

This beautiful passage from Isaiah is a foreshadowing of the light that Christ will bring. In fact, the Lord echoes the words of Isaiah: "The people who sit in darkness have seen a great light, on those dwelling in a land overshadowed by death light has arisen" (Mt 4:16). There are various terms related to light that at least partially describe what the Catholic school teacher does, ideally on a daily basis: illuminates, elucidates, enlightens, and brightens. Any enlightenment that the student thus achieves should be reflective (no pun intended) of the light of Christ. In other words, any and all knowledge that our students gain should help to equip them to serve others, both during and after they have finished their formal education. It is, of course, by serving their brothers and sisters that they give greater glory to God. Do you know Newtonian physics? You can serve God. Are you able to recite hundreds of digits of pi? You can serve God. Do you know how to paint a masterpiece? You can serve God. Magnify Christ's light.

JULY 23

> For he is the living God, enduring forever, whose kingdom shall not be destroyed, whose dominion shall be without end.
>
> **—Daniel 6:27**

The words of this passage were decreed by King Darius when Daniel had survived the lion's den, showing the preeminence of the true God of the Israelites. There will be various points within our lives in which we are readily aware of God's presence. A teacher does not have to be held captive in a den full of lions in order to hope for the Lord's intervention. (After all, being enclosed in a classroom with twenty-five wily young adults is adequately perilous; thank God for his grace.) So too should we invite our students to realize God's presence in their own lives. The Lord is readily willing to reveal himself to us, and he often does so through the good acts of others. In other words, we see God in the virtuous acts of our neighbors, our brethren. Remind your students that placing the Lord first allows him to exhibit how he reigns among us forever.

JULY 24

> Your eyes are too pure to look upon wickedness, and the sight of evil you cannot endure.
>
> **—Habakkuk 1:13a**

Our students should know how much God wants them to show their love for him, and how the primary way to exhibit this love is through their holiness and good deeds that truly benefit humanity. After all, the Lord does not "look upon wickedness" favorably and instead wants us to be holy: "For I, the LORD, am your God. You shall make and keep yourselves holy, because I am holy" (Lv 11:44a). There are numerous opportunities for youth to live out the holiness to which the Lord calls us all. This can be through personal sanctity (prayer, alms, fasting, and other small sacrifices), modesty (dressing appropriately), purity (abstinence until marriage), generosity (donating to clothing drives, feeding the less fortunate, and so forth), as well as other virtuous practices. Make sure to instill in your students knowledge of, and appreciation for, the four cardinal virtues: fortitude, justice, prudence, and temperance. Your students will veritably thank you for inspiring them to make Christian decisions.

JULY 25

> May the Lord direct your hearts to the love of God and to the endurance of Christ.
>
> **—2 Thessalonians 3:5**

All of us are in need of constant conversion. The summer is a worthwhile opportunity to ponder our need for personal conversion in order to be that much more spiritually fortified for the quickly approaching new school year. After all, you will be back in school in around a month, so along with thinking about how you are going to set up your classroom and have all your teaching supplies ready, it is time to get your "spiritual gear" fully prepared. Around this point in the summer, there is a healthy tension that has developed: although the upcoming school year is eminent, you still do have ample time to relax before things are in full academic swing. So, sit back and enjoy those reruns of *Keeping Up Appearances* on PBS. Finally finish that book that has been taking you far too long to read. Rest and recuperate. But also make the time each day to invite the Lord into your heart, thanking him for who he is, and begin to think of how you are going to extend that invitation to him continually throughout the coming school year.

JULY 26

> Why were you looking for me? Did you not know that I must be in my Father's house?
>
> **—Luke 2:49**

No, this was not Jesus providing a snide answer to Saint Joseph and the Blessed Virgin Mary. In this well-known episode from Luke's gospel, Mary and Joseph had taken Jesus to Jerusalem for the Feast of Passover. They were on their way back to their home in Nazareth when they realized that Jesus was missing, and returning to Jerusalem, they found him teaching in the Temple. Jesus had been missing for three days (see Lk 2:46; if you care to read the entire passage, it appears in Luke 2:41–52). Jesus offered this remark to Mary and Joseph because he had to assert his divine role. Adolescents frequently attempt to assert who they are, but their efforts are, let us just say, not always as "gracious" as the Lord's. It is important for the Catholic school teacher to counsel students on proper decorum as it relates to respect. Jesus was allowed to extend this quip because that is his prerogative as the Son of God. Similarly, we are called to be sure to model to our students the respect that we thus expect from them.

JULY 27

> One can put on gold and abundant jewels, but wise lips are the most precious ornament.
>
> **—Proverbs 20:15**

Remind your students frequently that riches and possessions are not what makes a person happy. Your sharing this with them may be one of few, if any, occasions for them to hear this within their young lives. The world beyond your school's walls will hardly offer such a declaration. The world often says that *less* is not more, *more* is more, that we are only worth the sum of our things, and that how many possessions and how much money we have amassed determines our overall worth as a person. To believe this would leave a person empty, unfulfilled, and ultimately spiritually imperiled. As a Catholic school teacher, no matter what subject you teach, make sure to lead your students to embrace Christ's gospel message: with our very being, we must serve and honor the Lord alone, by orienting both our words and actions toward the kingdom of God. Lead students to consider the transcendent by directing their thoughts toward eternity.

JULY 28

> I have much more to tell you, but you cannot bear it now. But when he comes, the Spirit of truth, he will guide you to all truth.
>
> **—John 16:12–13a**

Take the Holy Spirit seriously. In other words, listen to him. We are occasionally led to consider the Holy Spirit as an entity that is spiritually inaccessible, or otherwise unable to be considered as our true guide. The Catholic school teacher must actually rely on the Holy Spirit frequently, in order to be able to remain spiritually grounded. Of course, our openness to the movements of the Holy Spirit must be accompanied by our sound knowledge of doctrinal matters, in order to be able to make Christian choices based on allowing the Lord to work in our lives. The Holy Spirit will only inspire us to live according to the kingdom of God. The Holy Spirit would never encourage the foolish teacher to leave school early just to avoid traffic. Meanwhile, the wise teacher would contact that student who has seemed bothered by something, cooperating with the Holy Spirit's desire for the student's ultimate well-being. Pray, asking the Holy Spirit to abide with you, benefiting your community.

JULY 29

Do nothing out of selfishness or out of vainglory; rather, humbly regard others as more important than yourselves.

—Philippians 2:3

It is admittedly difficult to be selfless; it is not difficult in its effects (which are only good), but in its work of overcoming our ego. Egotism and pride are caustically deleterious for the Catholic school teacher in particular, because such selfishness not only impacts the teacher's relationship with God; it also takes away from the fruitfulness of students' and others' particular experiences. At some point each day, whether at the beginning of the day, in the middle, at the end, or anytime therein, reflect on your mindset as a Catholic school teacher. Is the kingdom of God the most important factor in the framework of your lessons? (This should be true for all teachers, not just theology teachers, campus ministers, and others who are unfortunately not allowed to wear capes due to faculty dress codes.) Your preference for God as the center of your teaching ministry is not resorting to instruction that is somehow "theocratic"; rather, it is having an undercurrent of glorification of the Lord. Get out of God's way and serve.

JULY 30

For sin is not to have any power over you, since you are not under the law but under grace.

—Romans 6:14

When it comes to sharing matters of faith with your students, make sure that you do not present a legalistic view of God. Now, of course, we must ensure that we remind them of the Lord's expectations in terms of following his will. After all, with the fullness of his divine being, Jesus reflected the Ten Commandments, and he likewise reminded us in Matthew 5:17: "Do not think that I have come to abolish the law or the prophets. I have come not to abolish but to fulfill." Following the Lord's commands must not mean following the rules for the rules' sake; after all, this was the very issue that underscored much of the friction between Jesus and the Pharisees. They had become so preoccupied with "the law" that they had forgotten that we follow the law because we love God, not vice versa. Therefore, it is important to remind your students that following God is not simply trying to follow the rules. Rather, we follow the rules because God has established morality and he knows what is best for us. The Father's rules thus protect his children.

JULY 31

> Trust in the LORD and do good that you may dwell in the land and live secure.
>
> **—Psalm 37:3**

At times, we need to hear very clearly what it is that God expects of us. "Trust" involves a great deal of relinquishment of our own will in order to cooperate with the Lord's will. Similarly, "doing good" involves acting in such a manner that we abide by the Lord's wishes, not necessarily our own. Today is the last day of July, and for the teacher, that means that in the next month the new school year will begin. The wise Catholic school teacher realizes that he or she does not know it all. Therefore, place a great deal of trust in God, so that he will lead and inspire you to be the most effective Catholic school teacher possible. Young students are not the subspecies of humanoid that we may be tempted to deem them; rather, they too want to be good and to please God. The better that teachers model Christian comportment for our students, the greater of an example our students will find. The world needs more examples of both trust and *trustworthiness*. Our students tend to look up to us; we cannot look down on them.

AUGUST 1

This is my commandment: love one another as I love you.

—John 15:12

Note Jesus' introductory phrase: "This is my commandment." Loving others is not a suggestion, a recommendation, or even simply an ideal—it is a requirement, a basic expectation on the part of every Christian. It is a commandment the Catholic school teacher must recall at every turn. Today is the first day of August, which means that school begins in just a few weeks. Are you ready to exhibit Christian love to *all* of your students, prior to any other consideration? The student who is failing your class? The student who tells you that your class is boring? The student who is self-centered and egotistical? The student who is constantly disruptive? The student who talks back? The student who rolls her eyes? The student who cusses under his breath? Love is hardly weakness. In other words, part of truly loving our students is acting according to the "tough" love that they require. For those students who need charitable correction, be the one to remind them of who Christ wants them to be, so that they can be as easily *loveable* as they are *loved.* Christian love is truly durable.

AUGUST 2

This is how all will know that you are my disciples, if you have love for one another.

—John 13:35

Those who claim themselves to be disciples of the Lord must make sure that their lives reflect their beliefs. The love that we have for others must be a testament to the greater love of him whom we follow, since "God is love" (1 Jn 4:8b). The Catholic school teacher must therefore remain a pillar of the community, ensuring that his or her actions are morally uplifting. After all, our students are watching. Their observance of our actions and mannerisms is reflective of their desire to have positive role models. There are plenty of negative role models in society, whether they come in the form of personalities on television, the radio, the Internet, and so forth, who have our students' attention. Hence, it is up to us to do our part to help Christ's light shine through, for the fullness of his love is what draws everyone, including the youth, to follow his divine will. Remind your students of what love truly is. Love supersedes mere emotion and requires sincerity, fidelity, and true selflessness—all attributes of the Lord Jesus Christ.

AUGUST 3

But you, brothers, do not be remiss in doing good.

—2 Thessalonians 3:13

Rare is the day in which you will find someone who feels guilty for having done something truly good, something that was able to build up the kingdom of God. God designed us to be oriented toward, and driven by, doing that which is verily good. For this reason, a clean conscience is the result of being a virtuous person. Remind your students of this always. Have them reflect on times in which they have done something good and then reaped the spiritual rewards. (Of course, we do not do good deeds in order merely to *feel* good, because we would then run the risk of slacking in our spiritual lives when we "don't feel like" being holy.) Endeavoring to have your students reflect on this important consideration is admittedly more conducive to the theology teacher or campus minister (given the inherent curricular milieu), but teachers in other subjects could, at a minimum, nudge students toward the good. God made us to imitate him, and since he is perfect, we can at least strive to live truly virtuously.

AUGUST 4

Worry weighs down the heart, but a kind word gives it joy.

—Proverbs 12:25

One word. With just one word, a person can either build someone up or tear someone down. As a Catholic school teacher, we are tasked with ensuring that our words are ultimately supportive of others within our school community. A school community has numerous stakeholders in various realms, and the most important figures whom we are tasked with supporting are our students. We should endeavor to allay their fears, worries, preoccupations, and concerns, in order to ensure that they are not being so encumbered or besieged by doubt that they are subsequently suffering within their spiritual lives. A student who is joyful because he or she senses God's presence is a student who is gaining the most worthwhile education imaginable. Our students have enough challenges and difficulties in their lives, and they are entitled to the joy of knowing Christ, just as we all are. Saying kind words is not some sort of indulgence; it is simply recognizing that others want to, and can, live according to true Christian joy.

AUGUST 5

For the LORD comforts his people and shows mercy to his afflicted.

—Isaiah 49:13b

All of us suffer. Suffering is a part of life. The pretentiousness of modern times attempts to claim that any type of suffering, discomfort, or inconvenience is to be avoided. The path of least resistance is the frequently selected route. Of course, we should seek treatment when physical or mental anguish is due to a treatable ailment. However, no matter how well we may feel at certain times, suffering will come in some form or another, sooner than later. When suffering does come, offer it up to the Lord. Another lesson is just as important. Although we will all face suffering to some degree throughout our lives, we must not cause undue suffering to others. What allegedly charitable teacher would announce to his students that it is time for their fiftieth essay of the quarter (excepting certain pertinent theological topics, which could afford such an academic adventure)? Pray for your students who are suffering and for all of their families as well. No suffering is in vain.

AUGUST 6

You listen, LORD, to the needs of the poor; you strengthen their heart and incline your ear.

—Psalm 10:17

The Catholic school teacher should readily look for opportunities to encourage his or her students to recognize the inherent human dignity of all people, including those living in material poverty. When we read through the gospels, particularly the Gospel of Luke, we are better able to comprehend the special place that those who are materially needy hold in the Lord's heart. You would also do well to remind your students that we are all called to practice the three evangelical counsels: poverty, chastity, and obedience. Although those in religious life take these three vows, even the laity are encouraged to adhere to these precepts as they relate to inviting us to remain closer to the Lord. It is particularly critical that teachers of subjects other than theology encourage students to treasure those living in poverty; in this way, students will realize that this expectation is not merely a principle propounded by theology teachers alone. Regarding obedience, your principal and other administrators might enjoy hearing of your interest in practicing this evangelical counsel.

AUGUST 7

His mercy is from age to age to those who fear him.

—Luke 1:50

This excerpt is from the famous "Canticle of Mary," also known as the Magnificat. (The entire passage can be found in Luke 1:46–55. You are encouraged to read the entire account in order to better fathom the context of this specific phrase.) Although sometimes it appears in a more veiled context, God the Father's mercy is clear within the Old Testament. Meanwhile, the Son of God's mercy is markedly evident throughout the New Testament. In particular, Mary, the Mother of the Lord, stressed how her Son's mercy is enduring. (If there were ever any doubt, remember that "Mother knows best"!) Are we as Catholic school teachers not expected to imitate the Lord by likewise being merciful toward the students in our charge? After all, the students of chemistry teacher Mr. Harry the Hammer might quake at his approach in the classroom and with his teaching style, but will they know compassion? Aim to teach mercifully.

AUGUST 8

> Let us not grow tired of doing good, for in due time we shall reap our harvest, if we do not give up.
>
> **—Galatians 6:9**

In mere weeks, the new academic year will begin. Days before that, you will return to school for in-service meetings, classroom decoration, dusting off your framed "Teacher of the Month" certificate, and many other activities that tell you that it is time to get back into the rhythm of school. Have you given serious consideration to how well this year can go? This can be a wonderful year, and you have the opportunity to make sure of that. But how can you categorize a superior year? It is one in which you are oriented toward the good and encourage your students to be so as well. If you prepare yourself, both mentally and spiritually, for a year of benevolence, then you will be in line with God's will and shall thus have the soulful resolve to have a verily monumental year. Persevere in your attempts to bring your students closer to the Lord. You may not reap the rewards during the time that you are within your school's walls, but your students will ultimately benefit. The wise students will go on similarly to serve future communities.

AUGUST 9

> We earnestly desire each of you to demonstrate the same eagerness for the fulfillment of hope until the end.
>
> **—Hebrews 6:11**

Whether or not people will readily admit it, or even realize it, we desire to be around people who are hopeful, even if we may initially find their bubbly positivity as grating as steel wool on a charcoal grill. Those who are hopeful lift up others. In other words, being positive reduces others' potential spiritual inhibitions. Meanwhile, those who have an attitude of hopelessness and negativity are all too ready to distribute their pessimism like a pushpin deftly administered to a balloon with a smiley-face design. Those Catholic school teachers who embrace their hope in the Lord are those who ultimately hold a Catholic school together. No matter what subject they teach, you can tell that others want to be around them: their colleagues enjoy their company, their students respect them, and the *Today* show wants to interview them. In the coming weeks, foster an eagerness to bring hope to your students, and your entire school community by extension. The Lord wants to grant to all of us "a future of hope" (Jer 29:11).

AUGUST 10

> What eye has not seen, and ear has not heard, and what has not entered the human heart, what God has prepared for those who love him.
>
> **—1 Corinthians 2:9**

This remarkable passage from Saint Paul's First Letter to the Corinthians comes from Isaiah 64:3: "No ear has ever heard, no eye ever seen, any God but you working such deeds for those who wait for him." As we prepare to begin the next school year, we have a lot of uncertainties, and we are unaware of what it holds. There are numerous variables that will inevitably be beyond the scope of our control. However, as Catholic school teachers, at the core of our teaching framework must be an abiding love in imitation of Christ. Hence, we must have faith that God will be there to guide and inspire us to be teachers who ultimately serve those in our midst with deep charity. Similarly, we must be at peace with others in our community: "Whoever does not love a brother whom he has seen cannot love God whom he has not seen" (1 Jn 4:20). In an era in which society only values the measurable and provable, your faith in God will inspire your students to model Jesus Christ, "the image of the invisible God" (Col 1:15).

AUGUST 11

Not that I say this because of need, for I have learned, in whatever situation I find myself, to be self-sufficient.

—Philippians 4:11

Teaching has the potential to be a rather lonely profession in various ways. Although you readily collaborate with your colleagues, whether those who teach in your department, your chairperson, administrators, or other school personnel, there are many day-to-day operations for which you are left to your own devices. It is important for the Catholic school teacher to be able to appreciate this solitude. In the first few centuries AD, the era of desert monasticism arose, in which those who sought to elude the (comparatively) bustling city life hastened to the desert, living the life of a hermit in order to be closer to God. The Catholic school teacher must not necessarily feel the call to don sackcloth and risk encountering scorpions in order to have an effective relationship with the Lord each day at school. However, be sure that you are capable of being resourceful when it comes to the lone moments that you will spend at school. Value this time in order to be able to be attentive to your students.

AUGUST 12

Praise the Lord, my soul; I will praise the Lord all my life.

—Psalm 146:2

Look for something beyond teaching that gives you joy. Of course, your status as a Catholic school teacher should be such a fulfilling role that you are certain that it is your true vocation from the Lord, and it should therefore fill your heart. However, ensure that you have some other interests. This participation in another hobby will buttress your ministry as a teacher. Even those in monastic life are conventionally commanded to spend around an hour per day doing something recreational. Do not worry: your recreation will not (or, at least, *should* not) consume you and, if maintained to a moderate degree, will restore your resolve when it comes to carrying out an effective apostolate within the classroom. Just make sure that your pastime is something that is morally uplifting and intellectually enriching, in order to ensure that it is ultimately benefiting you and the wider community. This is not to mention the "street cred" that you will gain from your students who find out that Ms. Smith is a world ukulele champion in her spare time.

AUGUST 13

> Grace be with all who love our Lord Jesus Christ in immortality.
>
> **—Ephesians 6:24**

Read that a second time: it says *immortality* (not *immorality*—had to make sure that you were paying attention!). How much time have you spent truly pondering and profoundly reflecting upon the implications of Christ's resurrection and ascension? Jesus rose from the dead. Forty days later, he went to heaven, by his own divine power. This is no minor matter. The paschal mystery (Jesus' passion, death, resurrection, and ascension) is the underpinning of any Catholic school's mission. Our work as Catholic school teachers has eternal implications. Soon, the materials in your science lab will be obsolete. The books in your English classroom will disintegrate and be consumed by bookworms (the entomological variety, rather than the respectably literate humanoid variety). The instruments in the band room will all rust (even the flutes, unfortunately). In years, all the current students will be replaced, as will the current teachers. This may seem dire, but the point is this: "Seek what is above" (Col 3:1).

AUGUST 14

The plans of the diligent end in profit, but those of the hasty end in loss.

—Proverbs 21:5

The Catholic school teacher must take great care in carrying out his or her lessons. This will not only benefit students in terms of receiving the most accurate presentation of academic material possible but also lead the teacher to reflect more deeply on what it actually means to "think with the end in mind." From a Christian viewpoint, "thinking with the end in mind" implies making sure that our students are not merely equipped with the intellectual readiness to engage with a world that is increasingly globalized but—and this is more important—also able to make recourse to the moral lessons reinforced by the Catholic school to make the world a better place. Making the world a better place does not simply mean facilitating access to materials. Rather, making the world a better place signifies offering your time, talent, and treasure to make sure that God's love is made manifest, thus ultimately allowing his greater glory to shine through. Be diligent, and do not rush through your daily planner as if to check off boxes.

AUGUST 15

And Mary said: "My soul proclaims the greatness of the Lord; my spirit rejoices in God my savior."

—Luke 1:46–47

This excerpt is from the "Canticle of Mary," or the Magnificat (Lk 1:46–55), which was Mary's response to Elizabeth at the time of the Visitation. Today is the Feast of the Assumption, in which we celebrate how God opted to raise Mary into heaven. (Although the dogma of Mary's Assumption is not explicitly mentioned in scripture, it has been ruminated upon theologically since the days of the early Church, and this consideration has been transmitted through the centuries by apostolic succession and Sacred Tradition.) Mary was no ordinary mother: she was the *Theotokos*, a Greek term meaning "God-bearer" and a name given to her at the Council of Ephesus in AD 431. Despite Mary's special status, she was never self-aggrandizing. Read through the Magnificat. Mary's prayers to God in heaven are more powerful than we are capable of fathoming. Strive to imitate Mary's deep humility this school year—she brings us closer to her Son.

AUGUST 16

> Jesus said to [Thomas], "Have you come to believe because you have seen me? Blessed are those who have not seen and have believed."
>
> **—John 20:29**

This proclamation from the Lord takes place when Thomas becomes the last of the eleven remaining disciples in Jesus' inner circle to witness the resurrected Lord. Of course, from this exchange we gained the term "Doubting Thomas." The Catholic school teacher is met with various circumstances that can lead to doubt. We are occasionally tempted to feel despair and not to recognize God's presence. On such occasions, we are not necessarily doubting God's existence, but something holds us back in terms of acknowledging that he is the fullness of who he says he is. Jesus is not just a really good guy. Jesus is not merely some semblance of a wise philosopher. Jesus is not simply a captivating orator, a moral giant, or a life coach. Jesus is God himself. If we do not have a solid embrace of this reality, our Catholic school community will not have the same opportunity to flourish spiritually. We must be able to address the Lord with the crucial words of Saint Thomas the Apostle: "My Lord and my God!" (Jn 20:28).

AUGUST 17

> You are lacking in one thing. Go, sell what you have, and give to [the] poor and you will have treasure in heaven; then come, follow me.
>
> **—Mark 10:21**

One of the demands (which actually turns out to be a blessing in disguise) that the Lord places on those who wish to follow him is that we must not lack dedication. This lack of dedication can be the fruit of a burdensome attachment to that which gets in the way of our relationship with God: "No one can serve two masters. He will either hate one and love the other, or be devoted to one and despise the other. You cannot serve God and mammon" (Mt 6:24; see Lk 16:13). The reality is that Catholic school teachers are, anecdotally, the lowest-paid profession commensurate to the level of education that is typically required for the position. A corporate executive could practically sneeze and earn a raise for one year that far eclipses our total income over the course of a decade. This is hardly a complaint, because we ought to remember that the acceptance of our vocation is a choice. The point is that the Lord calls us away from ourselves and our material comfort. So, answer him!

AUGUST 18

> But be content with what you have, for he has said, "I will never forsake you or abandon you."
>
> **—Hebrews 13:5**

This excerpt from Hebrews 13:5 is based on Deuteronomy 31:6, 8: "Be strong and steadfast; have no fear or dread of them, for it is the LORD, your God, who marches with you; he will never fail you or forsake you. . . . It is the LORD who goes before you; he will be with you and will never fail you or forsake you. So do not fear or be dismayed," as well as Joshua 1:5: "As I was with Moses, I will be with you: I will not leave you nor forsake you." In all of our duties as Catholic school teachers, we must rely on the Lord, because he will always accompany us. God's fidelity is abundant, and he wants to lead us to labor in concert with his divine will. Teachers in a wide variety of subject areas are often guilty of wanting to just "go it alone," hustling and bustling through each school day fueled by sheer obstinacy. Such an educational busybody is a prime candidate for burnout. If you want to keep your pedagogical flame lit, remain close to the Lord. Your students, as well as everyone else in your community, will benefit. God is there for you.

AUGUST 19

> If you keep my commandments, you will remain in my love, just as I have kept my Father's commandments and remain in his love.
>
> **—John 15:10**

The Catholic school teacher should know the Ten Commandments as the foundational framework of moral principles. The Ten Commandments provide the basic list of the Lord's expectations of us. However, make sure to aim to adhere to them not simply because they are God's law but because of your love for the Lord. At the core of our relationship with God is love, not spiritual litigiousness. The parent will readily understand this. You want your children not to eat that fifth jumbo-size chocolate bar not out of fear of getting sick or getting in trouble for eating too many but out of love for you, out of a desire to please you and to recognize, implicitly or otherwise, that you care for them. So it is with following God's law, as underscored by Jesus' teachings from the gospels. Let us recall what following Jesus entails: joy. After all, he follows up his proclamation in John 15:10 with this key affirmation: "I have told you this so that my joy may be in you and your joy may be complete" (Jn 15:11). God's law is lovely (in the true sense of the term).

AUGUST 20

> You belong to God, children.
>
> **—1 John 4:4a**

We should never pass up the opportunity to reflect on the totality of the implications of what it means to "belong" to the Lord. The Catholic school teacher is in a rather unique position, because we must remind our students that all of us belong to God, while also providing counsel, advice, and instruction to our students. In other words, we are expected to be know-it-alls while not ending up bigger than our educational britches. This is a factor no matter what particular subject comprises our expertise. Knowing that we are God's creation requires an exceptional degree of humility. So often we teachers are quite accustomed to being an authority figure, but allowing God to be himself implies having to submit to his will. Nevertheless, serving the Lord is rife with rewards because the sooner we realize the reality that he knows better than we do, the sooner we will better minister to all of our students. Let God be the tailor for your educational britches; he knows your exact size.

AUGUST 21

> All the paths of the LORD are mercy and truth toward those who honor his covenant and decrees.
>
> **—Psalm 25:10**

The Catholic school teacher must know, value, and appreciate God's mercy. We are all familiar with the magnitude of mercy. (This is not merely because we have experienced the summer break.) Verily, we have known forgiveness and reconciliation, and we are called to extend these to all whom we encounter. At the same time, we are expected to help our neighbor to be holy and virtuous. This duality of expectations is perhaps particularly encapsulated within Jesus' words as they appear in Luke 17:3: "Be on your guard! If your brother sins, rebuke him; and if he repents, forgive him." How does this relate to our students? Essentially, we must be prepared to proclaim the truth of the Lord, which of course necessarily includes his abundant mercy, and we best do this by following his will. Our students look to us as examples, and they want to be inspired. It is in our very nature to want to be inspired, not discouraged, through the process of learning. We should help our students ascertain the Lord's mercy and truth, all for his kingdom.

AUGUST 22

Therefore, take these words of mine in your heart and soul.

—Deuteronomy 11:18a

Catholic school teachers instruct students in a variety of academic subjects. The knowledge and learning that stem from the process of truly effective education is an impressive outcome, and one that can hardly be taken lightly. We must ensure that, at the very core of our teaching, our most important consideration is drawing our students closer to the Lord. This is an endeavor that can never be taken for granted. Just because your school is a Catholic institution does not mean that efforts must not continuously be made to improve and strengthen its Catholic identity. The measure of any Catholic institution should be this: If Jesus Christ were to walk into my school's main lobby, would he feel that this is a school in which his gospel is lived each day? The point made from this passage from Deuteronomy is key. For our students' well-being, we must have the Lord's law within our heart and soul.

AUGUST 23

May the Lord of peace himself give you peace at all times and in every way.

—2 Thessalonians 3:16a

It is quite rare for someone to detest peace. We are driven to embrace and delight in the prospect of true peace. However, the peace that we seek cannot be an illusory or pseudo-peace more affiliated with secularist pretensions than with the abiding peace that originates from the Lord: "Peace I leave with you; my peace I give to you. Not as the world gives do I give it to you. Do not let your hearts be troubled or afraid" (Jn 14:27). Look for ways to invite the Lord and his peace into your classroom "at all times and in every way." For example, if your students are being more energetic than a lab mouse who just downed a thimble of espresso on his way to his exercise wheel, you could either (1) yell and scream at them to get their attention (non-peacefully), or (2) speak to them in a calm, mature tone (peacefully). Model the truly peaceful behavior that you would like your students to emulate. When your students look back and remember you years from now, will they be able to recall someone who lived based on Jesus' peace?

AUGUST 24

Before they call, I will answer; while they are yet speaking, I will hear.

—Isaiah 65:24

God is our supreme sovereign. As our Father, he knows us better than we know ourselves. Similarly, he wants us to know him. God wants us to remain close to him by praying to him. The Lord's demands of prayer are interlaced between both the Old and New Testaments. God has emphasized repeatedly that it is through prayer that we are able to be more effective disciples: "Pray always without becoming weary" (Lk 18:1). Be sure to be sincere in your prayers to the Lord. Do not rush through your prayers or simply treat them as if they are something to finish so as to move on to better things. Prayer is conversing with the Lord God, not a chore to be completed during commercial breaks while watching *Wheel of Fortune*. Similarly, when praying at the beginning of class, make sure to slow down and pray very solemnly. Our students are perceptive and can tell if we are rushing. (But do not take too long, lest they try to use the extra time to finish their theology homework.) Take the time to "be still and know that [he is] God" (Ps 46:11). Pray!

AUGUST 25

> For there is no distinction; all have sinned and are deprived of the glory of God.
>
> **—Romans 3:22b–23**

This excerpt from Saint Paul's Letter to the Romans, depending on your openness to its implications, has the possibility of being either one of the most detracting scriptural passages you will ever consider, or one of the most enlightening. We are all in need of a redeemer. Comparing our capacity for morality to the Lord's would be akin to comparing an ice cube to a glacier—you would not come close. The reason that this passage is so important for the Catholic school teacher to recall and meditate upon profoundly is that we must never forget our place. We sin and make mistakes, and we must constantly pick ourselves up and seek the Lord's forgiveness and reconciliation. If we refuse to acknowledge this reality, then the Lord no longer holds a primary position as our God; our god instead becomes the self, replete with rampant hubris, stark hopelessness, and ultimately spiritual ruin. It is more than acceptable—it is *preferable*—for us to advise our students also to seek truly the Lord's forgiveness. Be a beacon of real hope to them.

AUGUST 26

> My brothers, show no partiality as you adhere to the faith in our glorious Lord Jesus Christ.
>
> **—James 2:1**

The Catholic school teacher would do well to recall that having faith in the Lord implies recognizing that his will is the primary consideration as it relates to how we go about our everyday activities, both in our personal lives and within our professional lives as educators. Keeping the Lord at the forefront of our existence is the only way for us to fill our role more completely as laborers in the Lord's service. To take matters further, we must also concede that the kingdom of God is both the ultimate *goal* of our mission and the *foundation* of our mission. As long as we maintain our relationship with the Lord insofar as we provide him with our due allegiance, we will be carrying out our educational duties and responsibilities more meaningfully, more devotedly, more sincerely, more appropriately, and more charitably. In the same way, we cannot assume that our students are some type of spiritual novice, unable to understand the Lord's prime position in the grand scheme of considerations. Encourage them to glorify Christ gladly.

AUGUST 27

> House of Jacob, come, let us walk in the light of the LORD!
>
> **—Isaiah 2:5**

At this point, you have either already started the new school year or are preparing for your first day. Remember always to look for opportunities to reflect on how walking with the Lord, striving to live according to his will, leads to a refreshingly new spiritual outlook.

When we follow the ways of the Lord, we see the world through different eyes—eyes that are more aware of the presence of God and his goodness. In other words, the more we stay close to the Lord and have the kingdom of God as our goal, the clearer the vision of our soul will be as it relates to effectively discerning the importance of remaining with the Lord and likewise encouraging others to follow him. Therefore, the Catholic school teacher must endeavor to draw his or her students to follow the Lord and to walk in his ways, in order for them to gain more effectively the inspiration and spiritual reinforcement to continue along that path. God does not just point out the way; he takes us by the hand and leads us where we truly want to be, whether or not we realize it: walking with him.

AUGUST 28

> You drew near on the day I called you; you said, "Do not fear!"
>
> **—Lamentations 3:57**

There are various points within the teacher's life in which we have to call on the Lord. We must not summon the Lord as a toddler beckons for a parent, demanding a chocolate-chip cookie when it is healthier to ask for a cup of fruit. Our addresses to the Lord must be in the form of soulfully, plaintively, humbly, and sincerely admitting that we can do nothing without him: "I have the strength for everything through him who empowers me" (Phil 4:13). During this school year, and in those to come, you as a Catholic school teacher will surely encounter various times in which you have genuine fear—fear that you are not being effective in the classroom, fear that you are not drawing your students closer to the Lord, fear that your students are not "connecting the dots" in terms of understanding what exactly this life is all about. God will not answer with thunderclaps or personal appearances, but your heart will hear his response eventually—and always right on time.

AUGUST 29

> On that day—oracle of the LORD—I will gather the lame,
> and I will assemble the outcasts.
>
> **—Micah 4:6**

It is important for students to understand that God's call to love the poor, the outcast, and the marginalized is not a mandate that ended at the time of the gospels. In other words, we too are called today to serve those in poverty. Jesus' love for the poor is a reminder of who he is and how he is close to all of us. It is crucial for the Catholic school teacher to remember this because then we will more effectively fathom the fullness of God's greatness, thereby honoring him and attempting to live according to his will. God calls to those who are outcast because he wants all of us to come to him. The tenets of faith necessarily underscore how all of us are in need of the Lord in terms of our redemptive aspirations. In fact, those who are in the most unfortunate circumstances are perhaps those who have the ability to better comprehend humankind's inability to attain our own salvation. Encourage your students to serve society's marginalized: the unborn, the indigent, the handicapped, the infirm, the elderly, and more—all those in need.

AUGUST 30

> Seek the LORD, all you humble of the land, who have observed his law;
> Seek justice, seek humility.
>
> **—Zephaniah 2:3**

There are various expectations when it comes to being a disciple of the Lord, many of which are encapsulated within this passage from the Book of Zephaniah. We must seek the Lord in our daily lives, making this desire our utmost aim, both in terms of *being* near him and likewise *remaining* near him. We must be humble, because humility is a virtue that leads us to recall that God's will, rather than our own will, must be at the forefront of our lives. (Also, make sure that you are not "that guy" who reminds everyone that humility is your best virtue; if so, you clearly have your work cut out for you.) We must observe the law, because Jesus came to reinforce the ultimate precedent of God's law (see Mt 5:17–18). We must seek justice because in so doing we serve the kingdom of God by veritably "hunger[ing] and thirst[ing] for righteousness" (Mt 5:6). It is in so aligning ourselves with God's will that we are able to serve even more effectively as Catholic school educators. Let us approach him and follow.

AUGUST 31

> Out of the depths I call to you, Lord; Lord, hear my cry! May your ears be attentive to my cry for mercy.
>
> **—Psalm 130:1–2**

Well, here you are. There is no turning back. The summer is definitely behind you. There is no hope for an extended break of the same duration that you recently experienced, at least until about mid-June of next year. Do not appear in the faculty room today with tears of strife streaming down your face, desiring the sensation of warm sand beneath your weary feet. The summer vacation is definitively over, and you must move forward. There will be days (hopefully not today—hopefully not already, so soon!) in which you are in the depths as a teacher. The Lord doubtlessly hears your cry and receives your plea. He knows how best to address our every need, of course in a better way than we could ever hope to know. Keep in mind, over the course of the next nine months (do you need to get some tissues now?), that God is always available to hear our calls for assistance. In imitation of the Lord, be sure also to heed your students when they need your help. Have a good academic year ahead, and ask God to help you along.

SEPTEMBER 1

The LORD is slow to anger, yet great in power.

—Nahum 1:3a

God's limitless power means that he can do as he sees fit. There is no supreme legislature to counteract his will (despite the occasional effort by some more misguided human institutions). There is no higher sovereignty to which he must report. It is reasonably within our human nature to suspect that such unchecked power would entail God to wield this potency. Yet, how does God use his power? Simply, he loves us. His "slow[ness] to anger" indicates his compassion and that he has our best interest at heart. God's position does not imply that he is somehow ignorant of what he has expected of us; after all, he calls us to strive constantly to be holier and thus closer to him. In imitation of the Lord, the Catholic school teacher should recall that the power of our position is fulfilled in being protective and nurturing. We should never take advantage of our responsibilities in serving the kingdom of God. Strive to make daily efforts to reflect on how you can further respect the Lord's power (while not "speeding up" his anger)!

SEPTEMBER 2

To me every knee shall bend; by me every tongue shall swear.

—Isaiah 45:23b

God's words through the prophet Isaiah are also referenced within the New Testament, perhaps most prominently in Philippians 2:9–11: "Because of this, God greatly exalted him and bestowed on him the name that is above every name, that at the name of Jesus every knee should bend, of those in heaven and on earth and under the earth, and every tongue confess that Jesus Christ is Lord, to the glory of God the Father." Hopefully, at some point this school year—ideally sooner than later—you will have a school-wide Mass (if you have not already). Make sure that you encourage your students to understand why it is so important to remain reverent at Mass: because the Holy Eucharist is the "source and summit" (*CCC* 1324) of the sacraments that the Lord gave us; it is the fullness of his divine being. It is especially important that teachers other than theology teachers participate in liturgical celebrations because it will mean a great deal more coming from you than from us "talking heads" in the theology classroom. Lead your students to give the Lord his due!

SEPTEMBER 3

The greedy see their share as not enough; greedy injustice dries up the soul.

—Sirach 14:9

The Catholic school teacher literally cannot afford to be greedy (at least in terms of his or her salary). Anecdotally, those who are the most generous tend to be the most fulfilled, while those who possess more tend continuously to want more. Look for opportunities to give within your school community, whether in terms of your time, talent, or treasure. Regarding your time, make sure that you do not waste the time of others. (During your planning period, do not let your time flitter away playing spider solitaire rather than grading those essays that are so old they were printed using a dot matrix printer.) In terms of your talent, look for unique ways to enhance your community. (Who knew that you could sign a late slip using calligraphy?) In terms of your treasure, although Catholic school teachers are admittedly of modest means, look for ways to give financially. (Buy those students' raffle tickets to support the school's missionary trip abroad.) Show your students how to serve others for Christ!

SEPTEMBER 4

> But you, LORD, are a shield around me; my glory, you keep my head high.
>
> **—Psalm 3:4**

There will be days in which you feel absolutely miserable, but you will have to push through and be there for your students. You cannot do this by yourself. Trying to go it alone is like trying to ride a bicycle with octagonal wheels; you might go a short distance, but you are bound to come to a halt eventually because of the physical exhaustion of using a poorly designed machine. Note here that a theology teacher attempted to use a mathematical analogy. (You would have a better chance of seeing Halley's Comet twice than seeing such a feat occur again!) Allow the Lord to provide you with the strength that you will never be able to muster solely. Students are quite perceptive, and they can tell if you are not at your best for any variety of reasons. Thank them if they happen to be compassionate toward you or if they ask if you are all right; do not simply brush them off, because they are truly inclined to being virtuous.

SEPTEMBER 5

> And Jesus said to the centurion, "You may go; as you have believed, let it be done for you."
>
> **—Matthew 8:13a**

Jesus, of course, spoke these words to the centurion in the midst of his healing of the centurion's servant. (If you have a minute, take the time to read the entire account in Matthew 8:5–13.) How often do we really believe what we ask of Jesus? Do we simply say the words, cynically conceiving that there is no way that the Lord could possibly respond to our prayers? There are various episodes within the gospels in which Jesus encourages his would-be followers to have faith. In fact, there are far too many occasions to mention in one reflection here. As Catholic school teachers, the prayers that we offer to the Lord will not necessarily be answered in the way that we would like. But remember, we are not God. Whether you are a first-year teacher or have taught since there were only thirteen states to memorize for your history test, we are no closer to being God than a grain of sand is to being a boulder—much less, in fact. Have faith and let God do what he does, because he is the ultimate source of strength for all of our students and for us as well.

SEPTEMBER 6

> Children, be on your guard against idols.
>
> **—1 John 5:21**

Although we know that we must avoid making idols, it is important for us to beware of how easily things, even immaterial entities, can become other gods. Although it is good for anyone, perhaps especially teachers, to enjoy recreation, we must make sure that pastimes, hobbies, and other manifestations of recreation do not become our focus. For example, if you became a teacher for the vacations, then you are in the wrong profession, and you may have been more geared toward being a pilot. (After all, operating a multi-ton metal tube filled with three hundred people sitting inches away from highly combustible jet fuel, rocketing through thin air at five hundred miles an hour, six miles above solid ground, is still somehow less daunting than the task of helping to mold the mind and heart of even one student, let alone multiple students.) Make sure that your recreation, in terms of how you spend your free time, does not cloud your professional obligations as an educator. Let your students flourish.

SEPTEMBER 7

> And a voice came from the heavens, "You are my beloved Son; with you I am well pleased."
>
> **—Mark 1:11**

This announcement from God the Father to God the Son takes place in the midst of Jesus' baptism in the Jordan River by John the Baptist. (To read the full account, see Mark 1:9–11, as well as Matthew 3:13–17, Luke 3:21–22, and John 1:31–33.) Since the actual Feast of the Baptism of the Lord takes place in January, reflecting on this passage in September may seem awry, but it is worthwhile to take a moment early in the school year to meditate on a particular aspect of this passage. Note how God the Father praises God the Son. In imitation of the Lord, the Catholic school teacher must remember to remain positive in terms of building up students. Even God the Father took the time to do this with Jesus because he saw fit to acknowledge who he was. (Make sure not to lead students to believe that they are somehow deities, no matter their attempts to avow this.) Choose words that will encourage students to lead lives in accord with God's will, and only say to them that which you would feel confident saying in the Lord's presence.

SEPTEMBER 8

> And it shall be that everyone shall be saved who calls on the name of the Lord.
>
> **—Acts 2:21**

This excerpt has allusions to various passages that are worth noting, including Joel 3:5 ("Then everyone who calls upon the name of the LORD will escape harm") and Romans 10:13 ("For everyone who calls on the name of the Lord will be saved"). Given this passage's prominence, it is worthwhile to consider its implications. Our salvation is from the Lord, for we cannot achieve this on our own, with a mere vocalization. Of course, the actions of our lives must accompany our words: "Not everyone who says to me, 'Lord, Lord,' will enter the kingdom of heaven, but only the one who does the will of my Father in heaven" (Mt 7:21); "Why do you call me, 'Lord, Lord,' but not do what I command?" (Lk 6:46); "Be doers of the word and not hearers only, deluding yourselves" (Jas 1:22). As Catholic school teachers, both within our personal and professional realms, we must be sure not to draw "near with words only and [honor him] with [our] lips alone, though [our] hearts are far from [him]" (Is 29:13).

SEPTEMBER 9

> [Jesus] was amazed at their lack of faith.
>
> **—Mark 6:6**

Jesus had feelings, sentiments, and other kinds of emotional expression; as we read in this passage, he "was amazed." This passage is set within a section of chapter 6 of the Gospel of Mark (Mk 6:1–6) known as Jesus' "rejection at Nazareth," when even those who had known the Lord himself for much of his life were hesitant to recognize his truly divine nature. As we learn from the equivocation of Jesus' associates, do not let the Lord be similarly "amazed at [your] lack of faith." In other words, we as Catholic school teachers should have the same approach as the Twelve: "And the apostles said to the Lord, 'Increase our faith'" (Lk 17:5). There are various ways to increase your faith in the Lord within the realm of the Catholic school. For example, you might take the time to recall why you value the privilege of being able to teach in a Catholic school and what brings you back every day—namely, to enhance your faith by seeing Christ in your students. Make sure that you aim to "amaze" Jesus with your great faith!

SEPTEMBER 10

> The way of fools is right in their own eyes, but those who listen to advice are the wise.
>
> **—Proverbs 12:15**

Catholic school teachers receive a lot of different types of information from various sources: fellow classroom teachers, administrators, students, parents, professional organizations, and various other outlets from which we are responsible for receiving, absorbing, retaining, and recalling information. This information is not necessarily conflicting, but it is still copious at the very least. Make sure to use all of the information that you receive to synthesize the content from these avenues and thus form a picture of how to best serve your community. If you close yourself off to the reception of relevant information, then you begin down the road to foolishness, believing that you are capable of subsisting professionally without any need for the input of your colleagues or other community stakeholders. Be sure to listen to the feedback of others, because everyone has a different perspective. This does not imply that everyone else is always right, but heed their valuable outlook. Recall that all wisdom can be spread.

SEPTEMBER 11

We call upon your name, we declare your wonderful deeds.

—Psalm 75:2b

The Catholic school teacher would do well to remind his or her students constantly of the marvelous works that the Lord has done for us. The Lord is always willing to show himself to us even in the midst of difficulties, trials, tribulations, tragedies, and other realities that accompany our fallen human nature. When we are dealing with such challenges, we must rely especially on the Lord to see us through. However, this does not necessarily mean he will provide us with some sort of temporal comfort; rather, we must ask the Lord to strengthen and fortify us so that we can be that much more prepared to serve him and thus bring greater glory to his kingdom. Similarly, look for various opportunities to ask your students to detail the times in their lives that they have taken note of the Lord's presence. This is an eye-opening endeavor, because it draws everyone (teachers and students alike) to realize that, even when we are faced with particular dilemmas, God reliably stays in control and wants us all to keep our eyes fixed on him.

SEPTEMBER 12

I say this so that no one may deceive you by specious arguments.

—Colossians 2:4

Saint Paul knew how to formulate good arguments. *Argument,* as it is used here, is conceived as an engagingly convincing discussion regarding certain matters of faith; it does not mean that Paul and Peter went to fisticuffs over who would arise as the victor in a game of "Is the pope Catholic?" In other words, Paul knew his stuff. He was familiar with the Mosaic Law and the scriptural messianic prophecies, in order to prove to prospective Christians (following his own famous conversion) that Christ was indeed the Messiah. To benefit your students, make sure that you look for various opportunities to instill in them a love for the truth, ensuring that they know both how to live and how to articulate gospel principles. But what if you teach a subject other than theology? Is not this expectation solely for theology teachers? There are no worries here. Just as theology teachers would do well to encourage students to know about molecular biology so as to show the wonder of life, teachers of other subject areas can tip their hats to theological topics.

SEPTEMBER 13

But as for me, I will look to the LORD, I will wait for God my savior; my God will hear me!

—Micah 7:7

This passage from Micah is compared to both Isaiah 8:17 ("I will trust in the LORD, who is hiding his face from the house of Jacob; yes, I will wait for him") and Joshua 24:15 ("As for me and my household, we will serve the LORD"). We must make sure to do our best to serve the kingdom of God in our daily duties as Catholic school teachers. One of the best ways to "look to the Lord" is by patiently serving our students. It is vital for us to recall that our role as Catholic school teachers is inherently one in which we have to be patient and wait to see the good work that God does in our students. Although we must necessarily remind our students that they are called to holiness—not only in their futures, but also now—we ought to bear in mind also that, in many cases, we will not see the germination of the seeds that we are planting. Nonetheless, seeing them grow in holiness is God's ultimate prerogative, and not ours. The work of the Holy Spirit is impressive to behold. Keep faith in the Lord, and your students will readily benefit.

SEPTEMBER 14

> No one is like you, LORD, you are great, great and mighty is your name.
>
> **—Jeremiah 10:6**

How often do you stop during the school day and reflect, even if just briefly, on how unique Catholic schools are? They are institutions that are far more than just bricks stacked together, a cafeteria that does not sell meat on Fridays during Lent, and a boiler that will eventually have to be replaced, requiring the inevitable fundraiser. A Catholic school is an institution in which the community places God at the forefront of every segment of student life. This, of course, does not mean having such overt expressions of faith that they become disdainful. For example, the football team can, and should, pray together before a game, but this does not mean that they have to fill the cooler with holy water and douse every passerby. God is who he is, and we would do well to honor him for who he is, particularly by following the example of selfless love that Jesus Christ provided us. Let us, in imitation of him, love one another in order to truly underscore and cherish our schools' Catholic identity.

SEPTEMBER 15

> But now I am standing trial because of my hope in the promise made by God to our ancestors.
>
> **—Acts 26:6**

Saint Paul knew persecution. However, he likewise knew that he could endure any suffering as long as he had Christ in his heart. Although Paul was imprisoned on various occasions, his captivity was not justifiable from a Christian standpoint. He had committed no offense against God; rather, his only alleged violation was against secular power. It is important to give students an adequate understanding of what is meant by the Christian conceptualization of "justice." Justice is not vengeance, retribution, or "getting even"; rather, the goal of justice is forgiveness, repentance, reconciliation, and bringing others to know God's love. Saint Paul had no sort of animosity toward his captors, and he even inspired some of them to conversion. The Catholic school teacher should encourage his or her students to pray for those who are persecuted for professing their faith in the gospel, whether in the United States or abroad. Students should be aware of the difficulties that come with discipleship and how our persecuted brethren need support.

SEPTEMBER 16

Grace and truth came through Jesus Christ.

—John 1:17

It is important for the Catholic school teacher to reflect on how Jesus is God himself. Jesus was not merely some sort of medicine man, shaman, sage, tie-dye-touting guru, or television personality sponsoring a telethon. Jesus is the Messiah. Jesus provides us with "grace and truth," but we must make sure not to take his offer of redemption for granted. Look for opportunities to have your students reflect on just how awesome and amazing it is that God himself came down to be with us. He did not merely remain in heaven, looking at us through some sort of cosmic water globe. Jesus came down to show us how to live in the midst of a world that is not necessarily open to the light of truth or grace. Depending on the particular course that you teach, look for ways to have your students reflect on Jesus' divine attributes. This could even be in the form of having students compose a short prayer to thank the Lord for all that he has done, particularly thanking him for his example and opportunity for salvation. Thank God!

SEPTEMBER 17

Whoever is ashamed of me and of my words, the Son of Man will be ashamed of when he comes in his glory and in the glory of the Father and of the holy angels.

—Luke 9:26

The intention of this passage is clear: the Christian is expected to profess Christ even in the midst of ridicule at best or outright persecution at worst. This passage correlates with its appearance in Matthew 10:33 ("But whoever denies me before others, I will deny before my heavenly Father") and Mark 8:38 ("Whoever is ashamed of me and of my words in this faithless and sinful generation, the Son of Man will be ashamed of when he comes in his Father's glory with the holy angels"). Fortunately, given your Catholic school setting, you have the opportunity to discuss, spread, and otherwise live out the Lord's command to share the gospel with others. Hence, it is important to remind students that the knowledge of Jesus Christ they gain as students in a Catholic school is a distinct gift that is not necessarily available in other places. Students are eager to serve the Lord, and they are readily looking for opportunities to live their faith. Proudly profess the Lord and thus teach your students, because your leading them to Christ will bring them to fulfillment.

SEPTEMBER 18

Indeed, the ways of each person are plain to the LORD's sight; all their paths he surveys.

—Proverbs 5:21

It is vital to remind students that the Lord is always with them. God is not watching us in the hopes that we somehow fail; rather, God wants us to come close to him and remain there. Therefore, it is important for us to admit our sinfulness and need of his redemption.

God knows us better than we know ourselves. Perfect Pam may think that she knows herself well enough to be able to go through life without needing to resort to any higher power (i.e., God) for true reconciliation, but she will soon realize her error. Encourage your students to comprehend how God remains vigilant over us, but not as a deific whack-a-mole player, looking forward to smashing us mercilessly into humility at least or compliance at most. Instead, God is with us because he wants us to follow his path of virtue and holiness. Hence, we must be sure to look to the example of Christ in terms of how he lived to know how we should thus conduct ourselves. Although we could never emulate God in his fullness, take some time to reflect: Is God pleased with what he sees?

SEPTEMBER 19

Bless the Lord, my soul; and do not forget all his gifts.

—Psalm 103:2

It is, very unfortunately, too common for us to approach prayer with an attitude of "What can we get out of it?" We cannot come to prayer as spoiled complainers, but we should come as humble servants. Is it possible for us to spend too much time either reflecting on the multitude of gifts with which the Lord has endowed us or thanking him for these reliable treasures? If we ever stop appreciating all that the Lord has done for us, our spiritual life and moral compass will start spiraling downward faster than the water plummets down the drain of the fifty-year-old water fountain in your school's lower hallway. Invite your students to consider ways in which the Lord has blessed them abundantly. Students are rather considerate, and they readily look for chances to think about how God has blessed them in a variety of ways. However, it is vital for us to make sure to emphasize to them that suffering does not necessarily mean that we have somehow fallen out of God's favor; hence, we should always beware of temporal prosperity as a goal of life.

SEPTEMBER 20

Let us approach with a sincere heart and in absolute trust.

—Hebrews 10:22a

It is very important for the Catholic school teacher to keep a clean heart. What does this mean? Make sure that you are not given to biting sarcasm and cynicism, because both of these drawbacks rob you and the community of true hope in the Lord. Make sure that your delivery of lessons to your students is done in a spirit of charity, rather than one of negativity and rancor. Just as the ideal is for Catholic school teachers to appreciate the ministry of teaching "with a sincere heart," so too should students have the opportunity to make themselves right with the Lord. If your school is blessed enough to have a priest on staff who can offer the sacrament of Reconciliation during school hours, make sure to encourage your students to take advantage of this opportunity. (Remember that even if a student is not of the Catholic faith, he or she can still go talk to the priest, in order for the priest to offer some spiritual conversation and prayer to help keep the student's heart oriented toward the Lord.) Trust that the Lord is who he has said he is.

SEPTEMBER 21

The child grew and became strong, filled with wisdom; and the favor of God was upon him.

—Luke 2:40

Jesus was no less God when he was young than when he was an adult. In other words, Jesus has possessed the fullness of his divinity for all time because God the Father, God the Son, and God the Holy Spirit have always existed in total unity. However, when it comes to our own students, we must remember that theirs is a process of ongoing conversion. Better said, all of us are constantly undergoing conversion. We will never arrive at a point in which we have attained the fullness of wisdom, because this is impossible for us to achieve as mere humans. If not even Siri or Google are capable of providing your average theology teacher with a satisfactory response to inquiries as to why we exist, then we can securely deduce that not even technology is capable of possessing all knowledge. A dilemma persists, however: knowledge is only useful insofar as it can be used to serve humanity and the Lord. It is by imitating the Lord that his favor rests on us. Let us therefore respect God's wisdom.

SEPTEMBER 22

You, Lord, are the one to be worshiped!

—Baruch 6:5

At this point, you are only a few weeks into the school year. However, you may have already experienced some stressful situations, some dilemmas, or some challenges, whether at the level of logistics, pedagogy, or otherwise. When things get particularly difficult, step back for a moment and recall that the Lord is always the goal; he is "the one to be worshiped." Test scores are not what ultimately matters. The ability to write in cursive (as impressive as that is, given its rueful decline in use) is not what ultimately matters. What matters is orienting our wills to the Lord, which will fulfill us and allow us to be effective in our teaching apostolate. Make sure that you likewise share with your students the vital importance of making sure to keep God first. This, of course, applies to any subject; in English class, for example, you could point out the Christian imagery that some authors employ; in health class, you could emphasize how we must respect our bodies in order to better magnify the Lord. Bring your students to the Lord.

SEPTEMBER 23

Now, therefore, fear the LORD and serve him completely and sincerely.

—Joshua 24:14a

Serving others is not something that is necessarily easy to do. Our orientation is often to want to be served, rather than to serve. However, this is in direct opposition to Jesus' position in Mark 10:45: "For the Son of Man did not come to be served, but to serve and to give his life as a ransom for many." If Jesus came to serve, and we are called to imitate him, you do not have to be a logician to fathom what the expectation is for us: we must serve likewise. However, note that this particular passage reminds us to serve the Lord first and foremost. There are numerous scriptural references to loving God above all, and our service to him and his kingdom stands as a reliable indication of our love for him. Remind your students of this latter point in particular, because the youth—despite the belief by others that they are the missing link between humanity and prehominid primates—are actually geared toward praising the Lord. Encourage your students to honor God by "serv[ing] him completely and sincerely" to supreme benefit.

SEPTEMBER 24

Do this is memory of me.

—Luke 22:19c

The reader will note that Jesus' command regarding the Eucharist, which he instituted for his twelve disciples and their spiritual posterity within the context of the Last Supper, is just that: a command, rather than a suggestion, recommendation, or hint. Be sure to provide students with the opportunity to reflect deeply on the Eucharist. This is admittedly an endeavor that will be the most applicable and relevant for the theology teacher, but Catholic school teachers of all subjects can still take the time to appreciate and respect this most important of the seven sacraments, since the Eucharist is Jesus himself, in the fullness of his body, blood, soul, and divinity. The Eucharist is present at Mass and during eucharistic adoration. Most Catholic schools offer school-wide Masses. If your school also offers eucharistic adoration, encourage your students to attend. Take your own presence and demeanor at school Masses seriously. Be reverent, upbeat, and respectful. In other words, act as if you are going to see the Lord Jesus—because you are!

SEPTEMBER 25

I bore you up on eagles' wings and brought you to myself.

—Exodus 19:4b

This passage, in which God is reminding the Hebrews, by way of Moses, that he led them out of slavery in Egypt, is effective beyond serving as the chorus of the well-known Catholic hymn "On Eagles' Wings." (As an aside, this song's nostalgia-inducing capabilities are rivaled only by "Be Not Afraid" and "Here I Am, Lord"). Note that the reference here regarding God's providence and protection relies on the imagery of an eagle. The eagle is readily recognized and referenced as being the archetype of glory, magnificence, and splendor. Therefore, the eagle is justifiably referenced, as opposed to the prospect of a vulture, an emu, an ostrich, and so on. The divinely inspired author of this passage uses the imagery of an eagle because the Lord is similarly splendid, regal, respectable, and awe-inspiring. Make sure that you invite your students to reflect on God's majesty because our souls will benefit from being constantly impressed by his glorious attributes.

SEPTEMBER 26

They are to slander no one, to be peaceable, considerate, exercising all graciousness toward everyone.

—Titus 3:2

Make sure to exercise Christian charity in all of your dealings with your colleagues. Avoid being like Negative Ned, who would rather scowl, grimace, and frown than actually offer a positive assessment of a benign situation. Do not imitate the approach of Flustered Felicia, who looks for an opportunity to criticize others like an oceanic whitetip shark prowls throughout the open sea, awaiting the passage of its next unsuspecting piscine victim. Have it in your mind each day, either while you are on your way to school or after you have arrived, that you are veritably going to build up your colleagues. Everyone has bad days, and it is easy to put up a defensive emotional wall in order to "be ready" for the next onslaught of challenges, but persevere. If you are incapable of letting your colleagues see the face of Christ, your entire community will soon suffer. Be a person of peace, supported by the Lord's grace and your desire to help others be close to the Lord. If you were your colleague, how would you view yourself?

SEPTEMBER 27

Those who shut their eyes to the cry of the poor will themselves call out and not be answered.

—Proverbs 21:13

This proverb is perhaps one of the more noteworthy passages within scripture that reminds us of how those living in poverty have a special place in the orientation of the kingdom of God. Its message is, of course, emphasized by Jesus within the gospels, particularly (although not exclusively, of course) in the Gospel of Luke, sometimes known as "the gospel of the poor." The Catholic school teacher should look for various opportunities to highlight the ways in which all of God's faithful are called to serve those living in abject poverty. This service should not merely be theoretical or conceptual; it must be practical and actual. Students must also know that serving those living in poverty should not be limited to occasions surrounding holidays. While Thanksgiving food drives, Christmas toy drives, Easter clothing drives, and other initiatives are remarkably excellent ways to serve the hungry, the homeless, and the otherwise indigent, make sure to endeavor to organize charitable initiatives all throughout the calendar year. Inspire your students in service.

SEPTEMBER 28

Return to me . . . and I will return to you.

—Zechariah 1:3

The condition of feeling far from God signifies that we need to return to him. However, God is so abundantly merciful that he readily seeks us out and actively endeavors to inspire our return. If you need a reminder, simply take a few minutes to review three of Jesus' perhaps more well-known parables from the fifteenth chapter of the Gospel of Luke: the parables of the lost sheep (Lk 15:1–7), the lost coin (Lk 15:8–10), and the prodigal son (Lk 15:11–32). There is no sin conceivable that God cannot forgive. There is no distance so far that you have fallen that God cannot pick you up again. There is no hopelessness so profound that the Lord cannot fill that hopeless void in your life. We as Catholic school teachers must always endeavor to remind our students of these realities (just as we must, of course, remind ourselves of them, lest we neglect our own spiritual lives). At the end of the day, we must remember the glorious capacity that God has to offer us redemption, which we cannot achieve through our own merits.

SEPTEMBER 29

Our help is in the name of the LORD, the maker of heaven and earth.

—Psalm 124:8

This passage is reflective of Psalm 121:2: "My help comes from the LORD, the maker of heaven and earth." It is important for the Catholic school teacher to recall that we must call on the Lord at various times within our careers as teachers. However, our calls to the Lord must not be in the form of vain, selfish, or shallow desires for temporal comforts, financial prosperity, or a life devoid of any suffering. Rather, the Christian journey is one that will inherently be fraught with difficulties and suffering. After all, a brief review of the gospels will reveal just how challenging it is to be a disciple of Christ. However, the Lord provides strength in order to encourage us to stay close to him and to rely on him as the very source of our strength. Hence, he, who is supernaturally powerful enough to have fashioned the very universe itself, has no problem helping us at all, since we are his most prized creation. We must remind our students likewise to call upon—but not whine to—the Lord during strife.

SEPTEMBER 30

Proclaim the word; be persistent whether it is convenient or inconvenient; convince, reprimand, encourage through all patience and teaching.

—2 Timothy 4:2

It would be worthwhile to reflect on the verses that immediately follow these words that appear at the beginning of the last chapter of Saint Paul's Second Letter to Timothy: "For the time will come when people will not tolerate sound doctrine but, following their own desires and insatiable curiosity, will accumulate teachers and will stop listening to the truth and will be diverted to myths. But you, be self-possessed in all circumstances; put up with hardship; perform the work of an evangelist; fulfill your ministry" (2 Tm 4:3–5). This passage is well worth considering for Catholic school teachers of all subjects because of its implications: no matter what we teach, we are given the important responsibility of being sincere insofar as we bring the gospel to our students. There are times during the school year when it may be either easier or more challenging to serve the kingdom of God. Many distractions get in the way. However, we must always keep in focus our crucial role: letting our students know God's love.

OCTOBER 1

> You say I am a king. For this I was born and for this I came into the world, to testify to the truth. Everyone who belongs to the truth listens to my voice.
>
> **—John 18:37**

This affirmation from Christ takes place within the midst of his dialogue with Pontius Pilate before Christ's passion. More specifically, this exchange takes place just prior to Christ's sentence of crucifixion, the tortuous execution method that the potentates within the Roman Empire reserved for the worst offenders—a sentence that in Jesus' case was delivered to someone who was not only innocent of the crime for which he was charged, but also innocent of *any* crime, *any* offense, *any* sin, *any* blemish of the soul. Early October may seem to be an unusual time to reflect on the reality of Christ's passion, since this is normally a spiritual exercise throughout Lent and Holy Week (Palm Sunday through Holy Saturday). However, it is critical to recall throughout the year Christ's ultimate sacrifice on the Cross for our sins, based on his love for us and our desire for salvation. No matter what subject you teach, aim for that same adoration for the truth to shine through, for the spiritual well-being of all our students.

OCTOBER 2

Grace, mercy, and peace will be with us from God the Father and from Jesus Christ the Father's Son in truth and love.

—2 John 1:3

The Second Letter of John is one of five short one-chapter books in the Bible. The Third Letter of John is another. In fact, these two books are each barely a paragraph in total length. Just like a verbose theology teacher (who allegedly exist, despite the contentions of present company), the introductions to 2 John and 3 John are actually longer than the content of the chapters themselves. This digression is hopefully worthwhile insofar as it inspires the reader to get to know scripture as well as possible—some of the books are so short that you can read them during a five-minute commercial break while watching *The Price Is Right*, a perfect program for a day off from school. The promises of "grace, mercy, and peace" are factors that we see laced throughout the gospels. The Christian lifestyle may not be in accord with society's standards, but persevere in living in line with God's will. Love the Lord and his will, in order to be more open to the "truth and love" that originate from proximity to God. Your students will thrive.

OCTOBER 3

Therefore, we must attend all the more to what we have heard, so that we may not be carried away.

—Hebrews 2:1

There is a certain potency of memory when it comes to recalling that which has been drilled into us throughout our lives. The same is true when it comes to students who learn something from their teacher after having been exposed to a lesson over and over again. The experienced teacher will readily assert that those colleagues of his or hers who have made the most impact on their students are those whose students can readily recall lessons that stuck with them. Therefore, the Catholic school teacher would do well to instill lessons in his or her students that will stay with them throughout their lives. Of course, the most enduring lessons are those that were delivered with truth and clarity. Offering lessons with the goal of bringing students to the Lord does not have to come in the form of reciting aphorisms repetitiously throughout the class; rather, be actively charitable and uplifting—over and over again.

OCTOBER 4

> They promise them freedom, though they themselves are slaves of corruption, for a person is a slave of whatever overcomes him.
>
> **—2 Peter 2:19**

The point can hardly be emphasized to a sufficient extent: students, particularly in modern times, must know the true expectations of freedom. Freedom does not signify doing whatever appeals to us, inconsiderate of the ultimate consequences. Freedom does not mean relishing in sin, devoid of any contrition, let alone of any reconciliation. In effect, freedom does not imply doing whatever we want. True freedom is having access to opportunities for morality. A basic review of the gospels reveals how repeatedly and emphatically Jesus calls us to repentance and sanctity—to turn away from our sins. We are never "good enough" in Jesus' eyes when it comes to our morality: "I tell you, unless your righteousness surpasses that of the scribes and Pharisees, you will not enter into the kingdom of heaven" (Mt 5:20); "So be perfect, just as your heavenly Father is perfect" (Mt 5:48); "If you love me, you will keep my commandments" (Jn 14:15). Youth are impressionable and prone to influence, so inspire them to holiness.

OCTOBER 5

For we are God's co-workers.

—1 Corinthians 3:9a

Of course, in this passage Saint Paul is not referring to God as some semblance of your colleague. (Could you imagine the pressure of having the Lord as a colleague? Talk about trying to match his standards; he would have the perfect lesson plans, not to mention evaluations that would be nothing less than divine!) Rather, Saint Paul is encouraging us here to make sure that our labors are in ultimate accord with the Lord's will. We have so many duties as teachers, and it is unfortunately very easy to get sidetracked and to lose focus of what our role as Catholic school teachers entails. Even in the midst of approaching the end of the first academic quarter (already), you may feel beleaguered and hesitant to be completely on board with what the Lord wants you to do with your life, particularly in light of your teaching ministry. Make sure to cooperate with the Lord's will; after all, going along with his will is the only way to achieve lasting fulfillment in your career and life. Also, remember that God is so mighty that he is ultimately even the boss of your principal!

OCTOBER 6

Rather, the law of the LORD is his joy; and on his law he meditates day and night.

—Psalm 1:2

How is your prayer life? How seriously do you take your conversations with the Lord? Remember that prayer is a two-way street; it involves both speaking to God *and* listening to what he has to say. It is easy to *talk* to God, but the difficulty may rest in *listening* to him, probably because of the unfortunate reality that we fear what his response might be. Look for ways to help your prayer. There are various types of prayer in the Christian tradition, and some of them may appeal to you more than others. Explore different types of prayer, with the ultimate goal being both to reach out to and to follow the Lord. For example, one reliable type of prayer is meditation on the Word of God, using scriptural readings to allow the Lord's will to flood your heart. The impactful Catholic school teacher is the teacher who opens himself or herself to the implications of the gospel, in order to serve the Lord more faithfully, and in order to bring students to know his abiding love. When listening to God, do not press "mute."

OCTOBER 7

> For by grace you have been saved through faith, and this is not from you; it is the gift of God; it is not from works, so no one may boast.
>
> **—Ephesians 2:8–9**

This passage has considerable meaning and importance insofar as it relates to several other scripture passages, including Romans 3:24—"They are justified freely by his grace through the redemption in Christ Jesus"—and Galatians 2:16—"Even we have believed in Christ Jesus that we may be justified by faith in Christ and not by works of the law, because by works of the law no one will be justified." Of course, we must still ensure that our works reinforce our faith, as we are reminded in James 2:14: "What good is it, my brothers, if someone says he has faith but does not have works? Can that faith save him?" Furthermore, and most famously, "For just as a body without a spirit is dead, so also faith without works is dead" (Jas 2:26). (When time permits, take a minute to read the full passage of James 2:14–26, rather than just these bookended excerpts. This will provide you with an even more extensive understanding of its implications.) The lesson itself is such a critical consideration for the Catholic school teacher, because we have daily opportunities both to believe and to act. Do both for your students.

OCTOBER 8

> When the crowds saw this they were struck with awe and glorified God.
>
> **—Matthew 9:8**

This excerpt from Matthew's gospel is placed immediately after Jesus' healing of a paralytic, hence the reaction of the crowd. You will notice the crowd's impression: they were so amazed at this miracle that they had just witnessed that, rather than standing by with mouths agape, they realized who had brought about the miracle—God himself—and they glorified him accordingly. The Lord manifests himself in various ways over the course of the academic year, so we must make sure not only to bear witness to these occasions but also to give glory to God whenever possible. To be clear, we should not feel slighted or abandoned by the Lord if we do not immediately discern his presence. This is particularly true when it comes to expecting temporal comforts, which are always an illusory goal; we should not expect such donatives, lest we fall into the trap of harboring some semblance of a faulty "theology of prosperity." Suffering is part of life (which Jesus knew exceedingly well). Let us reliably thank God for his many gifts and encourage our students to do likewise.

OCTOBER 9

> Jesus did this as the beginning of his signs in Cana in Galilee and so revealed his glory, and his disciples began to believe in him.
>
> **—John 2:11**

Turning water into wine at the wedding feast at Cana was Jesus' first miracle. (If you are unfamiliar with the occurrence, you should probably read its account in John 2:1–12 prior to continuing with this reflection.) Here, in what is one of Jesus' most well-known miracles, as the theology teacher will readily recognize, we see the allusions to the sacraments of Baptism, the Eucharist, and of course, Matrimony. Hence, the Catholic school teacher, no matter what subject he or she teaches, would do well to acquire at least a basic knowledge of the seven Catholic sacraments, all of which are scripturally based: Baptism, Confirmation, Eucharist, Reconciliation, Anointing of the Sick, Holy Orders, and Matrimony. Also, as John 2:11 indicates, once Jesus had begun performing miracles, his followers began to more fully comprehend who he was so that they could spread his Good News. In other words, they had to witness his divinity. Encourage your students to note the significance of Jesus' divinity.

OCTOBER 10

> Jesus said, "No one who sets a hand to the plow and looks to what was left behind is fit for the kingdom of God."
>
> **—Luke 9:62**

Jesus was rather demanding on his first disciples. For the Catholic school teacher, he is arguably even more demanding. However, we rest assured that following him is rife with, not necessarily temporal, but definitely eternal, rewards, as we are reminded by his richly uplifting words as they appear in Matthew 11:28–30: "Come to me, all you who labor and are burdened, and I will give you rest. Take my yoke upon you and learn from me, for I am meek and humble of heart; and you will find rest for your selves. For my yoke is easy, and my burden light." In other words, as far as this passage concerns our vocation as Catholic school teachers, we should ensure that we take our duties seriously. Following and living the gospel is not a part-time job; it is a full-time commitment with rewards that are more transcendent than the fleeting joys of a summer vacation and more impactful than any number of accolades that we might receive during our career. Ultimately, we must do our part to direct our students' steps toward the Lord God.

OCTOBER 11

> Lord, God of heaven, great and awesome God, you preserve your covenant of mercy with those who love you and keep your commandments.
>
> **—Nehemiah 1:5**

This may come as a surprise to some at worst, or a reminder to some at best, but God wants us to follow his commandments. Without any measure of a doubt, this expectation includes the Ten Commandments. God's commands are further elucidated by Jesus himself within the gospels, which provide us with an opportunity to more profoundly, more significantly, and more richly begin to fathom the beautifully complementary nature of his teachings on morality. Jesus' moral expectations should not be conceived as some sort of burden or load; rather, they allow us to remain in God's good graces, further underscoring how our time here on earth is ultimately oriented toward eternity—ideally an eternity in his presence. Thus, it is important for us as Catholic school teachers to encourage our students to acquire and maintain a familiarity with Christ's teachings, as well as with their remarkable splendor. Students and teachers alike should live as if we wanted to earn a gold-star sticker from the Lord, which is really a place in heaven.

OCTOBER 12

> Blessed are all who take refuge in him!
>
> **—Psalm 2:11c**

The Lord wants us to come to him with all that is in our hearts. If there is something there that honors him, he will reinforce it. If there is something there that offends the kingdom of God, he will ask us to continue our ongoing personal conversion and reform our ways in order to approach him once more. A key reason that "the God of Abraham, the God of Isaac, and the God of Jacob" (Ex 3:6) was understood to be the one, true God was his spiritual proximity to his Chosen People. In other Near Eastern civilizations, there was not this same dynamic in terms of the ability to approach the deity in a paternal way, as a child approaches his or her father. Jesus showed us this new approach by referring to the figure of God the Father as "Abba" ("Daddy") (see Mk 14:36). Encourage your students to understand God to be their true Father. For the youth, there might be some palpable angst when they think of their own parents, but remind them of God's abundantly abiding mercy, patience, and fidelity.

OCTOBER 13

> Observe, my son, your father's command, and do not reject your mother's teaching.
>
> **—Proverbs 6:20**

At this point in the academic year, you are probably near the time of parent-teacher conferences, preparing to discuss your students' progress with their parents. Make sure that you separately encourage your students to honor and respect their parents. Not only is this the fourth commandment, but it is likewise that which will ultimately lead to your students' overall well-being in their lives beyond your school's walls. The person who disrespects his or her mother or father is the person who can never be fully satisfied or content in himself or herself. Do not merely encourage your students to honor them; teach them why! At the time of parent-teacher conferences or during any other conversation during the year that deals with a student's progress in your course, be sure to provide constructive feedback. This will show that you have their best interest at heart, allowing them to better use their intellect to serve the kingdom of God. Build up your students, in imitation of how God ultimately attempts to build up spiritually all of his followers.

OCTOBER 14

> Are they not all ministering spirits sent to serve, for the sake of those who are to inherit salvation?
>
> **—Hebrews 1:14**

Why are people frequently stunned to learn that angels exist? Perhaps it is due to how they have been characterized by Hollywood's feature films, television shows, and one too many greeting cards with images of fluffy white plumes, rather than the immaterial, incorporeal entities of pure spirit who are more like God's personal telegram service (see the considerably worthwhile news delivered in Luke 1:26–38!). In fact, depending on the translation of the Bible, the term *angel* (which means "divine messenger") actually appears more than two hundred times in all of sacred scripture, in nearly equal proportions between the Old Testament and the New Testament. The Catholic Church celebrates the Feast of the Archangels (Michael, Gabriel, and Raphael, the only angels given names in scripture) on September 29 and the Feast of the Guardian Angels on October 2 of each year. The Catholic school teacher would do well to learn the Church's teachings on angels because they are truly present among us to help us along our spiritual trek toward the Lord.

OCTOBER 15

> Answer me when I call, my saving God.
>
> **—Psalm 4:2a**

The Lord answers every prayer that we offer. However, *he* knows how best to answer each prayer. Sometimes our prayers are vain, and we need to be taught humility. Sometimes our prayers are selfish, and we need to be taught selflessness. Sometimes our prayer life is lazy, and we need to be taught spiritual perseverance. Praying for a bright yellow sports car and not getting one does not mean that God does not love you; it means that you do not need a bright yellow sports car. Perhaps the Lord knows that what will bring you ultimate fulfillment is using that money, which perhaps you were going to use to buy something extra for yourself, to contribute to the needs of someone truly struggling to make ends meet. Make sure to help your students realize this as well because secular society surely has no interest in bringing anyone to look beyond the mere material world. Encourage your students to seek the Lord with sincerity, and he will address their prayers for their true benefit.

OCTOBER 16

> As you go, make this proclamation: "The kingdom of heaven is at hand."
>
> **—Matthew 10:7**

This passage is the third allusion within Matthew's gospel to Jesus' affirmation of the proximity of the kingdom of God (the other two being John the Baptist's announcement in Matthew 3:2 and the inception of Jesus' Galilean ministry in Matthew 4:17). The Catholic school teacher has a very rewarding opportunity to draw out his or her students' talents and abilities by reminding them that the Lord wants us to serve him in the present, rather than later in life or whenever we believe the suitable time has come to begin taking our souls and the implications for eternity seriously. No matter their subject area, teachers can lead their students to use their gifts to serve humanity, all for the glory of God. For example, a student who excels in biology could one day develop a vaccine for a dangerous pestilence, bringing relief and emphasizing the human dignity of all people in the Lord. Persuade students to respond to God's call for true charity!

OCTOBER 17

Behold, now is a very acceptable time; behold, now is the day of salvation.

—2 Corinthians 6:2b

Do not delay opportunities to share with students anything inspirational related to God's goodness. (Of course, this must be within reason. For example, you would not justifiably interrupt the proctoring of a lengthy midterm examination in order to share the Holy Father's most recent tweet.) In a particular way, this emphasis on exemplifications of God's goodness is easy for teachers of any subject area to undertake. There are some readily apparent examples in any subject that you could employ to aid your students to fathom just how good God is. Of course, the Lord wants to draw us to his salvation, and he thus continuously manifests his goodness; we simply have to remain open to the prospect of witnessing the immaterial manifestations of his bounteous love for us. Guide your students to him. After all, in a decade, they may not necessarily remember all of the lessons that you taught them while you were their teacher—but they will remember and continue to know God's love.

OCTOBER 18

And they shall dwell securely, for now his greatness shall reach to the ends of the earth.

—Micah 5:3b

Every student in a Catholic school should have at least a basic level of global awareness. It is inexcusable, in the globalized world of the twenty-first century, for students not to know critical elements about the world around them. However, their knowledge of the world should not be merely geopolitical; rather, their knowledge of the world should reflect dimensions of different cultures and backgrounds so that students have a grasp of various aspects of our human family. Likewise, exposing students to cultures beyond their "comfort zone" should lead them to better appreciate all of humanity, in such a way that they are better able to recognize the manners in which we can serve our fellow man and God by extension. Teachers of subjects such as foreign languages and social studies in particular (to name two of many) have a unique opportunity to instill in their students an interest in knowing about the world, all the while recalling that this world is verily not our final home: "You do not belong to this world" (Jn 15:19).

OCTOBER 19

[Jesus] said, "Abba, Father, all things are possible to you."

—Mark 14:36a

Jesus asks that we imitate him in all that we do. Our imitation of him hardly signifies that we will ever come anywhere close to replicating his divinity. However, because Jesus is God himself, he invites us to imitate him so that we can do our best to labor for the kingdom of God and draw others to him. Jesus' appellation of God the Father as "Abba" is quite telling in terms of how we can make recourse to God as our sovereign Lord, based on his familiarity and closeness. We must try to have that same love for the Lord, since we are able to refer to him in such a familial and proximate way. We should likewise ensure that our love for the Lord is reflected in our daily habits as Catholic school teachers. The closer that we are to the Lord, the more that our mission as educators in a Catholic school environment will be realized—because every Catholic school is ultimately oriented toward serving the Lord. Indeed, "all things are possible" through God; we just need to have faith that he knows what is truly best for us all.

OCTOBER 20

If you love me, you will keep my commandments.

—John 14:15

Even a cursory overview of the gospels reveals that Jesus has much to say about love. However, "love" in the (post)modern sense of the term can be rather misdiagnosed at best or misapplied at worst. There are various dimensions to love, and its categorical aspects must be evaluated in order to arrive at a more accurate sense of the term. Note that Jesus has never allowed any sort of "anything goes" permissiveness on the part of humanity. Quite the opposite, as we see in John 14:15. In too many passages to list in a small paragraph such as this one, we see Jesus calling us to repent, to turn away from our sins, to follow him, to accept his forgiveness and mercy, and likewise to offer this measure of reconciliation to others. There are many different menacing types and forms of temptation, but we must keep the Lord's love at the forefront of each day. When it comes to our students, we have the privilege of teaching them just how much God loves them, and how they can reflect this rich love by living in a virtuous and truly righteous manner.

OCTOBER 21

Have pity on me, LORD, for I am weak.

—Psalm 6:3a

"Is it really so early in the school year?" "It feels as if we have been in school for months already!" "The Thanksgiving break is still a month away!" If you are culpable of having of any of these thoughts, do not worry; you are actually normal (beyond the scope of most theology teachers). It is typical for teachers to feel tired. However, there is a vast distinction between tiredness and burnout. Even exhaustion does not necessarily denote burnout, because some of the hardest-working teachers will end up quite tired, due to the sheer physical and mental toll that teaching can take. However, we must be sure to recall that we can never go it alone; we must rely on the Lord for the resolve to be able to continue serving him by way of serving others within our communities. In order to fend off burnout, make sure that you have a rich prayer life. Jesus prayed to God the Father in some of his most challenging trials during his earthly ministry. We are hardly any exception, particularly because we are called to follow and thus imitate the Lord.

OCTOBER 22

> Fear of the LORD is the beginning of knowledge; fools despise wisdom and discipline.
>
> **—Proverbs 1:7**

How seriously do you take the advice of your elders? This includes your own family members, whether living or deceased. There is a certain characteristic mystique about our ancestors, in terms of what they experienced and contributed, or in other words, what they did with their lives. This can also be true of those who have gone before us who were not necessarily family members. These include teachers from prior generations, past administrators, and so forth. Remember that you have a wellspring of wisdom from the past. Whether you are a novice teacher or a veteran teacher, you have a lot to learn from those who have preceded you. Also, particularly within a Catholic school, we can draw on the gift of apostolic succession in the Catholic Church, beginning with Christ's establishment of the papacy with Saint Peter (see Mt 16:18). Knowing your past will only enrich your future. Instill this same mindset in all your students. Who does not like to learn? Keep learning!

OCTOBER 23

Jesus returned to Galilee in the power of the Spirit, and news of him spread throughout the whole region.

—Luke 4:14

Have you ever taken the time to wonder what it must have been like to hear about Jesus in person? What would it have been like to be a villager in an off-the-beaten-path hamlet in Galilee who heard that the Messiah had arrived, was making his way around the region, preaching the Good News, calling sinners to repentance, and performing miracles? Do you think that you would have sought out Jesus? Doubtlessly, Jesus' appeal supersedes that of any mere celebrity. Can you imagine what it must have been like to have your perspective shift from despair to actual hope? (Of course, if you had asked Jesus for an autograph, you would probably be unable to read his Aramaic script.) We should always have that same wonder and awe of the Lord—the same glimmer should enter our eyes when we encounter Jesus in prayer and the sacraments as entered the eyes of those who beheld the Lord or at least heard about him in the first-century Holy Land. Jesus is no longer walking physically among us, but we should look for him in the sacraments, through our prayer, and in our students' kindness. Let yourself be "starstruck" by Christ.

OCTOBER 24

For they do not know the way of the LORD, the justice of their God.

—Jeremiah 5:4b

The Catholic school teacher should foster in his or her students a natural and healthy curiosity in terms of learning about the Lord. Provide your students with a hunger for matters of faith. Throughout salvation history, there have been countless writings about the Lord and his goodness. Familiarize yourself with texts about the Lord that accurately reinforce who he is and that otherwise provide an image of God and his awesome nature. This is a valid consideration for teachers of a variety of subjects, because there are numerous conceivable opportunities to allow students to consider the extent of God's goodness. For example, in physics class, students could be invited to fathom the grandeur of the universe and how God's laws operate reliably throughout its realms. Students in physical education or health class could reflect on how taking care of one's body is part of human dignity. Ultimately, lead students to know God and how his creation is verily oriented toward justice and order.

OCTOBER 25

Keep my commands and live.

—Proverbs 7:2a

The Lord's laws are designed to be life-giving. Far from being a litany of "No, no, no," the doctrines of the Catholic Church, as reinforced by the Ten Commandments, are hardly either oppressive or suppressive in the accurate senses of the terms; rather, they are exceptionally supportive and ultimately uplifting, insofar as they fortify our attempt to live holy lives and thus draw ourselves closer to the Lord. If it were difficult to follow God's law, then he would have made us robots, automatons, or cyborgs, rather than living, breathing entities with free will. Of course, our free will must be used to bring God honor with our actions, rather than to do whatever we would like (or think that we would like) to do. Thus, the Catholic school teacher has the unique opportunity to share with his or her students the beauty of God's will and his law. In your courses, encourage your students to meditate on the numerous aspects of the Church's social teachings, in order to show your students how they can follow them more easily. Stay fortified!

OCTOBER 26

> O LORD, our Lord, how awesome is your name through all the earth!
>
> **—Psalm 8:2a**

It is good to be able to take some time and meditate on the Lord and his goodness. This may seem to be a tritely simplistic affirmation, but the more mature Catholic school teacher will readily recognize that those who are the most positive and the most grateful are those who are the most fulfilled—in other words, the *happiest*. At some point during the school day, whenever convenient, take the time to sit, even if only for one or two minutes, and do nothing (other than pray silently, if possible). Do not read; do not use technology; do not try to catch up on e-mails. Simply sit and bask in the presence of the Lord for one to two minutes. Admittedly, your school's chapel would be the best setting for this, but if you cannot make it to the chapel, find another quiet spot, perhaps in your school's library or another area where silence is possible. You should probably not attempt this in the faculty room, especially if there is deep conversation underway (hopefully centered on profound philosophical and theological ponderings).

OCTOBER 27

> But whoever drinks the water I shall give will never thirst; the water I shall give will become in him a spring of water welling up to eternal life.
>
> **—John 4:14**

Water is an essential element of all life. In this scriptural scenario, in which Jesus has an almost unheard of dialogue with a Samaritan woman at a well (see Jn 4:4–42), the Lord is emphasizing that the salvation that he offers is similarly vital: just as water is an essential element that is necessary for our very subsistence, so too is Jesus' offer of redemption required for the ultimate achievement of eternal life. The youth often think that they are invincible and that little, if anything, can imperil their sheer existence. Although some students might doubt their prospects for survival after they have to explain to Mom and Dad that they failed Mr. McClain's theology test, many young people do not account for matters related to eternity. Of course, a teacher should never have a "doom and gloom" perspective, but it is important to draw students to consider the reality of eternity, albeit with a positive outlook. Invite students to fathom the opportunity that the Lord has given us in terms of his offer of eternal salvation.

OCTOBER 28

> You are the LORD, you alone.
>
> **—Nehemiah 9:6a**

Make sure that Jesus Christ holds the prime position within your Catholic school community. If the Lord and his interests do not comprise the most considerable factor in your school's framework, then there is reason to worry regarding what is, in fact, the ultimate mission of your school. Of course, this does not imply that your school will have some semblance of theocratic educational operations or some other manifestation of functional rigidity. Rather, it means that students should have the opportunity to reflect on, and recognize, the larger picture. This larger picture is, of course, that serving the Lord and carrying out his divine will are the enduring goals of a Catholic school education, through which students will have the unique opportunity to act continuously in a manner that will contribute to the flourishing of God's kingdom. In other words, students should leave our Catholic educational institutions with a missionary spirit, in order to bring the Lord into a world that so greatly needs him, to abide in peace, justice, mercy, and forgiveness, which God is eager to bestow.

OCTOBER 29

For it is loyalty that I desire, not sacrifice.

—Hosea 6:6

These words from Hosea are reinforced by Jesus in Matthew 12:7: "I desire mercy, not sacrifice." Let us reflect for a moment on the reality that there are occasionally ways in which we believe that we are serving God but we are actually doing the very opposite, ending up serving merely ourselves in the process. Jesus reminds us: "Not everyone who says to me, 'Lord, Lord,' will enter the kingdom of heaven, but only the one who does the will of my Father in heaven. Many will say to me on that day, 'Lord, Lord, did we not prophesy in your name? Did we not drive out demons in your name? Did we not do mighty deeds in your name?' Then I will declare to them solemnly, 'I never knew you. Depart from me, you evildoers'" (Mt 7:21–23). So, in light of this seemingly demanding exhortation, is Jesus somehow especially difficult to please? Not precisely. However, we must recognize and promote his true nature, not any inventive or fanciful constructs of who he is. Know the Word of God, teaching your students to do likewise.

OCTOBER 30

O Lord, you are my God, I extol you, I praise your name.

—Isaiah 25:1a

This passage continues: "For you have carried out your wonderful plans of old, faithful and true" (Is 25:1b). Effectively, we must remember to have faith in the Lord, that what he has promised will come to fruition, in light of his divine providence. Whether we feel up to it or not, we must remember to honor the Lord and give him praise.

Doing so is a manifestation of spiritual self-discipline, pursuant to the understanding that discipline means doing what is best for all, even if that means temporal discomfort or inconvenience. *Self*-discipline has a similar designation, whereby we have to master ourselves and contain our own wills in order to allow God's will to unfold. As Catholic school teachers, we must likewise remind our students of the vast importance of self-discipline—that is, self-control. After all, they will be on their own in the world sooner than later. They must have some framework of spiritual vigor, facilitating a reinforced desire to serve the Lord, no matter the circumstances. Praise God!

OCTOBER 31

> From within people, from their hearts, come evil thoughts. . . . All these evils come from within and they defile.
>
> **—Mark 7:21, 23**

Jesus did not shy away from talking about sin. Why? Because he came in order to offer us redemption, inviting us to turn away from our sinful ways and seek true reconciliation with him, which he freely offers and freely gives. The world celebrates sin, but Jesus calls us to something greater. He reminds us that this world is not our ultimate home: "If you belonged to the world, the world would love its own; but because you do not belong to the world, and I have chosen you out of the world, the world hates you" (Jn 15:19). Let us also recall how Christ categorizes sin: "Amen, amen, I say to you, everyone who commits sin is a slave of sin" (Jn 8:34). This is not even to mention that Jesus began his public ministry by calling us to repentance (see Mk 1:15 and Mt 4:17). In the midst of a society that not only condones sin but also glamorizes it, make sure to embrace virtue, goodness, righteousness, and holiness, endeavoring to teach your students to do likewise. They will surely appreciate your guidance in the long run. Look heavenward.

NOVEMBER 1

> When [Jesus] saw the crowds, he went up the mountain, and after he had sat down, his disciples came to him. He began to teach them.
>
> **—Matthew 5:1–2**

Today is the Solemnity of All Saints, more commonly known as "All Saints' Day." (As a relevant aside, All Saints' Day immediately precedes All Souls' Day.) All Saints' Day is an opportunity for us to recognize and honor all those courageous and heroic men and women who are in heaven for all eternity because they ultimately oriented their earthly lives toward the Lord's will. One of the best ways to envision the significance of All Saints' Day is to think of the Communion of Saints as "God's Hall of Fame": those who fulfilled the rigors of life on earth and made it to heaven. Today's gospel reading is the Beatitudes (Matthew 5:1–12). Take some time today (or every day) to meditate on each of the Beatitudes, which are reflections of the Ten Commandments, and you will note the wonderful promises that our Lord makes for those who selflessly follow his will. Remember also that the saints are happy to intercede for you. The saints "have God's ear" without the human distractions and time limitations with which we contend.

NOVEMBER 2

Jesus said to Simon, "Do not be afraid; from now on you will be catching men."

—Luke 5:10

The Catholic school teacher has a unique opportunity to evangelize. It is important to note that "to evangelize" does not imply "to proselytize." In other words, the lover of the gospel will naturally desire to spread the Good News of Jesus Christ because it is both Christ's command and, ideally, our ultimate desire. No matter what course you teach, make sure to encourage your students to find ways in their own lives in which they can learn more about the gospel and therefore do their part in carrying out the Lord's grace-imbued will. Of course, Jesus reminds us that we "will be catching men"; however, we should not approach evangelization as if it were some sort of competition. To share the gospel does not mean to be a bounty hunter for those who are not necessarily currently close to the Lord. The only "wanted" poster to which we should respond is one in which the Lord is offering the reward—not in monetary reimbursement, but with the priceless prospect of eternal life. As Jesus reminds us all, "Do not be afraid." Have faith in him.

NOVEMBER 3

Give ear to my words, O Lord; understand my sighing.

—Psalm 5:2

There is no emotion that any human has ever experienced that Jesus did not likewise experience. Christ always knows everything that we are dealing with in our lives. He knows our trials, our difficulties, our weaknesses, our challenges, our temptations, and so forth (not to mention the more uplifting experiences that we have). Sometimes, particularly during those busy and stressful times that we educators are bound to encounter within the course of the teaching profession, there are no words to express how we feel, and all that will suffice is an ineffable sigh. Allow that sigh to transition into a prayer to the Lord. He wants us to be complete (a feat that can only be achieved by his presence in our lives), so he will readily come to our aid when we call on him. Jesus is more than some sort of talk show host or radio personality—he is uninterested in ratings or publicity. He simply wants us to come to him, admitting what is imperiling our souls, in order to conform our lives to him. Speak to the Lord because he is constantly listening.

NOVEMBER 4

Listen to instruction and grow wise, do not reject it!

—Proverbs 8:33

The Catholic school teacher should do everything possible to continue growing in wisdom. No person in his or her right mind would believe that he or she has achieved all of the wisdom possible; if so, he or she will be making himself or herself out to be a false god. This is overwhelmingly ill-advised. Bradley the Brainiac may be convinced of his superabundant knowledge, but sooner than later, he will be humbled through a discovery of the limitations of his human knowledge. Of course, the best source for enduring wisdom is sacred scripture. Determine a way of incorporating scripture reading into your daily routine. Make sure to inspire others to do likewise. Recognize that there are additional (that is not to say "alternative") sources of wisdom available, including your colleagues. Listen to those who have specialized knowledge in particular areas, and discern how their knowledge can serve as a complement to your own knowledge. Doing so will allow you to serve humanity here on earth and thus better contribute to the kingdom of God. Let the Lord be the only truly wise one.

NOVEMBER 5

> Holy, holy, holy is the LORD of hosts! All the earth is filled with his glory!
>
> **—Isaiah 6:3**

This passage from the Book of Isaiah provides the Catholic school teacher with a reminder of who remains at the forefront of any Catholic school's educational philosophy and missionary framework: a God who is holy, whose glory fills the earth, and who loves us so much that he sent his only-begotten Son to die a horrible death for the redemption of us sinners. In essence, God's holiness is that which a Catholic school has the privilege and the opportunity to highlight, in order to provide an outlook from which students can develop into servants of others, all for the greater glory of God. Have your students reflect on the various ways in which the education that they are gaining will benefit others. Teachers in various subject areas can rely on this reality to lead their students to devise ways to serve the Lord creatively beyond school walls. The next time that you hear the "Holy, Holy, Holy" sung at Mass, profoundly reflect on the implication of this assertion, seeing the Lord for who he is.

NOVEMBER 6

> Amen, amen, I say to you, whoever hears my word and believes in the one who sent me has eternal life.
>
> **—John 5:24a**

It is always an intriguing endeavor to look at how God the Son and God the Father communicate within the gospels. Primarily, we have God the Son speaking to God the Father. One reason that Jesus Christ, as true God and true man, is so remarkable to us mere humans is that he provided us with the perfect example of how to live entirely according to his Father's will. Jesus was God incarnate.

Jesus was literally the embodiment of goodness. He came into the world with a mission that was vital for humanity, and he carried out his mission fully. Jesus was far more than an earthly ruler; in fact, to be frank, he was hardly an earthly ruler at all, in terms of his having no secularly regal title. Let us recall his exchange with Pontius Pilate prior to his crucifixion: "So Pilate said to him, 'Then you are a king?' Jesus answered, 'You say I am a king. For this I was born and for this I came into the world, to testify to the truth. Everyone who belongs to the truth listens to my voice," (Jn 18:37). Listen to and heed the Word!

NOVEMBER 7

> Lord my God, in you I trusted; save me; rescue me from all who pursue me.
>
> **—Psalm 7:2**

Teachers can often feel "pursued" by various factors: striving to have the perfect lesson plans, grading a stack of essays taller than the obelisk in St. Peter's Square and then feeling the pressure to return all of them before the Parousia, responding to more e-mails per day than there are molecules of hydrogen and oxygen in the Pacific, responding to students' questions that are so challenging that they would not even be raised during the Prime Minister's Questions in the British Parliament, and so forth. In essence, although we may occasionally feel beleaguered by all of our expectations, we must slow down (or stop altogether) and remember that our vocation is one of service—to our Catholic school community and, by extension, ultimately to the Lord. Continue to trust in the Lord, and hone your ability to discern between the issues that pursue you but are part of our mission as Catholic school teachers and those issues that pursue you but must be eradicated—those that sideline us. Trust in the Lord, who will always win.

NOVEMBER 8

We give thanks to God always for all of you, remembering you in our prayers.

—1 Thessalonians 1:2

It is worthwhile to reflect on the remainder of this passage in order to arrive at a better understanding of the broader implications of Saint Paul's hope-filled address to the Church in Thessalonica: "unceasingly calling to mind your work of faith and labor of love and endurance in hope of our Lord Jesus Christ, before our God and Father, knowing, brothers loved by God, how you were chosen" (1 Thes 1:2–4). It is very important for the Catholic school teacher to remember to be grateful for his or her colleagues. No matter what role you fill within a Catholic school, remember to show a deep appreciation for everyone with whom you work and minister. After all, the support that you show to them will build up your community in numerous ways, and the students will greatly benefit. Do not worry about colleagues who do not reciprocate your enthusiasm. Instead, pray for Bitter Belinda eventually to come to know the joy that only God can inspire in us. Pray to thank the Lord for your colleagues and for the opportunity to minister alongside them.

NOVEMBER 9

The LORD, your God, loves you.

—Deuteronomy 23:6b

We often need to be reminded of this reality. Particularly when we look at the God of the Old Testament, we are occasionally led to think of God as entirely preoccupied with justice to the exclusion of mercy, similar to how when we look at the God of the New Testament, we are occasionally led to think of Jesus as entirely preoccupied with mercy to the exclusion of justice. This is hardly the case, by any measure of accurate and worthwhile theological study. As we remember from this passage, the Lord loves us and has our best interest at heart. Our students must be reminded of this reality. Too often, there is a pervasive image of God that is devoid of the literal *dying* love that he has for us. Meditating on God's love for us will reliably draw us to spread his love to others, especially those who do not sense his presence in their lives. The Catholic school community has a unique role in terms of transmitting God's love to society broadly. Remind others that God greatly loves them.

NOVEMBER 10

> Or do you hold his priceless kindness, forbearance, and patience in low esteem, unaware that the kindness of God would lead you to repentance?
>
> **—Romans 2:4**

God's love for us does not somehow mean that God is okay with us just as we currently are. We never come to God "good enough"; there is always some element (in fact, usually more than one) that he wants to change in us in order to draw us closer to himself and away from our sins. Hence, it is vital for the Catholic school teacher to be able to share this reality with students, lest they somehow believe that God's love for us gives us a carte blanche to live in any fashion we wish, devoid of morality and inconsiderate of God's call for repentance that must accompany our aspirations for redemption and salvation. Look for ways to lead your students to reflect on how they can live their lives in accordance with God's will. This is an endeavor that teachers in all courses can undertake, particularly since this opportunity would actually afford students the chance to tap into their cross-curricular knowledge in such a way that would allow them to better discern the ways in which the Lord is calling them to use their love in his service.

NOVEMBER 11

When the Lord saw her, he was moved with pity for her and said to her, "Do not weep."

—Luke 7:13

Jesus always knows what we are dealing with. Reading this excerpt from the passage of the raising of the widow's son (Lk 7:11–17) reminds us that Jesus had emotions, just as we do. Of course, Jesus had the fullness of control over his emotions, as we should likewise strive to have, lest they run rampant. However, he did have such emotions as sympathy, empathy, compassion, and other sentiments that would have allowed him to relate to everyone, in all of their miseries, joys, and everything in between. (On a side note, referring to Jesus in the past tense here is indicative of his actions during his earthly ministry, although he of course continues to have these qualities.) It is vital that we seek the Lord when we are in need. We must likewise remind our students to seek him in order to bring about resolutions to their various dilemmas. After all, the youth reliably have more drama occurring on a day-to-day basis than that which was present within Shakespeare's Globe Theatre at its height. Jesus can relate to us more than any other person could.

NOVEMBER 12

Whoever follows instruction is in the path to life, but whoever disregards reproof goes astray.

—Proverbs 10:17

We all make mistakes, but it comes down to whether or not we are willing to learn from them. Learn from mistakes, both others' and your own. In order truly and definitively to learn from our mistakes, we must be sure to follow the instruction of those who have wisdom to share with us. Broadly speaking, everyone has some semblance of wisdom to share. (Here is a case in point: toddlers possess the wisdom to slowly sneak away after evidencing for their father which pens and markers leave the most indelible marks on the walls.) There are various members of our school community from whom we can gain advice: administrators, veteran teachers, and other stakeholders in our community. Of course, our ultimate instruction stems from the Lord, the Author of life himself. We must humbly remain open to his reproof, in order to serve him as faithfully as possible and thus allow our students to better fathom his fully immutable wisdom.

NOVEMBER 13

> The Lord is a stronghold for the oppressed, a stronghold in times of trouble.
>
> **—Psalm 9:10**

Make sure that your school makes every effort to serve those who are living in poverty. Whether this is through making meals for the homeless, going on a service trip (whether domestic or international), organizing a canned-food drive, holding a clothing drive, and so on, make sure that your school emphasizes the need to care for the less fortunate, particularly those living in abject poverty. Another way of respecting human dignity is highlighting the gifts of immigrants and other populations that are frequently at risk for marginalization due to their current set of socioeconomic circumstances. In our economically oppressed brother and sister, we see the face of Christ, since he too was born into poverty, lived in poverty throughout his life, and for all intents and purposes *knew* poverty. Effectively, God stepped into humanity in impoverished conditions. The Messiah, the Savior, the Lord, has a special place in his heart for the disadvantaged, and it is a privilege for the Catholic school to serve others.

NOVEMBER 14

As they were proceeding on their journey someone said to him, "I will follow you wherever you go."

—Luke 9:57

In Matthew's version of this gospel passage, we see that the "someone" mentioned in Luke 9:57 is a scribe. Pay close attention to his words: "A *scribe* approached and said to him, '*Teacher*, I will follow you wherever you go' (Mt 8:19, emphasis added). Jesus would occasionally scold the scribes, not so much for their portrayal of God's love or their concept of what love constitutes, but rather for their hesitancy in putting that love into practice. The Catholic school teacher must meditate on the significance of this expectation. Jesus readily reminds his would-be followers that living the Christian life will be rife with challenges. However, he likewise reminds us of what following his will entails: the ultimate gift of eternal life. Jesus has never turned anyone away, but all who come to him must be willing to leave behind any impediment, whether in the form of certain sins, cowardice, or other spiritual defects. Fortunately, the Lord helps to strengthen us.

NOVEMBER 15

Whoever pursues justice and kindness will find life and honor.

—Proverbs 21:21

The Catholic school teacher has a special opportunity to underscore for students what is meant by true "justice" and "kindness." Within the Christian outlook, justice denotes making the universe right (or as right as possible), for the ultimately enduring benefit of the kingdom of God. There are many opportunities to exhibit to students what justice entails. As one example, justice comes in the form of marching to support the sanctity and dignity of all human life, including that of the unborn, the seriously infirm (including the terminally ill), the elderly, those facing capital punishment, and those in other circumstances. Justice also comes in the form of teaching students about religious liberty and how to speak out against efforts to abbreviate reasonable expressions of faith within the public square. Society's casual marginalization of faith makes it an occasional challenge for the Catholic Church and other faith groups to aid the otherwise overlooked members of society. Justice comes in many forms, and genuine kindness fosters lasting peace.

NOVEMBER 16

> The aim of this instruction is love from a pure heart, a good conscience, and a sincere faith.
>
> **—1 Timothy 1:5**

The "instruction" that Saint Paul was referring to here is not convincing a class full of children that knowing cursive is a valuable life skill (although it is). Rather, this "instruction" seeks to ensure that the transmission of faith provides an accurate depiction of Christ's teachings. Saint Paul warns against teaching "false doctrines" (1 Tm 1:3), "myths" (1 Tm 1:4), and so forth, that "promote speculations rather than the plan of God that is to be received by faith" (1 Tm 1:4). In other words, we teachers must be very cautious with our intent. Of course, students should have an array of educational experiences, because they need to dialogue with society beyond our schools' walls. However, if anyone intentionally leads a student away from an accurate portrayal of who Jesus Christ is and what he teaches, his or her agenda will reveal itself and unravel. If an ideology can be titled, there is inherently some aspect of spuriousness to it. We must take seriously the gift and privilege entrusted to us to draw our students to God.

NOVEMBER 17

Grace to you and peace from God our Father and the Lord Jesus Christ.

—Galatians 1:3

Throughout the course of the school day, be sure to be pleasant with everyone whom you encounter, whether your students, colleagues, visitors to the community, or enemies who are currently unaware that they will one day be your friend. The Catholic school teacher has a distinctive role in that he or she is on the "front lines" of the spiritual community. You can either make someone else's day with a smile or ruin it with a grimace. It is not juvenile to consider the question: What expression would you prefer to see on others' faces when you come across them as you traverse the hallowed corridors of your Catholic school? Many saints made it to heaven in great part because of the Christian demeanor with which they drew others to God. Think of Saint André Bessette, C.S.C., a Holy Cross brother who charitably and patiently shared the witness of the gospel with those who entered l'Oratoire Saint-Joseph du Mont-Royal in Québec, where he often sat as a doorkeeper. Many miracles are attributed to his intercession. He greeted others with Christ's love.

NOVEMBER 18

So Jesus said to them, "My time is not yet here, but the time is always right for you."

—John 7:6

It is important to read the full account from which this passage comes, in order to better understand its full scope and context. Take a moment to read about Jesus' dialogue with his kinsmen in the midst of the Feast of Tabernacles in John 7:1–13 in order to gain a better understanding of what is transpiring here. The key factor to take away from Jesus' affirmation is his point that "the time is always right for you." In other words, we are called to profess the gospel with our very lives. There is not a point at which we can decline to spread the Good News. After all, lest we lose focus of what Christian commitment entails, Jesus reminds us: "No one who sets a hand to the plow and looks to what was left behind is fit for the kingdom of God" (Lk 9:62). As Catholic school educators, our devotion to the Lord will have a paramount impact on students' overall well-being and will signify that we are serving them in terms of the overarching goals of Catholic education. Let us ask the Lord to guide us to use our time well to build up his kingdom.

NOVEMBER 19

I will grant safety to whoever longs for it.

—Psalm 12:6b

Note a particular feature of the Lord's promise in this psalm of David: "to whoever longs for it." Clearly, matters of faith are very profound; however, those who are open to the Lord and his will are those who are more likely to live a good life in word and action and follow him. The free will that God has given us is an indicator that he wants us to follow him. God does not want us to use our free will to have a lackadaisical orientation toward him, typified by only following the segments of his will with which we feel comfortable. Whoever tries to live according to this mindset will falsely believe that God could not care less about how we use our time here on earth. Our openness to the Lord's gift of faith signifies that we are willing to seek his safety when we feel beset by whatever is imperiling our proximity to him and his will. As you encounter the numerous challenges that characterize the teaching career, seek the safety of the Lord, and pray that your students will likewise seek out his refuge whenever they may feel besieged.

NOVEMBER 20

> Afterward [Jesus] journeyed from one town and village to another, preaching and proclaiming the good news of the kingdom of God.
>
> **—Luke 8:1**

This passage is related to a previous passage within Luke's gospel that likewise testifies to the Lord's pedestrian activities: "But [Jesus] said to them, 'To the other towns also I must proclaim the good news of the kingdom of God, because for this reason have I been sent'" (Lk 4:43). Any teacher who has had the "adventure" of picking up his or her supplies and teaching in more than one classroom can perhaps appreciate more than most what Jesus' earthly ministry must have entailed in terms of what the sheer magnitude of his ambulatory enterprise must have comprised. For the approximately three years of Jesus' earthly ministry, he walked around a great deal of the region of Galilee, particularly around Capernaum and his hometown of Nazareth. There were probably many long, exhausting days, as those who followed Jesus (particularly his twelve disciples) would have soon realized. Sometimes students are very tired from staying up late studying, difficulties at home, and other reasons. Encourage them to persevere, offering up all their trials to the Lord.

NOVEMBER 21

> When pride comes, disgrace comes; but with the humble is wisdom.
>
> **—Proverbs 11:2**

There are few sources, at least within the realms of the media and pop culture, from which students will hear that being humble will lead to them being successful in life, at least "successful" in what matters to God. The world says that you have to be beyond social reproach, that you have to be prominent and popular, that you have to go along with peer pressure—the list goes on and on. However, living in accordance with God's will reliably translates into having a humble outlook on life. Pride is dangerous, and it is actually the root of all sin, since it involves placing our will directly opposite to the Lord's. Humility can be a challenge to instill in students. For some students, humility comes in the form of enrollment in an allegedly "easy" theology course, only to be instructed otherwise. We adults especially must beware of the onset of sinful pride.

NOVEMBER 22

Then they abandoned their nets and followed him.

—Mark 1:18

It is not easy for us to leave something behind. It is in our human nature to want to retain that which allegedly means something to us. Anyone who has raised toddlers is aware of this reality; after all, taking a piece of candy away from a three-year-old, who acquired it because of an admittedly impressive intersection of cleverness and mischief, will lead to an inundation of tears that could serve as a living rival of Niagara Falls. Those who would become Jesus' twelve apostles had to leave behind what legitimately mattered to them. Many of them would have had to leave behind their wives, children, and other family members for the time that it took to help the Lord spread the Good News. Of course, as in the above passage, many had to leave behind their livelihood as well. Teachers, particularly Catholic school teachers, must leave behind a fair amount when we step up to the plate to minister to our students. However, the Lord will provide, especially in the life to come. (Read Mark 10:29–30 for reassurance.)

NOVEMBER 23

I have indeed been taken possession of by Christ [Jesus].

—Philippians 3:12

In these iconic words of Saint Paul, we see a very clear image that exhibits to us the reality of what happened to Saint Paul over the course of his fullness of conversion to Christ and the gospel: he allowed the Lord's will to become his own. This is what all followers of Christ are likewise called to embody: a commitment to the Lord's will, to the exclusion of our own. Of course, this degree of commitment must be renewed, just as we must undergo an ongoing conversion to the Lord. Look for ways to foster further devotion to Christ and the gospel within your teaching ministry. Commensurate to that perspective, allow your students to inspire you because, after all, the youth have a special place in the Lord's heart, and they are interested in following his will, which becomes easier when they have your guidance. Similarly, allow your colleagues and others in your Catholic school community to provide you with inspiration. Your dedication to accepting the Lord's will significantly clarifies your outlook and allows you to be ultimately effective.

NOVEMBER 24

Today is holy to the LORD your God. Do not lament, do not weep!

—Nehemiah 8:9b

Imagine if we treated every day as if it were holy. Actually, you do not have to imagine that prospect, because every day is indeed holy. Let us recall the words of Psalm 118:24: "This is the day the LORD has made; let us rejoice in it and be glad." The Catholic school teacher has the opportunity to remind his or her students of this reality daily. With today being November 24, those of us who teach in the United

States are in the midst of Thanksgiving. The holiness of each day tells us that it is a gift from the Lord, as well as a chance to proclaim his goodness for all that he has given us. Today is an opportunity to sanctify our lives and to inspire others to sanctify their own. Look for ways to be thankful for each day, and encourage your students to do likewise. A heart full of gratitude for the Lord is never so overflowing that he will not continue to fill it with his gracious love, which he lavishes on his faithful. Rejoice!

NOVEMBER 25

> O Lord, your name is forever, your renown, from generation to generation!
>
> **—Psalm 135:13**

Every generation from the time of Christ through now has passed on knowledge of the paschal mystery. Technically, this is something that should continue to the end of time. It is no secret that many young people do not necessarily have a strong drive to learn about history. You may witness this in the manner that fifteen-year-old Cool Carl's eyes glaze over as he listens to his grandmother Nadine the Nostalgic recounting what life was like back in the "olden days." While some youth do appreciate historical precedent, many do not. Of course, as people get older, we tend to find greater value in learning about the past. Moving beyond mere history to salvation history per se, the Catholic school teacher must be sure to relay accurately the value of learning about the Lord. After all, the setting of a Catholic school is the only place in which a fair amount of students are given knowledge of Christ and the gospel. The Good News cannot skip a generation, so share it!

NOVEMBER 26

> Blessed be the God and Father of our Lord Jesus Christ, the Father of compassion and God of all encouragement.
>
> **—2 Corinthians 1:3**

It is critical for the Catholic school teacher to convey to students the significance of "compassion." We are all called to be compassionate, in the sense that it is through alleviating the suffering of others that we imitate Christ, since having compassion toward others allows us to better appreciate the human dignity that we all have as a gift from God. Compassion is necessarily intertwined with mercy, because both afford us the opportunity to think more deeply about how we would like others to act toward us if we were in a similarly disadvantaged situation. As Catholic school teachers, having compassion on our students will be most effective if it comes in the form of leading them to reflect on the Lord as our source of true compassion (not to mention mercy). After all, the Lord owes us nothing, but gives us everything—most especially the possibility of eternal life basking in his glory. Similarly, encouragement is important, since we are all on this journey known as life, and we can rely on our brethren for veritably prayerful support.

NOVEMBER 27

> A good person brings forth good out of a store of goodness.
>
> **—Matthew 12:35a**

Our students must be aware that being virtuous and holy is only worthwhile if a person plans on using that virtue and holiness in order to acquire even more of the same. There is no maximum extent of goodness that we can attain. After all, lest we forget how demanding the Lord is, here are two reminders of his standards for our spiritual comportment: "So be perfect, just as your heavenly Father is perfect" (Mt 5:48); and, "Enter through the narrow gate; for the gate is wide and the road broad that leads to destruction, and those who enter through it are many. How narrow the gate and constricted the road that leads to life. And those who find it are few" (Mt 7:13–14). Now, do not ever aspire to get into a holiness competition with Jesus, because that would be like comparing the aquatic displacement characteristics of a paramecium to those of a blue whale. Remind your students to strive relentlessly for spiritual greatness, thus fortifying their preparation to evangelize and serve humanity.

NOVEMBER 28

> The fear of the Lord is training for wisdom, and humility goes before honors.
>
> **—Proverbs 15:33**

They say that the true measure of a person is who he or she is when no one is watching. For the Christian, we know that God is always watching. However, he is not watching as a police officer who waits for Larry Leadfoot, a repeat offender, to speed past so that he can stop him and issue him a citation in order to dissuade him from future infractions and thereby keep our roads safer. Instead, God watches us as a dad and mom watch their children throughout the course of their lives, looking forward to their successes, achievements, and dreams fulfilled. However, it is important to understand that God's "dream" for us does not necessarily mean material or professional achievements; rather, it means our acceptance of the gift of redemption that he has extended to us. Humility, from all parties involved, will do more for a Catholic school community than any worldly achievement, because humility prepares the soul for God's grace by placing one's will aside for the sake of the Lord's. Teach your students that true wisdom is God-fearing.

NOVEMBER 29

And I have given them the glory you gave me, so that they may be one, as we are one.

—John 17:22

It would be a challenge to discern the significance of Jesus' words here devoid of their precise context, so the reader would do well to review John 17:1–26 in order to arrive at an accurate grasp of what is transpiring in this particular passage. The unity that Christ calls for obviously transcends that which can be conceptualized within one faith community, but it is still clearly worthwhile to consider the implications for the Catholic school community. As Catholic school educators, we must make every effort to foster unity. There are students from a variety of faith traditions, ethnic backgrounds, socioeconomic strata, both genders, as well as other distinctions, but we teach them all, understanding and embracing their shared human dignity. Individual distinctions do not mean that we can or must somehow water down the gospel's intent. Christ is the ultimate Teacher, and in his unity with God the Father and God the Holy Spirit we witness the fullest measure of unity imaginable. Allow God to do his work in all of us.

NOVEMBER 30

Every house is founded by someone, but the founder of all is God.

—Hebrews 3:4

God knows what he is doing. He is incapable of deception, let alone sin at all or error in any capacity. As we read in the Letter of James: "No one experiencing temptation should say, 'I am being tempted by God'; for God is not subject to temptation to evil, and he himself tempts no one" (Jas 1:13). Similarly, we read in Sirach: "Do not say:

'It was God's doing that I fell away,' for what he hates he does not do. Do not say: 'He himself has led me astray,' for he has no need of the wicked" (Sir 15:11–12). The point here is that God, "the founder of all," made us in order to love us, not to let us be led away from him as an indicator of our own fallen human nature. The Catholic school teacher would do well to remind his or her students of the various ways in which all that is good leads back to God—and, fortunately for us, there is a lot of good in the universe. To be fair, we are not necessarily referring to how a chocolate milkshake is "good" or how a rerun of *Gilligan's Island* is "good"; rather, we are referring to the goodness of seeing the Lord operating within the world, including in our students' virtue.

DECEMBER 1

> So be imitators of God, as beloved children, and live in love, as Christ loved us.
>
> **—Ephesians 5:1–2a**

This passage continues: "And [Christ] handed himself over for us as a sacrificial offering to God for a fragrant aroma." In the milieu of Advent, it is time to begin reflecting on how very much we have to look forward to in terms of Christ's coming into the world. This passage of Ephesians 5:1–2 may not immediately seem so, but it is significant in terms of serving as a brief, yet fitting, description of what Christ calls us to, as well as of who he is. Before we were born, or even conceived, Christ knew and loved us. The love with which God entered into the world in human form is the same love that pervades his desire for us to come close to him, as "imitators of God, as beloved children." However, we must readily recall that Jesus came into the world not only to show us how to live; he also showed us how to die to our own sins, when he took upon himself our sinfulness and was crucified and then rose from the dead, demonstrating his victory over sin and death. As we anxiously await the arrival of the Christ Child at Christmas, may the Lord God bless you and your Catholic school community throughout the days of Advent.

DECEMBER 2

> Give thanks to the Lord, invoke his name; make known among the peoples his deeds!
>
> **—Psalm 105:1**

Do not keep to yourself your gratitude for what the Lord has done for you. However, in all fairness, ensure that this does not translate into boasting. Therefore, be sure to share with others God's goodness and the ways in which he has showered blessings. For example, if God has healed your family member of a serious illness, share with your colleagues how grateful you are. Do not, on the other hand, approach a colleague who is likewise currently suffering from some dire malady, and tell him, in a carefree, nonchalant, and seemingly oblivious manner, how happy you are that your family member is doing so well. This could understandably come across in such a way that it ends up inspiring resentment or despair, possibly even resulting in your friend distancing himself from the Lord. In other words, be sensitive. Alternatively, be sure to choose your words and timing carefully when highlighting what God has done. Others, particularly those struggling with their own faith, need help, guidance, and inspiration on their journeys.

DECEMBER 3

> And with complete assurance and without hindrance he proclaimed the kingdom of God and taught about the Lord Jesus Christ.
>
> **—Acts 28:31**

In this last chapter of the Acts of the Apostles, we read an attestation from the author regarding how Saint Paul, the "Apostle to the Gentiles," continued to profess his faith in Christ. The "complete assurance" with which Saint Paul evangelized is a testament to how deeply he had undergone his conversion, which continued well into the years beyond when Jesus had first appeared to him on the road to Damascus. Saint Paul is commendable for the relentless approach that he had to preaching the Good News of Christ. The Catholic school teacher has the same chance to teach continuously about the Lord and his goodness. Although the youth may occasionally seem disinterested in particular aspects of faith, they are seeking truth. After all, this is one reason that students, and adolescents in particular, tend to question various realities. Encourage students to ask questions—as long as they are open to answers! Continue to seek out opportunities to act in imitation of Saint Paul the apostle by teaching "about the Lord Jesus Christ."

DECEMBER 4

By wisdom is a house built, by understanding it is established.

—Proverbs 24:3

Encourage your students to imagine what life will be like after they have completed their formal education. This does not just mean college; rather, encourage them to reflect on what life will be like once they have their own families, their careers, and so forth, decades from now. Although it may be a challenge for them to fathom this, have them "go back in time" from decades in the future back to now. Have them report on whether or not your school was effective in terms of not only providing them with a strong academic base, but also leading them to know God and how to serve his will. If your students can produce a favorable account, this is a good sign. If not, ask them what factors about your community could be enhanced. Of course, pickier students might comment on how they have suffered throughout high school because of the poor texture of the French fries in the cafeteria. Either way, pay close attention to the useful feedback from the students. This can be in the form of an "exit survey" or another document. Build up your school's legacy of wisdom!

DECEMBER 5

> But may all who seek you rejoice and be glad in you.
>
> **—Psalm 70:5a**

The Catholic school teacher has a special privilege when it comes to the teaching field: he or she is able to have sheer joy in sharing Christ's gospel. In other words, the Catholic school teacher is able to reference God, as well as to discuss important considerations regarding matters of faith, no matter what subject he or she teaches. Allowing the Lord into our lives brings us joy. Similarly, inviting the Lord into our curriculum brings joy to our students, because they thus have the opportunity to make true and enduring connections at the cross-curricular level. Whether the topic is within the realm of mathematics, science, social studies, English, foreign language, visual or performing arts, computer science, or any other course designation, be creative in terms of how to invite the Lord into your lesson. Our students are looking for Jesus, and he not only wants to be found but is looking for them as well. Let us join our students in celebrating the Lord's presence in their lives.

DECEMBER 6

> When the centurion who stood facing him saw how he breathed his last he said, "Truly this man was the Son of God!"
>
> **—Mark 15:39**

Although we are far from the Lenten season, it is worthwhile to take a moment to reflect on the paschal mystery. The words of this Roman centurion, which are likewise reflected in Matthew 27:54, are iconic in that they draw us to imagine what must have been on the minds of those who witnessed Christ's last moments prior to the Resurrection. Those who had always known who he was would have had their beliefs confirmed. Those who had been unsure would have likewise no longer questioned the reality of his identity. Meanwhile, those who had been unconvinced of who he was would have either come to recognize who he was or declined to accept it. What does this have to do with the Catholic school teacher? Essentially, we can have hearts full of hope as we look forward to the joy of Christmas. When Christ was coming into the world, only a few key figures would have known who he truly was. Now, as we prepare to celebrate Christmas, we can confidently proclaim in our Catholic schools: "Truly this man [is] the Son of God!"

DECEMBER 7

> Claim no honor in the king's presence, nor occupy the place of superiors.
>
> **—Proverbs 25:6**

As we continue in the Advent season, looking forward to the Christ Child's arrival at Christmas, we must likewise prepare our hearts. After all, Christmas is not about retail sales, surreptitious elves, wrapping gifts, and other fright-inducing prospects; it is about celebrating the coming into the world of a king, *the* King, in order to extend to us the possibility of salvation and eternal life. In the presence of the Lord, we do not have to seek any semblance of recognition. After all, it is in our humility that God works through us. Hence, God is the epitome of superiority, because he has the prerogative to be so. As Catholic school teachers, we must endeavor to remind our students of what we are looking forward to at Christmas. Unfortunately, there is a rampant prevalence of materialism, consumerism, and individualism that runs the risk of taking our attention away from the significance of Christmas. Yet, in the midst of this season of Advent, the Catholic school has an opportune role in reinforcing Christmas's true meaning.

DECEMBER 8

> And coming to her, she said, "Hail, favored one! The Lord is with you."
>
> **—Luke 1:28**

Today is the Solemnity of the Immaculate Conception of the Blessed Virgin Mary. Today we celebrate the dogma of the Virgin Mary's conception without the stain of original sin. It is always worthwhile to recall that God *chose* Mary to be Jesus' Mother, based on her virtue. Mary did not campaign to be Jesus' Mother or highlight her virtue in some way; rather, she lived a holy life and was already looking forward to the coming of the Messiah when the angel Gabriel appeared to her in order to share with her how she was in God's favor. It is always worthwhile for the Catholic school teacher to use the occasion of the Immaculate Conception to remind students of how faithful Mary was, in terms of following God's will before Jesus' virginal conception, as Jesus was growing up, throughout Jesus' public ministry, and in the midst of Jesus' paschal mystery: his passion, crucifixion, resurrection, and ascension. Let us remember to ask Mary to pray to God for us, because as our dear Mother, she always wants to help.

DECEMBER 9

> Better one day in your courts than a thousand elsewhere.
>
> **—Psalm 84:11a**

Students need our guidance when it comes to understanding various realities of life. For example, it is important to share with them that you were once young and that you survived your teenage years. The point here is that we must remember to share with students that the time that we spend here on earth will decide our prospects for eternity. Although the present life will reliably be replete with a high quantity of challenges, difficulties, trials, and other tribulations, we must recall, as well as instill in our students, that the Lord has oriented our hearts toward his kingdom. Therefore, take the occasion of Advent to share with your students how remarkable of a gift we have in the Lord and Savior Jesus Christ. The time that we spend in prayer to the Lord, and in service to his kingdom in various ways, will be multiplied, magnified, and otherwise returned to us, thereby allowing us the resources and opportunities to serve the Lord to an even greater extent. Jesus wants us to stay close to him and to honor him.

DECEMBER 10

> Your faith flourishes ever more, and the love of every one of you for one another grows ever greater.
>
> **—2 Thessalonians 1:3b**

Love magnifies itself. Love cannot be limited or misconstrued. However, it is critically important to understand what is meant by *love*, a reality that Christianity professes quite accurately in terms of its totality of underpinnings. Essentially, love should not be confused with other manifestations of sentiment. Notions that do not provide an accurate portrayal of actual love and what it signifies should be called out for what they are: misrepresentations of the paschal mystery. With Christmas on the way, let us continue to reflect on the awesome love that God has for us, and how his love for us became incarnate, as he took on our nature in order to show us how much he loves us. Have your students reflect on the various ways that the Lord has exhibited his love for us. You might be surprised by how eloquently they are able to explain how they are aware of God's love. Love is not shallow; it is profound. Likewise, love is not disturbing;

it is captivating. Allow God's love as seen at Christmas to enter your life.

DECEMBER 11

> But you, beloved, remember the words spoken beforehand by the apostles of our Lord Jesus Christ.
>
> **—Jude 1:17**

It is worthwhile to consider the reality of apostolic succession and its significance within Catholicism. Essentially, apostolic succession is what connects our current pope, bishops, and priests all the way back to the apostles. Apostolic succession is based on Jesus' establishment of the Church on Peter, the rock (see Mt 16:18). It is through the witness and testimony of the apostles that we know Jesus. We know about his early life by reading the infancy narratives in the Gospels of Matthew and Luke. How do we have the four gospels at all (as well as the other twenty-three books of the New Testament)? We have them because they were authored and compiled by the apostles and their peers. It is important for students to know about apostolic succession because of its implications for approximating ourselves even more closely to Jesus' earthly ministry and his paschal mystery. This may be a challenge beyond the theology classroom, but teachers are reliably creative!

DECEMBER 12

> But Jesus came and touched them, saying, "Rise, and do not be afraid."
>
> **—Matthew 17:7**

Catholic school teachers might have a healthy fear of a few things when it comes to teaching: a fear that the photocopier will malfunction on the morning that you have to make multiple copies; a fear that some of your social studies students will believe that the first commandment appears on the Bill of Rights; a fear that, even though the school year has gone by rather quickly, the Christmas break will not arrive until after your sanity has long departed. Jesus has a way of dispelling fears. However, fears can lead us to rely on the Lord for spiritual safety. When we feel beset by temptations, when we feel outward pressure, when we have been let down by low academic achievement on the part of students who, we know, just need to study more, and so forth, we can place our cares upon the Lord. However, we must recall that Jesus is not some sort of self-help magnate or maharishi; rather, he wants us to have some semblance of reasonableness in our daily dealings, so that we can use our resources to serve him.

DECEMBER 13

Help me, LORD, my God; save me in your mercy.

—Psalm 109:26

Although it may have a penchant for coming off as debilitation at least, or cowardliness at best, asking others for help is far from a sign of weakness. Likewise, when it comes to God, asking him for help is hardly an indicator of weakness, because it is requesting something diminutive from he who is the provider of all. The Catholic school teacher can, and should, readily call on the Lord for help. There are times during the school year when we might get inundated with work, or end up besieged by numerous responsibilities, or find ourselves overrun by adolescent drama, and many other things. Look to the Lord for help. Your prayer to him for assistance can also be accompanied by a meaningful reading of the scriptures. A fitting suggestion for when you feel distraught in some way is to read the Psalms. (For that matter, try reading through all 150 psalms over the course of a year.) Essentially, every human emotion discernible is featured within the Psalms. In the end, thank and praise the Lord for who he is and what he provides.

DECEMBER 14

> Discipline your children, and they will bring you comfort, and give delight to your soul.
>
> **—Proverbs 29:17**

This passage is, of course, directed at how a mother and a father are expected to provide discipline to their children. To be clear, discipline is not the same as punishment, nor is it even necessarily a penalty. Having discipline is a good thing; the term *self-discipline* is often used to describe the behavior of those students, parents, teachers, and others who are able to control themselves for the benefit of others. For example, teachers can help their students' parents by encouraging students to honor their mother and father for all that they do. Similarly, parents can be sure to devote themselves to their children in order to bring them closer to the Lord. In eleven days, we will be celebrating Christmas. Reflect for a moment on what type of temporal parents Mary and Joseph must have been to Jesus. Of course, Jesus would have provided them with a rather "comfortable" childhood, with the fullness of his perfect nature and whatnot. Remember to tell your students that discipline—and more particularly, self-discipline—is a good thing that will serve them for this life and the next.

DECEMBER 15

> So they went off and preached repentance.
>
> **—Mark 6:12**

Jesus' disciples followed him and, in imitation of him, invited others to repentance. We are all likewise called to repentance, so part of our ongoing personal conversion and reorientation of our lives to the Lord involves reforming our own ways first, and then subsequently helping others to reform theirs. (In order to better fathom Jesus' teachings on judgment, take a moment to read Matthew 7:1–5 and Luke 6:37–42.) Jesus calls us all away from our sins, and he further calls us to help others turn away from their own sins: "Be on your guard! If your brother sins, rebuke him; and if he repents, forgive him. And if he wrongs you seven times in one day and returns to you seven times saying, 'I am sorry,' you should forgive him" (Lk 17:3–4). When you have a moment, read the related passages of Matthew 6:14–15, Matthew 18:21–22, 35, and Mark 11:25. Preach repentance *and* forgiveness to your students, who deserve to know true reconciliation. Guiding your students to the Lord is your best possible gift to them.

DECEMBER 16

> No wisdom, no understanding, no counsel prevail against the Lord.
>
> **—Proverbs 21:30**

Wisdom, in and of itself, is hardly a bad thing. Knowledge or understanding is a quite good thing, particularly insofar as it is concerned with the opportunity to relate to others and to dialogue with them in matters of faith. However, the concern comes when mere knowledge is misconstrued as wisdom. Sylvester Smartypants might be able to rattle off all of the data contained within the periodic table of elements, but then issue an invective against his neighbor at the next opportunity. Wisdom and knowledge can readily serve humanity, but it is a combination of the two, when used with a reliance on God as the origin of true wisdom, that actually has the possibility of ultimately serving the kingdom of God. The Catholic school teacher should encourage his or her students not to depend simply on a sweeping acquisition of knowledge; rather, they should also use what they have learned to contribute to serving others for the greater glory of the Lord God.

DECEMBER 17

Be eager to present yourself as acceptable to God, a workman who causes no disgrace, imparting the word of truth without deviation.

—2 Timothy 2:15

This passage from Saint Paul's Second Letter to Timothy continues with: "Avoid profane, idle talk, for such people will become more and more godless, and their teaching will spread like gangrene" (2 Tm 2:16–17). This message may appear to be rather dire, but the implications are significantly worthwhile in terms of how Catholic school educators are called to be careful of what they say over the course of their professional teaching duties. Perhaps nowhere is this truer than within settings around the school community. Imagine how justifiably disturbed a student would be to overhear an otherwise respectable role model, such as a teacher, coach, or administrator, using language that is degrading, gossip-laden, or otherwise unfit for a Catholic institution. Alternatively, use language that is uplifting and worthy of appreciation by anyone who would happen to hear it. As a standard, only consider saying that which you would feel comfortable saying while standing before a crucifix. Ask yourself: Would the Lord want to hear this? (Because he does hear you.)

DECEMBER 18

But blessed are your eyes, because they see, and your ears, because they hear.

—Matthew 13:16

In order to appreciate fully what Jesus was saying here, you have to understand the context: he was addressing his disciples after having taught the parable of the sower and the purpose of parables. The Catholic school teacher should take care to ensure that he or she is not merely listening to students but actually *hearing* what they have to say. Young people are still learning how to communicate effectively that which they are experiencing as they navigate the ever-intertwined roads of life. They are actually quite interested in learning much more than celebrity news, pop culture sound bites, or what their current teachers looked like in their high school yearbooks. Listen, and then *hear* what students are trying to communicate, especially in terms of their relationship with the Lord. Likewise, make sure that you encourage your students to *hear*. This includes the need for them to hear the Lord speaking to their hearts. With all of the noise that attempts to drown out the Lord's voice, lead your students to hear God in order to follow him effectively.

DECEMBER 19

> Light shines through the darkness for the upright; gracious, compassionate, and righteous.
>
> **—Psalm 112:4**

Looking forward to celebrating the arrival of Jesus at Christmas means looking forward to celebrating who the Lord is. We would never do well to heed the forces of darkness; instead, we are justifiably drawn toward that which is light. In the same way, looking forward to the light of Christ means having hope in who he is and in the Good News that he brings. Therefore, the Catholic school teacher would do well to emphasize to his or her students all that we have to look forward to in the Lord. Leading up to that holy night in Bethlehem nearly two thousand years ago must have entailed a fair degree of anxiety for those who were looking forward to the Messiah. Of course, this would have been especially true for Mary and Joseph. However, they had great faith, and their faith was rewarded by bearing witness to the Incarnation. Provide your own students with a beacon of hope in Christ so that they can foster their relationship with the Lord Jesus Christ and thereby be steadily open to his Good News.

DECEMBER 20

> But you, be self-possessed in all circumstances; put up with hardship; perform the work of an evangelist; fulfill your ministry.
>
> **—2 Timothy 4:5**

We have various "hardships" to endure over the course of the academic year. These "hardships" can come in the form of having to stand and pace for hours each day, needing to grade multiple assignments, providing frequent communication, pursuing professional development (including advanced degrees), taking the time to autograph glossy photos for the "Teacher of the Month" fan base, and more. So as to avoid the perception of complaint, this litany of various hardships could be more sympathetically considered "duties," but they are still extensive. At this point in the Advent season, your vacation time either has already begun or is about to begin. Appreciate your break, and rather than using it merely to catch up on reruns of *The Golden Girls*, make sure to re-envision difficult circumstances at school as opportunities to serve. Hardships that truly eclipse those mentioned above will come, so be spiritually invigorated. Make sure that you concede that laboring for God will bring eternal rewards in the face of mere temporal challenges.

DECEMBER 21

> My spirit remains in your midst; do not fear!
>
> **—Haggai 2:5b**

Christmas is mere days away. During the Christmas break, teachers can unfortunately run the risk of entering into despair, asking questions such as these: Have my students learned all that I have tried my best to teach them over the last four months? Will they forget everything during the Christmas vacation? Are they aware of "the big picture"? Why didn't I get as much Christmas candy from my students this year—am I now as unpopular as Mr. McClain? Celebrating Christ's Nativity is an opportunity to reflect that, just as we are confident that Christ came into the world at all, we can likewise rest assured that God is still with us and will never leave us. In the days remaining until Christmas, as well as into the Christmas season, make sure that you take the time to thank God for abiding with us and for the opportunity to imitate the perfect example of the Lord in the midst of challenging times. Keep your focus on the Lord. Your confidence in him will thus enhance your students' own confidence in him.

DECEMBER 22

> Behold, we are going up to Jerusalem, and the Son of Man will be handed over to the chief priests and the scribes, and they will condemn him to death.
>
> **—Matthew 20:18**

This account in Matthew's gospel continues: "And [they will] hand him over to the Gentiles to be mocked and scourged and crucified, and he will be raised on the third day" (Mt 20:19). As we continue in Advent and quickly approach Christmas, let us reflect on the very reason why Christ came into the world at all: to purchase our salvation by offering his life for our sins and rising to show his victory over death. The paschal mystery must continue to be recalled by our students. Some students may have difficulty grasping why Easter is considered a holier day than Christmas. This is a worthwhile question, and one that deserves a fair degree of consideration. Ask such students which is more important: the first day of school or graduation day? This analogy may provide such inquisitive students with a better grasp of the paschal mystery in light of Jesus' Incarnation. Our students are always learning (as are we), so provide them with opportunities to reflect on the great expanse that is God's love.

DECEMBER 23

> Your mercy is before my eyes; I walk guided by your faithfulness.
>
> **—Psalm 26:3**

How great is the mercy that Jesus came into the world to bestow upon us! God's merciful aspects have been on display since the Old Testament. In the New Testament, the mercy that Jesus extends to us is effectively on the same redemptive continuum as the mercy of God the Father, as evidenced by a studious comparison of various passages within the Old Testament and the New Testament. Meditate on the glorious nature of God's mercy in light of the Incarnation. Remember that God has never owed us anything, but came to us in human form in order to refocus our attention on him and his Word. Hence, we cannot take God's mercy for granted, because we cannot take for granted that which is ultimately a gift. Instill in your students a semblance of respect for God's mercy. Otherwise, they run the risk of losing sight of the merciful Savior of us all, whom we rightly love and follow. Encourage your students to remain faithful on their path to, and with, the Lord Jesus.

DECEMBER 24

> Therefore the Lord himself will give you a sign; the young woman, pregnant and about to bear a son, shall name him Emmanuel.
>
> **—Isaiah 7:14**

The name *Emmanuel* is from the Hebrew for "God with us." Tomorrow, we will celebrate the Nativity of the Lord. Take some time today to reflect on the awesome gift that we have in Jesus, as well as on how he is so much more than a mere man—he is God himself. God is with us, but not in a sentimental, gushy sort of way; rather, he is with us in a way that extends to us the opportunity for salvation, so that we can spend eternity glorifying him in his presence. Throughout the remainder of your Christmas vacation, make sure actually to appreciate the vast beauty and overwhelming significance of Christ's Incarnation. Take time to appreciate, as well, how blessed we are that God chose to reveal himself to us, not in fear-fostering displays of cosmic bewilderment, but in the humble, simple circumstance of a tiny, vulnerable, destitute infant devoid of outward grandiosity. Prepare your heart to receive the Lord at Christmas tomorrow. Your celebration of Christ's holy birth should enliven in you a joy that your students also acquire when they return to school soon.

DECEMBER 25

> In the beginning was the Word, and the Word was with God, and the Word was God.
>
> **—John 1:1**

Merry Christmas! The Christ Child is born! This excerpt from the very beginning of John's gospel is a reflection of the opening lines of Genesis: "In the beginning . . ." (Gn 1:1). The next line from the beginning of John 1 succinctly, yet relevantly, provides us with a profoundly fitting understanding of the dynamic by which Christ came into the world: "He was in the beginning with God" (Jn 1:2). In other words, Jesus is not a production of God the Father akin to an item produced by Santa's elves at the North Pole. Rather, God the Son has always existed in conjunction with God the Father and God the Holy Spirit. Therefore, Jesus was not somehow "manufactured" and sent to earth—he came onto the scene of his own accord and of his own power. Throughout the day today, take a few moments to reflect on how you, as a Catholic school teacher, are going to continue to work to instill in your students an adoration of the

Lord and his divine will. Celebrate with joy today, as if it were the first Christmas.

DECEMBER 26

The slack hand impoverishes, but the busy hand brings riches.

—Proverbs 10:4

The reader of the gospels may notice something significant regarding Jesus' ministry: the ever-present perception that Jesus never stopped laboring. His rests were quite infrequent, and they usually entailed not some sort of vacation, but a quiet place for prayer and recuperation in order to be able to take back up the work of his ministry. The "riches" that the Lord bestows upon us are not wealth or prosperity in the temporal sense; rather, they are spiritual manifestations of his love for us that will continue to draw us ever closer to him and his will. As we continue in the Christmas season, and as you continue your vacation (hopefully), let us reflect on, and appreciate, all that the Lord has given us through his many blessings. Of course, we must count our blessings, including our family, our students, the expertise of our subject, as well as the opportunity to teach and live out our ministerial efforts within a Catholic school. Thank God for all of the true "riches" that he provides for us, riches that are effectively spiritually imperishable.

DECEMBER 27

The LORD is just and loves just deeds; the upright will see his face.

—Psalm 11:7

During your Christmas break (a gift further attesting to God's goodness), continue to meditate on the benevolence of the Lord in order to fortify your resolve and commitment to serving your students once everyone returns to school in the coming days. God wants his followers to perform good works that build up his kingdom. After all, we must recall that he gave us free will in order for us ultimately to orient our wills to his own, as we are reminded in John 3:30: "He must increase; I must decrease." The Lord promises the reward of eternity in his presence to those who have dedicated themselves to following his will, as well as to those who have dedicated themselves to bringing others to conversion—an ongoing conversion that must be central to any disciple's life. Your devotion to pleasing the Lord will inspire and encourage your students to do likewise, so persevere in your apostolate of teaching.

DECEMBER 28

The disciples went and did as Jesus had ordered them.

—Matthew 21:6

Obedience is not a term that easily fits into the vocabulary of many young people. However, we as Catholic school educators have all passed from infancy to the toddler years to childhood to adolescence to adulthood. Unless you were the shining exemplar of perfection (and none of us were), you probably had some modicum of preoccupation with yourself at some point along the way. But we survived ourselves, thanks be to God. The Catholic school teacher must have obedience to legitimate authority. Of course, the Lord Almighty is our justifiably authoritative figure. Similarly, our prelates (the pope and his bishops), along with our school administrators, are authorities in our lives who reliably have our best interest at heart. Trust that they know what they are doing. Along with obedience, make sure to incorporate the other two evangelical counsels (poverty and chastity) into your personal and educational framework. (Of important note, be sure to understand what these counsels truly mean, lest you exaggerate them!) Your aspired holiness will draw others to the Lord.

DECEMBER 29

> Now this is eternal life, that they should know you, the only true God, and the one whom you sent, Jesus Christ.
>
> **—John 17:3**

The entirety of the seventeenth chapter of the Gospel of John is commonly referred to simply as the "Prayer of Jesus." Take a minute to read through this segment of scripture slowly, methodically, and devotedly. In essence, whenever God the Son talks to God the Father within the gospels, we ought to pay careful attention to what he says. (No, Jesus does not have a multiple-personality condition; rather, the unity of the Holy Trinity signifies the complementarity of the three persons along with the fullness of their unity and divinity.) In this passage, Jesus displays for us yet again who he truly is, a reality that he emphasizes throughout John's gospel and the synoptic gospels of Matthew, Mark, and Luke (albeit not in so distinct of a manner as the Gospel of John). As Catholic educators, we should reflect on the remarkable unity of the Blessed Trinity, one God in three persons, in order to be able to lead our students to an increasingly greater desire to learn steadily more about God's awesome characteristics.

DECEMBER 30

> In all your ways be mindful of him, and he will make straight your paths.
>
> **—Proverbs 3:6**

As this calendar year draws to a close, you may have decided what your New Year's resolution is by now. Perennially, people decide to lose weight, watch less TV, read more, and gossip less. All of these are noble goals, but too often, our human nature leads us away from actually being able to keep up with the standards that we have set for ourselves. Make sure that any resolution that you make is not merely for the New Year; rather, make *resolutions* (emphasis on the plural) that you plan to keep year after year that will also glorify the kingdom of God. "In all your ways" consider what God wants you to do, on a daily basis, on an hourly basis—in fact, minute by minute. The great French saint and one of just four female Doctors of the Church, Saint Thérèse of Lisieux, had her "Little Way" in which she sought to fulfill the demands of God out of love in every action of any given moment and in every circumstance. Despite her great sufferings throughout her short life, she persevered. Let us thus inspire our students to persevere.

DECEMBER 31

> For the fruit of noble struggles is a glorious one; and unfailing is the root of understanding.
>
> **—Wisdom 3:15**

And so another calendar year draws to a conclusion. Tomorrow is a new year, but also a new day on which we shall glorify God. Let us pause to reflect on a brief exhortation from Saint Paul: "Finally, my brothers, rejoice in the Lord" (Phil 3:1a). Is this not the attitude with which we should approach every day? Should we not allow joy to fill our hearts whenever we are given an opportunity to share the gospel? Our students are a willing audience, because—as the Catholic school teacher must always recall—the youth are close to the kingdom of God. They want to please God and bring him honor. Allow the Lord to continue to inspire and invigorate you as an educator in the year to come, and beyond. Live in accord with God's will in order to be as effective of a faithful leader as possible. Walk with him and stay near him, because he will always do so for us as we face the challenges inherent to our earthly voyage and strive to live based on his will. As Jesus told the indefatigable apostle Saint Paul: "Take courage" (Acts 23:11a).

ACKNOWLEDGMENTS

Of the various segments of this book, this portion was admittedly the easiest to write, and I was actually able to type these salutatory pages in merely one sitting (although, in the interest of full disclosure, I did have to get up once, in order to check my copy of the 2006–2007 yearbook for Bishop McNamara High School, due to my disbelief that I am actually now in my tenth year of teaching there). The authorship of this section also happens to have been a miraculous achievement for a father of three children aged four and under. In essence, I have much for which (i.e., many for whom) to offer thanks. This litany of gratitude is not in any particular order of significance, but even if it were, we Catholic educators typically require an occasional dose of Matthew 19:30 and Matthew 20:16.

Thank you to my students over the years at Bishop McNamara High School, Prince George's Community College, and the Pre-College Programs at the University of Maryland. God bless you all in a special way—particularly after having withstood my exacting expectations.

Speaking of former students, thank you to my former Bishop McNamara students who are now teachers yourselves within the Catholic educational system, including Krista Scanlan at the Academy of St. Matthias the Apostle in Lanham, Maryland; Jasmine Wedge at St. Thomas More Catholic Academy in Washington, DC; and others who have given of themselves by returning to the classroom in order to accept the call to be courageous.

Thank you to all of the editorial staff at Ave Maria Press. Although I have had the privilege of providing consultation for your high school theology textbooks, I have (unfortunately) not yet experienced the honor of meeting you in person. I dearly look forward to such a prospect while we are still on this side of eternity. In a particular way, thank you to Mike Amodei, Executive Editor of Adolescent Catechesis, for your patience, advocacy, guidance, wisdom, and availability, all achieved while occupying your post as the "keeper of the memories" for the annals of collegiate and professional athletics nationwide. I am likewise thankful for the assistance of Susana Kelly, Senior Managing Editor, and the leadership inherent to Bob Hamma, Editorial Director, and Tom Grady, Publisher. The team at Ave Maria Press sets the standard for professionalism and service to the Church. My gratitude abounds for your ministry of Catholic literacy in the Holy Cross tradition.

Thank you to all of my colleagues at Bishop McNamara, especially my inspiring, dedicated peers in the Department of Theology: Katie Bacon, Nancy Cunningham, Hunter Gallagher, Martin Hipkins, Jim Monahan, and Paul O'Brien, as well as our hardworking staff in campus ministry: Sandy Herndon, Rachel Longest, and Peter Sanneman. Thank you to our department chair, Adam Greer, indeed, for tolerating my eccentricities, and to Abbie Greer, Principal at the Academy of St. Matthias—together a couple imbued with an outlook of servant leadership within Catholic education. (Back when Abbie was Abbie *Thompson*, then a teacher herself at Bishop McNamara, she told this first-year Spanish teacher on his first day of teaching to "just look like you know what you're doing, and you'll be fine." Well . . . I still have no idea what I am doing, but I guess I have gotten better at pretending.) Thank you sincerely to Dr. Marco Clark, President of Bishop McNamara (and his dear wife, Peggy Clark, herself an award-winning Catholic educator at St. Ambrose Catholic School in Cheverly), and Dr. Robert Van der Waag, Principal of Bishop

McNamara and professorial lecturer at Georgetown University, for relentlessly fostering our students' school-wide loyalty to the Pillars of Holy Cross. I wish that I could mention all of my more than one hundred colleagues at Bishop McNamara individually by name, but please know how much I treasure each and every one of you. Nonetheless, I must take a quick moment to appreciate those of you who took the time out of your already busy schedules to review my manuscript during its drafting stages: Gina Gómez-Bozzo, LaSandra Hayes, Kristian Owens, and Dr. Nancy Paltell.

Thank you to my vitally influential theology and philosophy professors at Seton Hall University (including Dr. Gregory Glazov and Dr. Dianne Traflet) and at the Franciscan University of Steubenville (including Dr. Scott Hahn, Dr. Michael Healy, Dr. Stephen Hildebrand, and Dr. Andrew Minto), as well as the staff of Franciscan University's Distance Learning Office (Virginia Garrison and Evelyn Minch) and the staff of the S.T.E.P. initiative offered by the University of Notre Dame's Institute for Church Life.

Thank you to Dr. Tom Burnford, Secretary for Education of the Archdiocese of Washington, for your worthwhile feedback in the midst of publication, as well as for leading our Catholic schools within the Archdiocese of Washington. Thank you likewise to Kelly Branaman, Associate Superintendent for Schools of the Archdiocese of Washington, for your reliably enthusiastic commitment to Catholic education. Thank you as well to Sara Blauvelt, Director for Catechesis of the Archdiocese of Washington, for your support of catechetical formation throughout the Archdiocese.

Thank you to Heather Gossart, esteemed President Emerita of Bishop McNamara High School, Senior Consultant for the National Catholic Educational Association, and unofficial matriarch during a critical era (and at the inception of a subsequently rewarding legacy) within the hallowed history of Bishop McNamara High School. Thank you for your breadth of wisdom over the years, for taking the time to review my manuscript, and for ultimately encouraging me to seek publication.

Thank you to Rick Middleton, a man of deep faith and a retired guidance counselor from Bishop McNamara, whose sagacious feedback on my reflections was as meaningful as were your Christ-centered words of inspiration to so many students, including myself, over your decades of service within Catholic education.

Thank you to Al Odierno, my English teacher during my freshman year at Bishop McNamara, and my eventual colleague. It was at least marginally intimidating to have my former English teacher reading my writing (even nearly two decades later), but your input was characteristically charitable.

Thank you to Steve Showalter, my eighth-grade religion teacher at St. Mary of the Assumption Catholic School in Upper Marlboro, Maryland, and now principal of St. Mary's, for your encouragement in light of my reflections. Also at St. Mary's, thank you to my fourth-grade teacher, Sr. Myra Gilbart, I.H.M., a tirelessly Christian servant, for your uplifting words of advice on my reflections. I hope that my religious considerations matched your justifiably demanding standards. Thank you for always making us work!

Thank you to Beth Blaufuss, President and CEO of Archbishop Carroll High School in Washington, DC, for your input regarding the applicability of using the reflections daily.

Thank you to my fellow members of the board of directors for the Forestville Pregnancy Center, in recognition of your fidelity in serving unborn babies and their parents. In a special way, thank you to board members Frank and Jeanette Zak, particularly in light of Jeanette's keen editorial eye and experience as a former science and computer teacher, and later as an assistant principal at St. Philip the Apostle Catholic School in Camp Springs, Maryland.

Thank you to other good friends, from an array of K–12 Catholic institutions across the United States, who took the time to read through my manuscript: Br. Nigel Ali, O.Carm.; Rick Nichols, S.J.; Fr. Daniel O'Mullane; and Fr. Jeffrey Samaha, holy men of God and experienced Catholic educators with a unique clerical perspective; Tonya Bubolz, a perennially considerate former colleague at Bishop McNamara and now religion teacher at St. Petersburg Catholic High School in Florida; Chris and Elizabeth Keplinger, good friends and teachers at DeMatha Catholic High School and St. Elizabeth Ann Seton High School, respectively; and Dr. Zan Raynor, David Szostak, Lauren Warner, and Lindsay Wilcox, all sharp intellectuals and seasoned Catholic teachers.

Thank you to Dr. Peter Murphy of the United States Conference of Catholic Bishops (USCCB) and Katie Murphy, Dr. Andy Lichtenwalner of the USCCB and Kristen Lichtenwalner, as well as Dr. Ray Fermo, for your kind measures of support. Your friendship is a blessed gift.

Thank you to our parish priests at Sacred Heart Catholic Church, masterful homilists Msgr. Charles Parry and Fr. Scott Holmer, both of whom have a sizable background in Catholic education, including Msgr. Parry's expertise in teaching the Acts of the Apostles and Fr. Holmer's years in the classroom at DeMatha Catholic High School.

Although, as I mentioned at the beginning of this section, there was not a precise order of gratitude posited here, I must concede that I have reserved my ultimate expression of thanks for my family members who have been adept guides within the realm of Catholic education and formation: my incredible wife, Bernadette, who watches our children at home every day in order primarily to instruct them in matters of faith while likewise occasionally teaching part-time, and who was so patient and supportive throughout my preparation of this book of reflections; Bernadette's parents, my dear in-laws, John and Patricia Snyder, for your tireless selflessness in terms of your volunteering efforts within Catholic schools, which has extended beyond your children's years in school—you are both models of service; my brother and sister-in-law, Jaris and Lauren McClain, who give us all hope through your example of good, holy, Catholic parenting (and I must also thank Lauren's mother, Barbara, for your consistent and faithful conviction as a Catholic school teacher); and my father, Charles McClain Sr., and his cherished wife, Beth McClain, two remarkable instructors in the faith who still hold the record for being my theology students' favorite guest presenters following your trip to the Holy Land, the very ground where God walked. Lastly, thanks are always due to my late mother, Leona McClain, who, alongside my father, served as my first teacher in the Catholic faith. *Gratias vobis ago!*

SUBJECT INDEX

Do you partially recall the content of a reflection that you read previously and want to revisit it, but do not remember the day? Do you need some further inspiration by reading other reflections related to a specific topic? Use this listing of topics to find such reflections, listed by their corresponding days.

SCRIPTURE INDEX

Do you have a favorite scriptural passage, perhaps remembering it from the reflections, and would like to know where it is referenced within the reflections? If so, use this listing of scriptural passages to find its corresponding day. Make sure consistently to endeavor to familiarize yourself with scripture beyond these reflections because they are only a brief sampling of the multiple noteworthy passages to inspire and uplift the Catholic school teacher. Let the Word of God be "a lamp for [your] feet, a light for [your] path" (Ps 119:105).

Revelation

Justin McClain has taught theology and Spanish at Bishop McNamara High School in Forestville, Maryland, since 2006. He also has served as an adjunct lecturer in Spanish for the pre-college programs at the University of Maryland, College Park, and taught English as a second language at Prince George's Community College.

McClain earned bachelor's degrees (2004) in Spanish language and literature and in criminology and criminal justice from the University of Maryland and master's degrees in Spanish language and culture (2008) from the Universidad de Salamanca (Spain) and in international history (2011) from Staffordshire University (England). He has studied philosophy and theology at the Immaculate Conception Seminary/School of Theology at Seton Hall University and Church history through the University of Notre Dame's Institute for Church Life/STEP initiative. He is pursuing a master's degree in theology and Christian ministry at Franciscan University of Steubenville

McClain was a consultant to the US Conference of Catholic Bishops' Secretariat of Cultural Diversity in the Church, Subcommittee on African-American Affairs in 2015. He is a high school theology textbook consultant for Ave Maria Press, where he also provides content for the *Engaging Faith* blog and high school newsletter. McClain serves on the boards of directors for the Forestville Pregnancy Center and the Prince George's County Historical Society. He is a member of the Maryland Historical Society. McClain is the author of *Stepping into the Darkness* and *Mientras el sol pasaba*. He and his wife, Bernadette, live in Bowie, Maryland, with their three children.